D0765533

Presented to ______________________

From ______________________

Date ______________________

I thank God every time I remember you.

PHILIPPIANS 1:3

Children's Favorite BIBLE STORIES

Compiled by Tama Fortner

A Division of Thomas Nelson Publishers

NASHVILLE   DALLAS   MEXICO CITY   RIO DE JANEIRO

Published in Nashville, Tennessee, by Tommy Nelson. Tommy Nelson is a registered trademark of Thomas Nelson, Inc.

Thomas Nelson, Inc., titles may be purchased in bulk for educational, business, fund-raising, or sales promotional use. For information please e-mail *SpecialMarkets@ThomasNelson.com.*

Library of Congress Cataloging-in-Publication Data

Fortner, Tama, 1969-
Children's favorite Bible stories / compiled by Tama Fortner.
p. cm.
Includes bibliographical references (p.   ) and index.
ISBN 978-1-4003-2103-2 (hardcover)
1. Bible stories, English. 2. Families--Religious life. I. Title.
BS551.3.F67 2012
220.95'05--dc23

2012030019

Printed in China

12 13 14 15 16 RRD 6 5 4 3 2 1

Teach This Little Child to Pray

Lord, teach this little child to pray,
And now accept my prayer;
Thou hearest every word I say,
For Thou art everywhere.

A little sparrow cannot fall
Unnoticed, Lord, by Thee;
And though I am so young and small,
Thou dost take care of me.

Teach me to do whate'er is right,
And when I sin, forgive;
And make it still my chief delight
To love Thee while I live.

—Jane Taylor

Contents

God Has a Message for . . . You!

God's Message

The Bible is God's message to you . . . his message of love. That message begins in the book of Genesis with the story of creation—and it continues all the way through the Bible to the book of Revelation and its amazing descriptions of how wonderful heaven will be.

The Old Testament

The Bible is divided into two parts: the Old Testament and the New Testament. The Old Testament tells the history of God's people, beginning with the story of creation in Genesis. Here, God tells us how he made us in his own image:

> So God created human beings in his image. In the image of God he created them. He created them male and female. *Genesis 1:27*

From the first moment of creation, God has kept watch over his people—and he still does today! Sometimes they please him, sometimes they sadden him, and sometimes they even anger him, but God always loves his people. Over and over again, throughout the Old Testament, we see God's faithful love and care—from Abraham to Moses, from Esther to Ruth, and from Daniel to David.

The New Testament

In the New Testament, God shows us just how high and wide and deep and strong his love for us really is. Here, God tells us of his greatest gift—the gift of his Son, Jesus:

> For God loved the world so much that he gave his only Son. God gave his Son so that whoever believes in him may not be lost, but have eternal life. *John 3:16*

The first four books of the New Testament (Matthew, Mark, Luke, and John) are called the Gospels. They tell about Jesus' life on earth, of the many lessons he taught and miracles he did, and of how he let himself be sacrificed on the cross so we could one day live with him in heaven.

The rest of the New Testament tells of how the early church began and how it spread throughout the world, carrying Jesus' message of love and forgiveness everywhere it went.

Not Just Stories

While the Bible has many stories, we must remember that these aren't just made-up stories, like "Cinderella" or "Jack and the Beanstalk." These stories are true. They are the real histories of real people and the real things that happened to them. Second Timothy 3:16 tells us that "all Scripture is given by God." That means that men wrote down the words of the Bible, but it was God who told them what to write.

God gave us the Bible to help us learn more about him, to teach us how to live better lives, and most of all, to show us how much he loves us.

What Does the Bible Mean to Me?

God has one great hope for your life—that you will choose to be his child so that you can be with him in heaven one day.

God knows that you aren't perfect. You can never be good enough to get to heaven all on your own. That's why he sent his Son, Jesus:

> This is how God showed his love to us: He sent his only Son into the world to give us life through him. . . . God sent his Son to be the way to take away our sins. That is how much God loved us, dear friends! *1 John 4:9–11*

So how do you choose to be God's child? God's own Word tells us:

> Change your hearts and lives and be baptized, each one of you, in the name of Jesus Christ for the forgiveness of your sins. *Acts 2:38*

Say a prayer and ask God to show you how to become his child. Your prayer might sound something like this:

> Dear God,
>
> I am learning so much about you and how you sent your Son to save me. Thank you for loving me so much. I want to learn to follow Jesus and to be like him in all I say and do. Please show me how.
>
> I know I mess up sometimes—forgive me when I do. And fill my heart with your love, so I can learn to love others as you love me.
>
> In Jesus' name, amen.

And then try to live your life as a child of God by loving "the Lord your God . . . with all your heart, all your soul, all your strength, and all your mind" and by loving "your neighbor as you love yourself" (Luke 10:27). You still won't be perfect, but you will be forgiven.

About This Book

The stories in this book are color-coded:

A story with a beige heading is from the Old Testament.

A story with a blue heading is from the New Testament.

- Going Deeper includes *Read It!* and *Do It!* sections that direct you to related readings with fun and educational family activities.

- Special Words teach the meaning of unusual or unfamiliar biblical terms.

- Did You Know? sections offer fun facts you may not have known before.

- The Quote of the Day shares bits of wisdom from some well-known people.

Family Prayer Time

Just as it is important to spend time alone with God, it is also important to spend time with God as a family. Going to church, singing his praises, and praying together will draw you not only closer to God but also closer to one another.

> They called to the Lord,
> and he answered them. *Psalm 99:6*

Let's Get Started!

Now you are ready to start your great adventure with God. So let's begin at . . . the beginning, with Genesis 1:1.

Shout to the Lord, all the earth.
Serve the Lord with joy.
Come before him with singing.
Know that the Lord is God.
He made us, and we belong to him.
We are his people, the sheep he tends.
Come into his city with songs of thanksgiving.
Come into his courtyards with songs of praise.
Thank him, and praise his name.
The Lord is good. His love continues forever.
His loyalty continues from now on.
—Psalm 100

Stories from the Old Testament

God Creates Light and Space

Genesis 1:1–8

God is eternal. That means God has no beginning and no end. The universe, our world, and everything in it—even time itself—began when God spoke it into being. Let's read about God's amazing creations in the very first book of the Bible, Genesis.

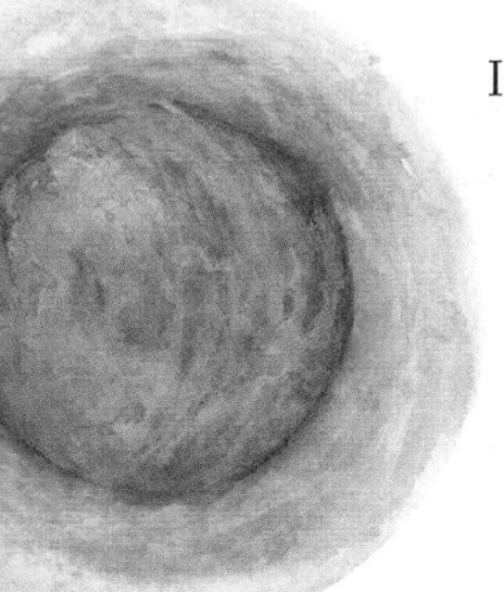

In the beginning God cre-
ated the sky and the earth.
2The earth was empty and
had no form. Darkness
covered the ocean, and
God's Spirit was moving
over the water.
3Then God said, "Let
there be light!" And there
was light. 4God saw that the light
was good. So he divided the light from the
darkness. 5God named the light "day" and
the darkness "night." Evening passed, and
morning came. This was the first day.
6Then God said, "Let there be something
to divide the water in two!" 7So God made
the air to divide the water in two. Some of
the water was above the air, and some of
the water was below it. 8God named the air
"sky." Evening passed, and morning came.
This was the second day.

Let's Pray

The heavens tell the glory of God.
And the skies announce what his hands have made.

—Psalm 19:1

Thank you, God, for the beauty of this world. Help me take good care of the beautiful things you have made. In Jesus' name, amen.

Going Deeper

Read It! Did you know that Jesus was present at creation? Read about it in John 1:1–2. The Word was Jesus!

Do It! What can you do this week to take care of God's creation? Take some time to help clean up a playground, recycle, or plant a tree.

Special Words:
God's Spirit *is sometimes translated as "a wind of God."*

Did You Know? There are volcanoes on Mars! The tallest, the Olympus Mons, is taller than three Mount Everests.[1]

God Creates Sea and Sky

Genesis 1:9–19

Have you ever stood at the edge of the ocean and imagined how deep the water must be? Have you ever wondered if the mountains really do touch the sky? God created this world as a home for every fish that swims, every bird that flies, and every animal that roams. And then God asked us to take care of it all! Let's read about how God prepared a place for every living creature.

Then God said, "Let the water under the sky
be gathered together so the dry land will
appear." And it happened. 10God named
the dry land "earth." He named the water
that was gathered together "seas." God saw
that this was good.
11Then God said, "Let the earth produce
plants. Some plants will make grain for
seeds. Others will make fruit with seeds in
it. Every seed will produce more of its own
kind of plant." And it happened. 12The earth
produced plants. Some plants had grain for
seeds. The trees made fruit with seeds in it.
Each seed grew its own kind of plant. God
saw that all this was good. 13Evening passed,
and morning came. This was the third day.
14Then God said, "Let there be lights in
the sky to separate day from night. These
lights will be used for signs, seasons, days
and years. 15They will be in the sky to give
light to the earth." And it happened.
16So God made the two large lights. He
made the brighter light to rule the day. He
made the smaller light to rule the night.
He also made the stars. 17God put all these
in the sky to shine on the earth. 18They are
to rule over the day and over the night. He
put them there to separate the light from
the darkness. God saw that all these things
were good. 19Evening passed, and morning came. This was the fourth day.

Let's Pray

Blessed be your wonderful name.
It is more wonderful than all blessing
and praise.
You are the only Lord.
You made the heavens, even the highest
heavens.
You made all the stars.
You made the earth and everything that is
on it.
You made the seas and everything that is
in them.
You give life to everything.
The heavenly army worships you.

—Nehemiah 9:5–6

Going Deeper

Read It! The One who created the waves can also control them. Read about how Jesus calmed the storm in Mark 4:35–39.

Do It! Go outside and see the beauty of God's sunset. Just imagine—God creates a new one every evening!

Special Words: Vegetation *means all the plant life on earth. The "sky" in verse 14 is sometimes called the "firmament." This is "the enormous area of sky and space where the stars and planets are set."*[2]

God Creates All Living Creatures

Genesis 1:20–25

What's your favorite animal? Is it a giraffe, an elephant, or a dolphin? On the fifth and sixth days of creation, God made the birds, the fish, and all the other living creatures. Then he put them in the homes he had created just for them, so that the whole world was filled with life!

Then God said, "Let the water be filled with living things. And let birds fly in the air above the earth."

21So God created the large sea animals.
He created every living thing that moves in
the sea. The sea is filled with these living
things. Each one produces more of its own
kind. God also made every bird that flies.
And each bird produces more of its own
kind. God saw that this was good. 22God
blessed them and said, "Have many young
ones and grow in number. Fill the water of
the seas, and let the birds grow in number on the earth." 23Evening passed, and
morning came. This was the fifth day.

24Then God said, "Let the earth be filled
with animals. And let each produce more
of its own kind. Let there be tame animals and small crawling animals and wild animals. And let each produce more of its kind." And it happened.

25So God made the wild animals, the tame
animals and all the small crawling animals to produce more of their own kind. God saw that this was good.

Let's Pray

"The Doxology"

Praise God, from whom all blessings flow;
Praise Him, all creatures here below;
Praise Him above, ye heavenly host;
Praise Father, Son, and Holy Ghost.
Amen.

—Thomas Ken

Going Deeper

Read It! All creatures of the earth were created to show God's glory. Read about it in Psalm 148.

Do It! Visit a zoo and check out the wonderful works of God!

Did You Know? The world did not appear by accident. It was by God's design. The order of creation is proof that God exists. Before creating the birds and fish and animals, God first created homes for them. And before creating people, he made sure we'd have everything we need. What a wonderful God!

God Creates People

Genesis 1:26–31

Even after all those different animals were created, there was something missing from God's creation—someone to glorify God and to take care of his creation. So God created the very first man, Adam.

Then God said, "Let us make human beings in our image and likeness. And let them rule over the fish in the sea and the birds in the sky. Let them rule over the tame animals, over all the earth and over all the small crawling animals on the earth."

27So God created human beings in his image. In the image of God he created them. He created them male and female. 28God blessed them and said, "Have many children and grow in number. Fill the earth and be its master. Rule over the fish in the sea and over the birds in the sky. Rule over every living thing that moves on the earth."

29God said, "Look, I have given you all the plants that have grain for seeds. And I have given you all the trees whose fruits have seeds in them. They will be food for you. 30I have given all the green plants to all the animals to eat. They will be food for every wild animal, every bird of the air and every small crawling animal."
And it happened. 31God looked at everything he had made, and it was very good. Evening passed, and morning came. This was the sixth day.

Let's Pray

You made my whole
being.
You formed me in my mother's body.
I praise you because you made me in an
amazing and wonderful way.
What you have done is wonderful.
—Psalm 139:13–14

Thank you, God, for making me me! *In Jesus' name, amen.*

Going Deeper

Read It! God created us to do good works. Read about how God wants us to live our lives in Ephesians 2:10.

Do It! Make a card and send it to someone for whom you are especially thankful!

Did You Know?
Scientists believe that there are more than 8 million different species on the earth. And they are finding new ones all the time![3]

Adam and Eve

Genesis 2:18–24

Have you ever been to a wedding? The very first wedding was in the garden of Eden, when God made Eve and gave her to Adam to be his wife.

Then the Lord God said, "It is not good for the man to be alone. I will make a helper who is right for him."
[19]From the ground God formed every wild animal and every bird in the sky. He brought them to the man so the man could name them. Whatever the man called each living thing, that became its name. [20]The man gave names to all the tame animals, to the birds in the sky and to all the wild animals. But Adam did not find a helper that was right for him. [21]So the Lord God caused the man to sleep very deeply. While the man was asleep, God took one of the ribs from the man's body. Then God closed the man's skin at the place where he took the rib. [22]The Lord God used the rib from the man to make a woman. Then the Lord brought the woman to the man.
[23]And the man said,

"Now, this is someone whose bones
came from my bones.
Her body came from my body.
I will call her 'woman,'
because she was taken out of man."

[24]So a man will leave his father and mother and be united with his wife. And the two people will become one body.

Let's Pray

"Prayer for the Family"

Lord, behold our family here assembled.
We thank You for this place in which we
dwell,
for the love that unites us,
for the peace accorded us this day,
for the hope with which we expect the
morrow;
for the health, the work the food, and
the bright skies that make our life
delightful;
for our friends in all parts of the earth.
Amen.

—Robert Louis Stevenson

Going Deeper

Read It! In the book of Mark, Jesus told us how important marriage is to God. Read what Jesus said in Mark 10:9.

Do It! Plan a family night—play games, head for the park, or prepare a meal together. Whatever you do, be sure to thank God for the blessing of your family.

Quote of the Day:
Love is patient and kind. Love is not jealous, it does not brag, and it is not proud. Love is not rude, is not selfish, and does not become angry easily. Love does not remember wrongs done against it. Love is not happy with evil, but is happy with the truth. Love patiently accepts all things. It always trusts, always hopes, and always continues strong. Love never ends.
—1 Corinthians 13:4–8

That Bad Snake!

Genesis 3:1–15, 23–24

Adam and Eve lived in the beautiful garden of Eden that God had created for their home. God told them they could eat from any tree in the garden—except the Tree of Knowledge of Good and Evil. Together, Adam and Eve took care of the garden and all the animals. But one day the evil one, in the form of a snake, ruined it all.

Now the snake was the most clever of all the
wild animals the Lord God had made. One
day the snake spoke to the woman. He said,
"Did God really say that you must not eat
fruit from any tree in the garden?"
2The woman answered the snake, "We may
eat fruit from the trees in the garden. 3But
God told us, 'You must not eat fruit from the
tree that is in the middle of the garden. You
must not even touch it, or you will die.'"
4But the snake said to the woman, "You
will not die. 5God knows that if you eat the
fruit from that tree, you will learn about
good and evil. Then you will be like God!"
6The woman saw that the tree was beautiful. She saw that its fruit was good to eat and
that it would make her wise. So she took
some of its fruit and ate it. She also gave
some of the fruit to her husband who was
with her, and he ate it.
7Then, it was as if the man's and the woman's eyes were opened. They realized they
were naked. So they sewed fig leaves together
and made something to cover themselves.
8Then they heard the Lord God walking in the garden. This was during the cool
part of the day. And the man and his wife
hid from the Lord God among the trees in
the garden. 9But the Lord God called to the
man. The Lord said, "Where are you?"
10The man answered, "I heard you walking in the garden. I was afraid because I was
naked. So I hid."
11God said to the man, "Who told you that
you were naked? Did you eat fruit from
that tree? I commanded you not to eat
from that tree."
12The man said, "You gave this woman to me.
She gave me fruit from the tree. So I ate it."
13Then the Lord God said to the woman,
"What have you done?"
She answered, "The snake tricked me. So
I ate the fruit."
14The Lord God said to the snake,
"Because you did this,
a curse will be put on you.
You will be cursed more than any tame
animal or wild animal.
You will crawl on your stomach,
and you will eat dust all the days of
your life.
15I will make you and the woman
enemies to each other.
Your descendants and her descendants
will be enemies.
Her child will crush your head.
And you will bite his heel." . . .
23So the Lord God forced the man out
of the garden of Eden. He had to work the
ground he was taken from. 24God forced the
man out of the garden. Then God put angels
on the east side of the garden. He also put
a sword of fire there. It flashed around in
every direction. This kept people from getting to the tree of life.

Let's Pray

You are my protection,
my place of safety in times of trouble.
God, my strength, I will sing praises to you.
God, my protection, you are the God who loves me.
—Psalm 59:16–17

Lord, please protect me from the evil one. In Jesus' name, amen.

Going Deeper

READ IT! The devil is still on the loose! Read about what he's up to—and what you can do about it—in 1 Peter 5:8–9.

DO IT! Look in magazines and newspapers for examples of people making good and bad choices. If the choice was a bad one, what should that person have done instead?

Did You Know?
The snake (or serpent) is the Bible's first and last animal villain? Check out Genesis 3 and Revelation 20:2.[4]

Cain and Abel

Genesis 4:2–12

Even though Adam and Eve had to leave the garden of Eden because of their sin, God was still with them. He blessed them with two sons: Cain, who became a farmer, and Abel, who tended sheep. Like most brothers, Cain and Abel didn't always get along. In fact, the story of Cain and Abel is also the story of the first murder!

Abel took care of sheep. Cain became a farmer.

3Later, Cain brought a gift to God. He brought some food from the ground. 4Abel brought the best parts of his best sheep. The Lord accepted Abel and his gift. 5But God did not accept Cain and his gift. Cain became very angry and looked unhappy.

6The Lord asked Cain, "Why are you angry? Why do you look so unhappy? 7If you do good, I will accept you. But if you do not do good, sin is ready to attack you. Sin wants you. But you must rule over it."

8Cain said to his brother Abel, "Let's go out into the field." So Cain and Abel went into the field. Then Cain attacked his brother Abel and killed him.

9Later, the Lord said to Cain, "Where is your brother Abel?"

Cain answered, "I don't know. Is it my job to take care of my brother?"

10Then the Lord said, "What have you done? Your brother's blood is on the ground. That blood is like a voice that tells me what happened. 11And now you will be cursed in your work with the ground. It is the same ground where your brother's blood fell. Your hands killed him. 12You will work the ground. But it will not grow good crops for you anymore. You will wander around on the earth."

Let's Pray

Open my eyes to see the wonderful things
in your teachings. . . .
Help me obey your commands
because that makes me happy.

—Psalm 119:18, 35

Going Deeper

Read It! The tenth commandment tells us not to be jealous or to envy what other people have. Read what God said in Exodus 20:17.

Do It! Have you ever wanted to take what someone else had? That's called *jealousy* or *envy*. When we are jealous, we forget to be thankful for what we *do* have. Thank God for something today.

Special Words:
The "best sheep" were the firstlings, or the first animals to be born in a flock. The "best parts" were the fat portions of the sheep.

Quote of the Day: Think about the things that are good and worthy of praise. Think about the things that are true and honorable and right and pure and beautiful and respected.
—Philippians 4:8

Noah Builds a Boat

Genesis 6:5–8, 10, 13, 17–22

Years passed, and the number of people on the earth grew and grew. But the people forgot about God. They stopped worshiping him, and their hearts were filled with evil. Only one man was faithful to God, but God was about to ask him to do something very difficult. Would Noah obey?

The Lord saw that the human beings on
the earth were very wicked. He also saw
that their thoughts were only about evil all
the time. 6The Lord was sorry he had made
human beings on the earth. His heart was
filled with pain. 7So the Lord said, "I will
destroy all human beings that I made on
the earth. And I will destroy every animal
and everything that crawls on the earth. I
will also destroy the birds of the air. This is
because I am sorry that I have made them."
8But Noah pleased the Lord. . . .

10Noah had three sons: Shem, Ham and
Japheth. . . .

13So God said to Noah, "People have made
the earth full of violence. So I will destroy
all people from the earth. . . . 17I will bring
a flood of water on the earth. I will destroy
all living things that live under the sky. This
includes everything that has the breath of
life. Everything on the earth will die. 18But I
will make an agreement with you. You, your
sons, your wife and your sons' wives will all
go into the boat. 19Also, you must bring into
the boat two of every living thing, male and
female. Keep them alive with you. 20There
will be two of every kind of bird, animal and
crawling thing. They will come to you to be
kept alive. 21Also gather some of every kind
of food. Store it on the boat as food for you
and the animals."

22Noah did everything that God commanded him.

Let's Pray

May God give you . . .
For every storm, a rainbow,
For every tear, a smile,
For every care, a promise,
And a blessing in each trial.
For every problem life sends,
A faithful friend to share,
For every sigh, a sweet song,
And an answer for each prayer.

—Traditional Irish Prayer

Going Deeper

READ IT! Hebrews 11 names Noah as one of the heroes of the faith. Read about Noah in verse 7.

DO IT! Make animal cracker sandwiches with peanut butter or frosting. Be sure to eat them two by two!

Did you know?

God told Noah how to build the boat (often called an ark). Genesis 6:15–16 says, "This is how big I want you to build the boat: 450 feet long, 75 feet wide and 45 feet high. Make an opening around the top of the boat. Make it 18 inches high from the edge of the roof down. Put a door in the side of the boat. Make an upper, middle and lower deck in it."

God Sends a Rainbow

Genesis 9:8–17

Poor Noah! Stuck inside the boat with all those animals and people. For forty days and forty nights it rained, and the boat floated on the water-covered earth. When dry land finally appeared and the dove returned with the olive branch, Noah's family was able to leave their floating home at last. As they left the boat, God made Noah and his family a promise—and he gave them a beautiful way to remember it.

Then God said to Noah and his sons, 9"Now
I am making my agreement with you and
your people who will live after you. 10And
I also make it with every living thing that
is with you. It is with the birds, the tame
animals and the wild animals. It is with all
that came out of the boat with you. I make
my agreement with every living thing on
earth. 11I make this agreement with you: I
will never again destroy all living things
by floodwaters. A flood will never again
destroy the earth."
12And God said, "I am making an agreement between me and you and every living
creature that is with you. It will continue
from now on. This is the sign: 13I am putting my rainbow in the clouds. It is the
sign of the agreement between me and
the earth. 14When I bring clouds over the
earth, a rainbow appears in the clouds.
15Then I will remember my agreement.
It is between me and you and every living thing. Floodwaters will never again
destroy all life on the earth. 16When the
rainbow appears in the clouds, I will see
it. Then I will remember the agreement
that continues forever. It is between me
and every living thing on the earth."
17So God said to Noah, "That rainbow is
a sign. It is the sign of the agreement that I
made with all living things on earth."

Let's Pray:

Thank the Lord because he is good.
His love continues forever.

—Psalm 107:1

Thank you, God, for each of your promises. I know that I can always trust in you. In Jesus' name, amen.

Going Deeper

Read It! All of creation declares how wonderful and amazing God is. Read about it in Job 12:7–8.

Do It! Why do you think God gave Noah and his family a reminder of his promise that they could see? What do you think of when you see a rainbow?

Special Words: Another word for God's agreement is covenant. *A covenant is a promise between God and his people. And God never breaks his promises!*

Abram, Sarai, and Lot

Genesis 12:1–7

Have you ever moved to a new home? Was it hard to leave behind old friends or your old school or church? In Genesis 12, God asked Abram—whom he later called Abraham—to move to a new home where he would bless him. This covenant (or promised blessing) was not only for Abram and his wife, Sarai, but for their children and for future generations as well. But first Abram had to leave behind everything he knew and move to a place he had never seen before!

Then the Lord said to Abram, "Leave your country, your relatives and your father's family. Go to the land I will show you.

2I will make you a great nation,
and I will bless you.
I will make you famous.
And you will be a blessing to others.
3I will bless those who bless you.
I will place a curse on those who harm you.
And all the people on earth
will be blessed through you."

4So Abram left Haran as the Lord had
told him. And Lot went with him. At this
time Abram was 75 years old. 5Abram took
his wife Sarai, his nephew Lot and everything they owned. They took all the servants they had gotten in Haran. They set out from Haran, planning to go to the land of Canaan. In time they arrived there.

6Abram traveled through that land. He went as far as the great tree of Moreh at Shechem. The Canaanites were living in
the land at that time. 7The Lord appeared to
Abram. The Lord said, "I will give this land to your descendants." So Abram built an altar there to the Lord, who had appeared to him.

Let's Pray

Lord, teach me your demands.
Then I will obey them until the end.
Help me understand, so I can obey your teachings.
I will obey them with all my heart.
—Psalm 119:33–34

Special Words:
Moreh *is Hebrew for "teacher."* Shechem *means "shoulder."*

Going Deeper

Read It! Did you know that Abram (Abraham) was called "God's friend"? Check it out in James 2:23.

Do It! As a family, talk about why it is important to obey God even when you don't understand his plan for you.

Abraham Believes

Genesis 17:1–8, 15–22

When a child is adopted, his or her last name is changed to match the new family's name. It is a sign of the family's promise to take care of that child. In the Bible, God sometimes changed a person's name too. In today's story, Abram and Sarai became Abraham and Sarah. This name change was a sign of God's promise to bless them and care for them and their children. The only trouble was that Abraham and Sarah had no children of their own. But with God nothing is impossible!

When Abram was 99 years old, the Lord appeared to him. The Lord said, "I am God All-Powerful. Obey me and do what is right. [2]I will make an agreement between us. I will make you the ancestor of many people."

[3]Then Abram bowed facedown on the ground. God said to him, [4]"I am making my agreement with you: I will make you the father of many nations. [5]I am changing your name from Abram to Abraham. This is because I am making you a father of many nations. [6]I will give you many descendants. New nations will be born from you. Kings will come from you. [7]And I will make an agreement between me and you and all your descendants from now on: I will be your God and the God of all your descendants. [8]You live in the land of Canaan now as a stranger. But I will give you and your descendants all this land forever. And I will be the God of your descendants." . . .

[15]God said to Abraham, "I will change the name of Sarai, your wife. Her new name will be Sarah. [16]I will bless her. I will give her a son, and you will be the father. She will be the mother of many nations. Kings of nations will come from her."

[17]Abraham bowed facedown on the ground and laughed. He said to himself, "Can a man have a child when he is 100 years old? Can Sarah give birth to a child when she is 90?" [18]Then Abraham said to God, "Please let Ishmael be the son you promised."

[19]God said, "No. Sarah your wife will have a son, and you will name him Isaac. I will make my agreement with him. It will be an agreement that continues forever with all his descendants.

[20]"You asked me about Ishmael, and I heard you. I will bless him. I will give him many descendants. And I will cause their numbers to grow very greatly. He will be the father of 12 great leaders. I will make him into a great nation. [21]But I will make my agreement with Isaac. He is the son whom Sarah will have at this same time next year." [22]After God finished talking with Abraham, God rose and left him.

Let's Pray

Happy are those who respect the Lord
and obey him.

—Psalm 128:1

God, help me always to walk in your ways. I want your love to change me from the inside out. In Jesus' name, amen.

Did You Know?
Abraham *means "father of a multitude."* *And* Sarah *means "noble lady."*[5]

GOING DEEPER

READ IT! Did you know that God will give you a new name when you get to heaven? Check it out in Revelation 2:17.

DO IT! What do you think your new, "heavenly" name will be? Perhaps it will have something to do with how you serve God—such as Lauren the Loving or Kenneth the Kind. Make up a "heavenly" name for your name.

Heavenly Guests

Genesis 18:1–15

Do you like having company for dinner? It's great to visit with friends, share stories, and maybe even get a special dessert. In this story, Abraham welcomed three very special visitors. Two of them were angels, and the third was God himself! And they had some very exciting news for Abraham and Sarah.

Later, the Lord again appeared to Abraham near the great trees of Mamre. At that time Abraham was sitting at the door of his tent. It was during the hottest part of the day. [2]He looked up and saw three men standing near him. When Abraham saw them, he ran from his tent to meet them. He bowed facedown on the ground before them. [3]Abraham said, "Sir, if you think well of me, please stay awhile with me, your servant. [4]I will bring some water so all of you can wash your feet. You may rest under the tree. [5]I will get some bread for you, so you can regain your strength. Then you may continue your journey."

The three men said, "That is fine. Do as you said."

[6]Abraham hurried to the tent where Sarah was. He said to her, "Hurry, prepare 20 quarts of fine flour. Make it into loaves of bread." [7]Then Abraham ran to his cattle. He took one of his best calves and gave it to a servant. The servant hurried to kill the calf and to prepare it for food. [8]Abraham gave the three men the calf that had been cooked. . . . While the three men ate, he stood under the tree near them.

[9]The men asked Abraham, "Where is your wife Sarah?"

"There, in the tent," said Abraham.

[10]Then the Lord said, "I will certainly return to you about this time a year from now. At that time your wife Sarah will have a son."

Sarah was listening. . . . [11]Abraham and Sarah were very old. Sarah was past the age when women normally have children. [12]So she laughed to herself, "My husband and I are too old to have a baby."

[13]Then the Lord said to Abraham, "Why did Sarah laugh? Why did she say, 'I am too old to have a baby'? [14]Is anything too hard for the Lord? No! I will return to you at the right time a year from now. And Sarah will have a son."

[15]Sarah was afraid. So she lied and said, "I didn't laugh."

But the Lord said, "No. You did laugh."

Let's Pray

Lord, who may enter your Holy Tent?
Who may live on your holy mountain?
Only a person who is innocent
and who does what is right.
He must speak the truth from his heart.

—Psalm 15:1–2

Help me, Lord, to live so that I may find a place in your Holy Tent. In Jesus' name, amen.

Did You Know?
Scientists now think there are more stars in the heavens than there are grains of sand on all the earth.

Going Deeper

Read It! Abraham did have a son—and his descendants were as many as the stars in the sky and the grains of sand on the seashore. Check it out in Hebrews 11:11–12.

Do It! Some problems seem impossible to fix. The next time you face an impossible problem, try turning it over to God in prayer. He will help you—and your faith will grow too!

Hagar and Ishmael

Genesis 21:1–19

Have you ever wanted to do something, but then your parents told you to clean your room first? Were you tempted to take a shortcut? When the Lord promised Abraham a son, he and Sarah tried to take a shortcut. Sarah gave her servant, Hagar, to Abraham to have a child. Hagar did have a son, and he was named Ishmael. But once Sarah had her own son, she wanted Hagar and Ishmael to disappear. What would Abraham do?

The Lord cared for Sarah as he had said. He
did for her what he had promised. 2Sarah
became pregnant. And she gave birth to a
son for Abraham in his old age. Everything
happened at the time God had said it would.
3Abraham named his son Isaac. Sarah gave
birth to this son of Abraham. 4Abraham
circumcised Isaac when he was eight days
old as God had commanded.

5Abraham was 100 years old when his son
Isaac was born. 6And Sarah said, "God has
made me laugh. Everyone who hears about
this will laugh with me. 7No one thought that
I would be able to have Abraham's child. But
I have given Abraham a son while he is old."

8Isaac grew and became old enough to
eat food. At that time Abraham gave a great
feast. 9But Sarah saw Ishmael making fun of
Isaac. (Ishmael was the son of Abraham by
Hagar, Sarah's Egyptian slave.) 10So Sarah
said to Abraham, "Throw out this slave
woman and her son. When we die, our son
Isaac will inherit everything we have. I don't
want her son to inherit any of our things."

11This troubled Abraham very much
because Ishmael was also his son. 12But
God said to Abraham, "Don't be troubled
about the boy and the slave woman. Do
whatever Sarah tells you. The descendants
I promised you will be from Isaac. 13I will
also make the descendants of Ishmael into
a great nation. I will do this because he is
your son, too."

14Early the next morning Abraham took
some food and a leather bag full of water. He
gave them to Hagar and sent her away. Hagar
carried these things and her son. She went
and wandered in the desert of Beersheba.

15Later, all the water was gone from the
bag. So Hagar put her son under a bush.
16Then she went away a short distance and
sat down. Hagar thought, "My son will die.
I cannot watch this happen." She sat there
and began to cry.

17God heard the boy crying. And God's
angel called to Hagar from heaven. He said,
"What is wrong, Hagar? Don't be afraid!
God has heard the boy crying there. 18Help
the boy up. Take him by the hand. I will
make his descendants into a great nation."

19Then God showed Hagar a well of water.
So she went to the well and filled her bag
with water. Then she gave the boy a drink.

Let's Pray

Happy are those who respect the Lord
and obey him.

—Psalm 128:1

Help me, Lord, to be a blessing to everyone I meet this day. In Jesus' name, amen.

Going Deeper

Read It! Matthew 1:1–17 traces Jesus' family all the way back to Abraham and Isaac. Read these verses and see how many of the names you know.

Do It! Ask your parents about your family tree. How far back can you trace your family?

Did you know? Ishmael *means "God hears,"* and Isaac *means "he laughs."*[6]

God Tests Abraham

Genesis 22:1–3, 6–14

In the Bible, the wilderness is often a place of testing. In this story, Abraham's faith was tested when God asked him to go into the wilderness and sacrifice his only son, Isaac—the child God had promised Abraham long ago. Would Abraham's faith be strong enough to enable him to obey God?

After these things God tested Abraham's
faith. . . .
2Then God said, "Take your only son,
Isaac, the son you love. Go to the land of
Moriah. There kill him and offer him as a
whole burnt offering. Do this on one of the
mountains there. I will tell you which one."
3Early in the morning Abraham got up
and saddled his donkey. He took Isaac and
two servants with him. He cut the wood for
the sacrifice. Then they went to the place
God had told them to go. . . .
6Abraham took the wood for the sacrifice
and gave it to his son to carry. Abraham
took the knife and the fire. So Abraham
and his son went on together.
7Isaac said to his father Abraham, "Father!"
Abraham answered, "Yes, my son."
Isaac said, "We have the fire and the
wood. But where is the lamb we will burn
as a sacrifice?"
8Abraham answered, "God will give us
the lamb for the sacrifice, my son."
So Abraham and his son went on together. 9They came to the place God had
told him about. There, Abraham built an
altar. He laid the wood on it. Then he tied
up his son Isaac. And he laid Isaac on the
wood on the altar. 10Then Abraham took his
knife and was about to kill his son.
11But the angel of the Lord called to him
from heaven. The angel said, "Abraham!
Abraham! . . . 12Don't kill your son or hurt
him in any way. Now I can see that you respect God. I see that you have not kept your
son, your only son, from me."
13Then Abraham looked up and saw a
male sheep. Its horns were caught in a
bush. So Abraham went and took the sheep
and killed it. He offered it as a whole burnt
offering to God. Abraham's son was saved.
14So Abraham named that place The Lord
Gives. Even today people say, "On the
mountain of the Lord it will be given."

Let's Pray

I love you, Lord, because you listen to my prayers. You pay attention to me. So I will pray to you for as long as I live! In Jesus' name, amen.

—Adapted from Psalm 116:1–2

Going Deeper

Read It! Jesus was also tested in the wilderness. Read about it in Matthew 4:1–11.

Do It! Although Abraham didn't have to sacrifice his son Isaac, God did sacrifice his own Son, Jesus, to save us. God did this because he loves us so much. What small things can you sacrifice for your friends and family this week just because you love them?

Quote of the Day:
God never made a promise that was too good to be true.
—Dwight L. Moody

A Wife for Isaac

Genesis 24:12–20

Choosing a husband or a wife is one of the most important decisions in life, so it's important to pick someone who shares your faith! Abraham knew this too. When Isaac became old enough to marry, Abraham wanted his son to find a good woman who would love the one true God, just as Isaac had been taught to do. So Abraham sent his trusted servant back to his hometown to find just such a girl. When the servant reached Abraham's hometown, the first thing he did was pray.

The servant said, "Lord, you are the God of
my master Abraham. Allow me to find a wife
for his son today. Please show this kindness
to my master Abraham. 13Here I am, standing by the spring of water. The girls from the
city are coming out to get water. 14I will say
to one of the girls, 'Please put your jar down
so I can drink.' Then let her say, 'Drink, and
I will also give water to your camels.' If that
happens, I will know she is the right one for
your servant Isaac. And I will know that you
have shown kindness to my master."
15Before the servant had finished praying, Rebekah came out of the city. She
was the daughter of Bethuel. (Bethuel was
the son of Milcah and Nahor, Abraham's
brother.) Rebekah was carrying her water
jar on her shoulder. 16She was very pretty.
. . . She went down to the spring and filled
her jar. Then she came back up. 17The servant ran to her and said, "Please give me a
little water from your jar."
18Rebekah said, "Drink, sir." She quickly
lowered the jar from her shoulder and gave
him a drink. 19After he finished drinking,
Rebekah said, "I will also pour some water
for your camels." 20So she quickly poured
all the water from her jar into the drinking
trough for the camels. Then she kept running to the well until she had given all the
camels enough to drink.

Let's Pray

Lord, help me to always be as faithful as Abraham's servant and as generous as Rebekah. In Jesus' name, amen.

Going Deeper

Read It! Read the whole story of Rebekah in Genesis 24:52–67. Imagine how brave Rebekah must have been to leave her family and meet a husband she did not know!

Do It! Parents, pray with your children that each will be blessed with a godly husband or wife.

Did You Know? *Camels store fat in their humps. This fat breaks down into water and energy so that camels can travel up to one hundred desert miles without water. When they do drink, camels can drink up to thirty gallons of water in thirteen minutes!*[7]

Jacob and Esau

Genesis 25:21, 24, 27–34; 27:1–4, 15–19

Do you ever try to take something that belongs to your brother or sister? When Rebekah was pregnant, God told her, "Two nations are in your body" (Genesis 25:23). Jacob was born moments after Esau, clutching his older brother's heel. This struggle went on throughout their lives. In today's story, Jacob stole not only his brother's inheritance but their father's blessing as well!

Isaac's wife could not have children. So Isaac prayed to the Lord for her. The Lord heard Isaac's prayer, and Rebekah became pregnant. . . .

24And when the time came, Rebekah gave birth to twins. . . .

27When the boys grew up, Esau became a skilled hunter. He loved to be out in the fields. But Jacob was a quiet man. He stayed among the tents. 28Isaac loved Esau. Esau hunted the wild animals that Isaac enjoyed eating. But Rebekah loved Jacob.

29One day Jacob was boiling a pot of vegetable soup. Esau came in from hunting in the fields. He was weak from hunger. 30So Esau said to Jacob, "Let me eat some of that red soup. I am weak with hunger." (That is why people call him Edom.)

31But Jacob said, "You must sell me your rights as the firstborn son."

32Esau said, "I am almost dead from hunger. If I die, all of my father's wealth will not help me."

33But Jacob said, "First, promise me that you will give it to me." So Esau made a promise to Jacob. In this way he sold his part of their father's wealth to Jacob. 34Then Jacob gave Esau bread and vegetable soup. Esau ate and drank and then left. So Esau showed how little he cared about his rights as the firstborn son. . . .

27:1When Isaac was old, his eyes were not good. He could not see clearly. One day he called his older son Esau to him. Isaac said, "Son."

Esau answered, "Here I am."

2Isaac said, "I am old. I don't know when I might die. 3So take your bow and arrows, and go hunting in the field. Kill an animal for me to eat. 4Prepare the tasty food that I love. Bring it to me, and I will eat. Then I will bless you before I die." . . .

15[Rebekah] took the best clothes of her older son Esau that were in the house. She put them on the younger son Jacob. 16She took the skins of the goats. And she put them on Jacob's hands and neck. 17Then she gave Jacob the tasty food and the bread she had made.

18Jacob went in to his father and said, "Father."

And his father said, "Yes, my son. Who are you?"

Special Words:
A birthright *was the inheritance given to the oldest son after his father's death. It included most of the father's property as well as the title of head of the family.*[8]

19 Jacob said to him, "I am Esau, your first son. I have done what you told me. Now sit up and eat some meat of the animal I hunted for you. Then bless me."

Did You Know?
Esau's descendants were called the Edomites. They were enemies of Israel throughout history (2 Kings 8:20–22).

Let's Pray

Lord, you bless your children with such a wonderful inheritance—heaven! Thank you for loving me so! In Jesus' name, amen.

Going Deeper

Read It! When you become a Christian, God promises you an inheritance in heaven. Read about God's promise in 1 Peter 1:3–4.

Do It! Exodus 20:12 says to "honor your father and your mother." Did Jacob honor his father? Parents, share with your children how you honor your parents now and how you did so when you were a child. Children, how can you show honor to your mom and dad this week?

ALL THINGS BRIGHT AND BEAUTIFUL

All things bright and beautiful,
All creatures great and small,
All things wise and wonderful:
The Lord God made them all.

Each little flower that opens,
Each little bird that sings,
He made their glowing colors,
He made their tiny wings.

The purple-headed mountains,
The river running by,
The sunset and the morning
That brightens up the sky.

The cold wind in the winter,
The pleasant summer sun,
The ripe fruits in the garden;
He made them every one.

The tall trees in the greenwood,
The meadows where we play,
The rushes by the water,
To gather every day.

He gave us eyes to see them,
And lips that we might tell
How great is God Almighty,
Who has made all things well.

—Mrs. Cecil F. Alexander

Jacob and Rachel

Genesis 29:1–3, 16–28

Esau was furious with Jacob for stealing his birthright! He was so angry that he wanted to kill Jacob. To escape his brother's anger, Jacob ran away to his mother's family. While he was traveling there, he stopped at a well. There he met Rachel, his uncle's daughter. Jacob wanted to marry Rachel, but his uncle had other plans. In today's story, Jacob—the trickster—gets tricked!

Jacob continued his journey. He came to the land of the people of the East. 2He looked and saw a well in the field. Three flocks of sheep were lying nearby, because they drank water from this well. A large stone covered the mouth of the well. 3All the flocks would gather there. The shepherds would roll the stone away from the well and water the sheep. Then they would put the stone back in its place. . . .

16Now Laban had two daughters. The older was Leah, and the younger was Rachel. 17Leah had weak eyes, but Rachel was very beautiful. 18Jacob loved Rachel. So he said to Laban, "Let me marry your younger daughter Rachel. If you will, I will work seven years for you."

19Laban said, "It would be better for her to marry you than someone else. So stay here with me." 20So Jacob worked for Laban seven years so he could marry Rachel. But they seemed to him like just a few days. This was because he loved Rachel very much.

21After seven years Jacob said to Laban, "Give me Rachel so that I may marry her. The time I promised to work for you is over."

22So Laban gave a feast for all the people there. 23That evening Laban brought his daughter Leah to Jacob. . . . 24(Laban gave his slave girl Zilpah to his daughter to be her servant.) 25In the morning Jacob saw . . . Leah! He said to Laban, "What have you done to me? I worked hard for you so that I could marry Rachel! Why did you trick me?"

26Laban said, "In our country we do not allow the younger daughter to marry before the older daughter. 27But complete the full week of the marriage ceremony with Leah. I will give you Rachel to marry also. But you must serve me another seven years."

28So Jacob did this and completed the week with Leah. Then Laban gave him his daughter Rachel as a wife.

Let's Pray

The goodness of an innocent person
makes his life easier.
But a wicked person will be destroyed by
his wickedness.

—Proverbs 11:5

Lord, help me to always choose what is honest and good, and to run away from what is evil. In Jesus' name, amen.

Special Words:
In verse 17, weak
(rak *in Hebrew) could*
also be translated
ordinary.

Going Deeper

Read It! God did not intend for a man to have more than one wife. Read God's plan for marriage in Genesis 2:24 and Matthew 19:4–6.

Do It! Talk with your parents about some important things to look for in a spouse—things like faithfulness to God, kindness, and gentleness. What are your top five characteristics?

Jacob Wrestles with God

Genesis 32:1–8, 22–30

Angels are the messengers of God, and the Bible is full of stories about them. Jacob was especially blessed because he got to see angels twice! First, he dreamed of angels going up and down a ladder (Genesis 28:10–13). And in this story, he met angels a second time as he traveled with his family to make up with his brother, Esau. But most amazing of all is how Jacob spent a night wrestling with God!

When Jacob also went his way, the angels
of God met him. 2When Jacob saw them, he
said, "This is the camp of God!" So Jacob
named that place Mahanaim.

3Jacob's brother Esau was living in the
area called Seir in the country of Edom.
Jacob sent messengers to Esau. 4Jacob told
the messengers, "Give this message to my
master Esau: 'This is what Jacob, your servant, says: I have lived with Laban and have
remained there until now. 5I have cattle,
donkeys, flocks, and male and female servants. I send this message to you and ask
you to accept us.'"

6The messengers returned to Jacob and
said, "We went to your brother Esau. He is
coming to meet you. And he has 400 men
with him."

7Then Jacob was very afraid and worried. He divided the people who were with
him into two camps. He also divided all the
flocks, herds and camels into two camps.
8Jacob thought, "Esau might come and
destroy one camp. But the other camp can
run away and be saved." . . .

22During the night Jacob rose and crossed
the Jabbok River at the crossing. He took
his 2 wives, his 2 slave girls and his 11 sons
with him. 23He sent his family and everything he had across the river. 24But Jacob
stayed behind alone. And a man came
and wrestled with him until the sun came
up. 25The man saw that he could not defeat
Jacob. So he struck Jacob's hip and put it
out of joint. 26Then the man said to Jacob,
"Let me go. The sun is coming up."

But Jacob said, "I will let you go if you will
bless me."

27The man said to him, "What is your
name?"

And he answered, "Jacob."

28Then the man said, "Your name will
no longer be Jacob. Your name will now be
Israel, because you have wrestled with God
and with men. And you have won."

29Then Jacob asked him, "Please tell me
your name."

But the man said, "Why do you ask my
name?" Then he blessed Jacob there.

30So Jacob named that place Peniel. He
said, "I have seen God face to face. But my
life was saved."

Let's Pray

He has put his angels in charge of you.
They will watch over you wherever you go.

—Psalm 91:11

Dear Lord, thank you for creating angels to watch over me. In Jesus' name, amen.

Special Words: Israel *means "He strives with God."* Peniel *means "face of God."*[9]

GOING DEEPER

READ IT! God's angels were busy in the New Testament too! They tended to Jesus after Satan tempted him in the wilderness (Matthew 4:11), freed Peter from prison (Acts 12:6–11), and warned Paul of a shipwreck (Acts 27:23–24).

DO IT! Make angel cookies. As you eat them, talk about some of the other people in the Bible who met angels. Don't forget Mary and Joseph!

Joseph the Dreamer

Genesis 37:3–8, 12–13, 18–28

When you get something nice, like a birthday present, do you ever tease your brother or sister with it? Although Jacob (also called Israel) loved all his children, he loved Joseph best. Jacob gave Joseph a beautiful coat that was a sign to his older brothers of how important Joseph was to their dad. No wonder they hated their little brother! They hated him so much they decided to get rid of him . . . forever!

Joseph was born when his father Israel, also called Jacob, was old. So Israel loved Joseph more than his other sons. He made Joseph a special robe with long sleeves. 4Joseph's brothers saw that their father loved Joseph more than he loved them. So they hated their brother and could not speak to him politely.

5One time Joseph had a dream. When he told his brothers about it, they hated him even more. 6Joseph said, "Listen to the dream I had. 7We were in the field tying bundles of wheat together. My bundle stood up, and your bundles of wheat gathered around mine. Your bundles bowed down to mine."

8His brothers said, "Do you really think you will be king over us? Do you truly think you will rule over us?" His brothers hated him even more now. They hated him because of his dreams and what he had said. . . .

12One day Joseph's brothers went to Shechem to herd their father's sheep. 13Jacob said to Joseph, "Go to Shechem. Your brothers are there herding the sheep."

Joseph answered, "I will go." . . .

18Joseph's brothers saw him coming from far away. Before he reached them, they made a plan to kill him. 19They said to each other, "Here comes that dreamer. 20Let's kill him and throw his body into one of the wells. We can tell our father that a wild animal killed him. Then we will see what will become of his dreams."

21But Reuben heard their plan and saved Joseph. He said, "Let's not kill him. 22Don't spill any blood. Throw him into this well here in the desert. But don't hurt him!" Reuben planned to save Joseph later and send him back to his father. 23So when Joseph came to his brothers, they pulled off his robe with long sleeves. 24Then they threw him into the well. It was empty. There was no water in it.

25While Joseph was in the well, the brothers sat down to eat. When they looked up, they saw a group of Ishmaelites. They were

Quote of the Day: Content makes poor men rich; discontent makes rich men poor. —Benjamin Franklin

traveling from Gilead to Egypt. Their camels were carrying spices, balm and myrrh.
26Then Judah said to his brothers, "What will we gain if we kill our brother and hide his death?
27Let's sell him to these Ishmaelites. Then we will not be guilty of killing our own brother. After all, he is our brother, our own flesh and blood." And the other brothers agreed.
28So when the Midianite traders came by, the brothers took Joseph out of the well. They sold him to the Ishmaelites for eight ounces of silver. And the Ishmaelites took him to Egypt.

Let's Pray

When I am jealous of what others have, Lord, please help me remember all that I have. In Jesus' name, amen.

Going Deeper

Read It! Jesus warned about jealousy and other sins that come from inside a person's heart. Read about it in Mark 7:20–23.

Do It! Family movie night! Rent and watch together the movie *Joseph and the Amazing Technicolor Dreamcoat*.

Joseph and His Brothers

Genesis 41:46–49, 53–54; 42:1–8; 45:3–5

Have you ever gotten into trouble for something you didn't do? Was it hard to forgive those who got you into trouble? Joseph was betrayed—first by his brothers who sold him to slave traders bound for Egypt. And then his owner's wife betrayed him too, and he ended up in prison! Yet somehow Joseph never lost his trust in God, and God took care of Joseph. He even became the second most powerful man in all of Egypt! But what would Joseph do when he saw his brothers again?

Joseph was 30 years old when he began serving the king of Egypt. And he left the king's court and traveled through all the land of Egypt. 47During the seven good years, the crops in the land grew well. 48And Joseph gathered all the food produced in Egypt during those seven years of good crops. He stored the food in the cities. In every city he stored grain that had been grown in the fields around that city. 49Joseph stored much grain, as much as the sand of the seashore. He stored so much grain that he could not measure it. . . .

53The seven years of good crops came to an end in the land of Egypt. 54Then the seven years of hunger began, just as Joseph had said. In all the lands people had nothing to eat. But in Egypt there was food. . . .

42:1Jacob learned that there was grain in Egypt. So he said to his sons, "Why are you just sitting here looking at one another? 2I have heard that there is grain in Egypt. Go down there and buy grain for us to eat. Then we will live and not die."

3So ten of Joseph's brothers went down to buy grain from Egypt. 4But Jacob did not send Benjamin, Joseph's brother, with them. Jacob was afraid that something terrible might happen to Benjamin. 5Along with many other people, the sons of Jacob, also called Israel, went to Egypt to buy grain. This was because the people in the land of Canaan were hungry also.

6Now Joseph was governor over Egypt. He was the one who sold the grain to people who came to buy it. So Joseph's brothers came to him. They bowed facedown on the ground before him. 7When Joseph saw his brothers, he knew who they were. But he acted as if he didn't know them. He asked unkindly, "Where do you come from?"

They answered, "We have come from the land of Canaan to buy food."

8Joseph knew they were his brothers. But they did not know who he was. . . .

45:3He said to his brothers, "I am Joseph. Is my father still alive?" But the brothers could not answer him, because they were very afraid of him.

4So Joseph said to them, "Come close to me." So the brothers came close to him. And he said to them, "I am your brother Joseph. You sold me as a slave to go to Egypt. 5Now don't be worried. Don't be angry with yourselves because you sold me here. God sent me here ahead of you to save people's lives."

Let's Pray

God, be merciful to me
because you are loving.
Because you are always ready to be merciful,
wipe out all my wrongs.
Wash away all my guilt
and make me clean again.

—Psalm 51:1–2

Did You Know? Joseph named his firstborn son Manasseh, which means "causing to forget." Joseph's second son was named Ephraim, which means "doubly fruitful."[10]

Going Deeper

Read It! Jesus told us why it is so important to forgive others. Read about it in Matthew 6:14–15.

Do It! In Matthew 5:44, Jesus said to "love your enemies. Pray for those who hurt you." How do we see this happen in the story of Joseph and his brothers?

Baby in the Basket

Exodus 2:1–10

More than four hundred years ago, the first Americans settled in a colony at Jamestown, Virginia. Think of how much has changed since then! Four hundred years is a very long time, and that's how long the Hebrew people remained in Egypt. Over time, a new king who did not know Joseph came to power in Egypt. The Egyptians forced the Hebrews to become their slaves. But the numbers of the Hebrew people grew so large, the king worried that his slaves would rise up against him. So the king ordered that every Hebrew baby boy be killed. But God heard the cries of his people and had a plan to deliver them. And it all began with a baby in a basket!

There was a man from the family of Levi.
He married a woman who was also from the
family of Levi. 2She became pregnant and
gave birth to a son. She saw how wonderful the baby was, and she hid him for three
months. 3But after three months, she was
not able to hide the baby any longer. So she
got a basket made of reeds and covered it
with tar so that it would float. She put the
baby in the basket. Then she put the basket
among the tall grass at the edge of the Nile
River. 4The baby's sister stood a short distance away. She wanted to see what would
happen to him.

5Then the daughter of the king of Egypt
came to the river. She was going to take a
bath. Her servant girls were walking beside
the river. She saw the basket in the tall
grass. So she sent her slave girl to get it.
6The king's daughter opened the basket
and saw the baby boy. He was crying, and
she felt sorry for him. She said, "This is
one of the Hebrew babies."

7Then the baby's sister asked the king's
daughter, "Would you like me to find a
Hebrew woman to nurse the baby for you?"

8The king's daughter said, "Yes, please."
So the girl went and got the baby's own
mother.

9The king's daughter said to the woman,
"Take this baby and nurse him for me. I will
pay you." So the woman took her baby and
nursed him. 10After the child had grown
older, the woman took him to the king's
daughter. She adopted the baby as her
own son. The king's daughter named him
Moses, because she had pulled him out of
the water.

Let's Pray

Lord, you have been our home
  since the beginning.
Before the mountains were born,
  and before you created the earth and the
    world,
you are God.
  You have always been, and you will
    always be.

—Psalm 90:1–2

Because you are God, I will trust your plan for my life. In Jesus' name, amen.

SPECIAL WORDS: The king of Egypt was also called Pharaoh, which means "great house." The Levites—from the tribe of Levi—were the priests and the helpers for the priests of the Hebrew people."

GOING DEEPER

READ IT! Moses was adopted into the family of the king of Egypt. God adopts us into his family through Jesus. Read about it in Ephesians 1:4–6.

DO IT! Family Movie Night! Watch *Prince of Egypt* (for younger kids) or *The Ten Commandments* (for older kids and adults).

The Burning Bush

Exodus 3:1–8, 10

Did you ever do something wrong, then run away so you wouldn't get into trouble? As a young Egyptian prince, Moses became so angry with the way the Hebrew slaves were being treated that he killed an Egyptian slave master. When the king became angry, Moses ran away and started a new life in the wilderness as a shepherd. For forty years Moses tended his father-in-law's flocks in the wilderness of Sinai. Then one day, out on the mountain, Moses saw something amazing!

One day Moses was taking care of Jethro's sheep. Jethro was the priest of Midian and also Moses' father-in-law. Moses led the sheep to the west side of the desert. He came to Sinai, the mountain of God. [2]There the angel of the Lord appeared to Moses in flames of fire coming out of a bush. Moses saw that the bush was on fire, but it was not burning up. [3]So Moses said, "I will go closer to this strange thing. How can a bush continue burning without burning up?"

[4]The Lord saw Moses was coming to look at the bush. So God called to him from the bush, "Moses, Moses!"

And Moses said, "Here I am."

[5]Then God said, "Do not come any closer. Take off your sandals. You are standing on holy ground. [6]I am the God of your ancestors. I am the God of Abraham, the God of Isaac and the God of Jacob." Moses covered his face because he was afraid to look at God.

[7]The Lord said, "I have seen the troubles my people have suffered in Egypt. And I have heard their cries when the Egyptian slave masters hurt them. I am concerned about their pain. [8]I have come down to save them from the Egyptians. I will bring them out of that land. I will lead them to a good land with lots of room. This is a land where much food grows. This is the land of these people: the Canaanites, Hittites, Amorites, Perizzites, Hivites and Jebusites. . . . [10]So now I am sending you to the king of Egypt. Go! Bring my people, the Israelites, out of Egypt!"

Let's Pray

My whole being, praise the Lord.
  All my being, praise his holy name.
My whole being, praise the Lord.
  Do not forget all his kindnesses.

—Psalm 103:1–2

Lord, I praise you! In Jesus' name, amen.

Going Deeper

Read It! Moses spoke to God. In the New Testament, Jesus taught his disciples how to talk to God. Find out how in Matthew 6:5–15.

Do It! God wanted Moses to lead his people to the promised land. But first, God wanted him to stand up to the king of Egypt. How would learning to stand up for what is right help Moses when he became leader of the Hebrew people?

Did You Know?
Moses was eighty years old when God sent him from the desert and placed him before the king of Egypt. God can use you at any age if you will let him!

"Let My People Go!"

Exodus 10:21–29; 11:1–7

In this story, when Moses and his brother, Aaron, went before the king of Egypt, they had the power of God with them. Through these two men, God sent nine different warnings, from turning the Nile River to blood to covering the land in darkness. But the king's heart was hard; he would not let the Hebrew people go. So God sent the most terrible warning of all.

Then the Lord told Moses, "Raise your hand
toward the sky, and darkness will cover the
land of Egypt. It will be so dark you will be
able to feel it." 22So Moses raised his hand
toward the sky. Then total darkness was
everywhere in Egypt for three days. 23No
one could see anyone else. And no one
could go anywhere for three days. But the
Israelites had light where they lived.

24Again the king of Egypt called for
Moses. He said, "All of you may go and worship the Lord. You may take your women
and children with you. But you must leave
your sheep and cattle here."

25Moses said, "You must let us have animals to use as sacrifices and burnt offerings. We have to offer them to the Lord
our God. 26So we must take our animals
with us. Not a hoof will be left behind. We
have to use some of the animals to worship the Lord our God." . . .

27But the Lord made the king stubborn
again. So he refused to let them go. 28Then
he told Moses, "Get out of here! Don't come
here again! The next time you see me, you
will die."

29Then Moses told the king, "I'll do what
you say. I will not come to see you again."

11:1Now the Lord had told Moses, "I have
one more way to punish the king and the
people of Egypt. After this, the king will send
all of you away from Egypt. When he does,
he will force you to leave completely. 2Tell
the men and women of Israel to ask their
neighbors for things made of silver and
gold." 3The Lord had caused the Egyptians
to respect the Israelites. The king's officers
and the Egyptian people already considered
Moses to be a great man.

4So Moses said to the king, "This is what
the Lord says: 'About midnight tonight I
will go through all Egypt. 5Every firstborn
son in the land of Egypt will die. The firstborn son of the king, who sits on his throne,
will die. Even the firstborn of the slave girl
grinding grain will die. Also the firstborn
farm animals will die. 6There will be loud
crying everywhere in Egypt. It will be worse
than any time before or after this. 7But not
even a dog will bark at the Israelites or their
animals.' Then you will know that the Lord
treats Israel differently from Egypt."

Let's Pray

But let everyone who trusts you be happy.
  Let them sing glad songs forever.
Protect those who love you.
  They are happy because of you.
Lord, you bless those who do what is right.
  You protect them like a soldier's shield.

—Psalm 5:11–12

Did You Know?
The Bible says that about 600,000 men left Egypt during the Exodus. If women and children are added, then all together about 2,500,000 Hebrews followed Moses out of Egypt.[12]

Going Deeper

Read It! Did you know that Moses talked to Jesus in the New Testament? Read about it in Matthew 17:1–3.

Do It! God took the children of Israel on a great adventure. Plan an adventure with your family—a backyard scavenger hunt, a day in the park, or even a family vacation.

Passover

Exodus 12:21–32

Nine times Moses said to the king of Egypt, "Let my people go!" Each time the king refused. So God sent the final, most terrible plague, and the firstborn son of each Egyptian family died. But the Hebrew children were safe. They had followed Moses' special instructions so that the Lord knew to "pass over" their homes.

Then Moses called all the elders of Israel together. He told them, "Get the animals for your families. Kill the animals for the Passover. [22]Take a branch of the hyssop plant and dip it into the bowl filled with blood. Wipe the blood on the sides and tops of the doorframes. No one may leave his house until morning. [23]The Lord will go through Egypt to kill the Egyptians. He will see the blood on the sides and tops of the doorframes. Then the Lord will pass over that house. He will not let the one who brings death come into your houses and kill you.

[24]"You must keep this command. This law is for you and your descendants from now on. [25]Do this when you go to the land the Lord has promised to give to you. [26]When your children ask you, 'Why are we doing these things?' [27]you will say, 'This is the Passover sacrifice to honor the Lord. When we were in Egypt, the Lord passed over the houses of Israel. The Lord killed the Egyptians, but he saved our homes.'" So now the people bowed down and worshiped the Lord. [28]They did just as the Lord commanded Moses and Aaron.

[29]At midnight the Lord killed all the firstborn sons in the land of Egypt. The firstborn of the king, who sat on the throne, died. Even the firstborn of the prisoner in jail died. Also all the firstborn farm animals died. [30]The king, his officers and all the Egyptians got up during the night. Someone had died in every house. So there was loud crying everywhere in Egypt.

[31]During the night the king called for Moses and Aaron. He said to them, "Get up and leave my people. You and your people may do as you have asked. Go and worship the Lord. [32]Take all of your sheep and cattle as you have asked. Go. And also bless me."

Let's Pray

Thank you, Lord, for blessing me with your love and protection. In Jesus' name, amen.

Did You Know?
Passover is still celebrated by Jewish families in honor of when God "passed over" the Hebrew families in Egypt. It is a seven-day feast during Nisan (the first month in the Jewish calendar), which is around March and April.

Going Deeper

Read It! Did you know that the Passover meal was Jesus' last meal before he went to the cross? Read about it in Matthew 26:17–35.

Do It! Have lamb chops and matzo bread for dinner tonight! This is what Jewish families eat when they celebrate Passover. You can find recipes for these dishes and others online.

Miracle by the Sea

Exodus 14:5–8, 9–10, 13–18, 21–22, 26–28

Have you ever seen a body of water that was so big you couldn't see from one side to the other? The Israelites needed to cross just such a body of water—and fast! After they left Egypt, the king of Egypt changed his mind about letting them go. He wanted his slaves back and sent his army after them! The Israelites found themselves trapped between the Red Sea and the Egyptian army. How would they ever escape?

The king of Egypt was told that the people of Israel had already left. Then he and his officers changed their minds about them. They said, "What have we done? We have let the people of Israel leave. We have lost our slaves!" 6So the king prepared his war chariot and took his army with him.

7He took 600 of his best chariots. He also took all the other chariots of Egypt. . . . And they chased the Israelites. They caught up with the Israelites while they were camped by the Red Sea. . . .

10The Israelites saw the king and his army coming after them. They were very frightened and cried to the Lord for help. . . .

13But Moses answered, "Don't be afraid! Stand still and see the Lord save you today. You will never see these Egyptians again after today. 14You will only need to remain calm. The Lord will fight for you."

15Then the Lord said to Moses, "Why are you crying out to me? Command the people of Israel to start moving. 16Raise your walking stick and hold it over the sea. The sea will split. Then the people can cross the sea on dry land. 17I have made the Egyptians stubborn so they will chase the Israelites. But I will be honored when I defeat the king and all of his chariot drivers and chariots. . . . 18Then Egypt will know that I am the Lord." . . .

21Moses held his hand over the sea. All that night the Lord drove back the sea with a strong east wind. And so he made the sea become dry ground. The water was split. 22And the Israelites went through the sea on dry land. A wall of water was on both sides. . . .

26Then the Lord told Moses, "Hold your hand over the sea. Then the water will come back over the Egyptians, their chariots and chariot drivers." 27So Moses raised his hand over the sea. And at dawn the water became deep again. The Egyptians were trying to run from it. But the Lord swept them away into the sea. . . . 28Not one of them survived.

Let's Pray

The Lord gives me strength and makes me sing.
He has saved me.
He is my God,
and I will honor him.

—Exodus 15:2

Going Deeper

Read It! God also parted the waters of the Jordan River—three times! Read about it in Joshua 3:14–17; 2 Kings 2:8; and 2 Kings 2:13–14.

Do It! The parting of the Red Sea was a huge miracle, but even today God performs miracles all around us. What miracles do you see in the world around you?

Bread from Heaven

Exodus 16:1–8, 13–15

Think of a time when you were very hungry and couldn't wait for dinner. Now imagine that when suppertime came, there wasn't anything to eat. When this happened to the Israelites, God gave them food in a most unusual way!

Then the whole Israelite community left
Elim. They came to the Desert of Sin. This
place was between Elim and Sinai. They
came to this place on the fifteenth day of
the second month after they had left Egypt.
2Then the whole Israelite community
grumbled to Moses and Aaron in the desert. 3The Israelites said to them, "It would
have been better if the Lord had killed us in
the land of Egypt. There we had meat to eat.
We had all the food we wanted. But you have
brought us into this desert. You will starve
us to death here."

4Then the Lord said to Moses, "I will
cause food to fall like rain from the sky.
This food will be for all of you. Every day
the people must go out and gather what they
need for that day. I will do this to see if the
people will do what I teach them. 5On the
sixth day of each week, they are to gather
twice as much as they gather on other days.
Then they are to prepare it."

6So Moses and Aaron said to all the
Israelites: "This evening you will know
that the Lord is the one who brought you
out of Egypt. 7Tomorrow morning you will
see the greatness of the Lord. He has heard
you grumble against him. We are nothing. You are not grumbling against us, but
against the Lord." 8And Moses said, "Each
evening the Lord will give you meat to eat.
And every morning he will give you all the
bread you want. He will do this because he
has heard you grumble against him. You are
not grumbling against Aaron and me. You
are grumbling against the Lord." . . .

13That evening, quail came and covered the camp. And in the morning dew
lay around the camp. 14When the dew was
gone, thin flakes like frost were on the desert ground. 15When the Israelites saw it,
they asked each other, "What is that?" They
asked this question because they did not
know what it was.

So Moses told them, "This is the bread the Lord has given you to eat."

Let's Pray

Bless me, O Lord,
and let my food
strengthen me to serve thee,
for Jesus Christ's sake.
Amen.

—*The New England Primer*

Did You Know? Manna resembled coriander seed and tasted like honey (Exodus 16:31). Look in the pantry or at the grocery store to see what coriander seed looks like.

Going Deeper

Read It! Jesus told us that he is the true Bread of Life. Read about it in John 6:30–35.

Do It! Don't forget your "daily bread." Read something from God's Word every day.

Water in the Desert

Exodus 17:1–6

When you get thirsty during a long trip, do you get cranky? The Israelites did! No sooner had God provided the food they needed than they began to complain again. "Give us water," they demanded. And once again God answered their prayers.

The whole Israelite community left the Desert of Sin. They traveled from place to place as the Lord commanded. They camped at Rephidim. But there was no water there for the people to drink. [2]So they quarreled with Moses. They said, "Give us water to drink."

But Moses said to them, "Why do you quarrel with me? Why are you testing the Lord?"

[3]But the people were very thirsty for water. So they grumbled against Moses. They said, "Why did you bring us out of Egypt? Was it to kill us, our children and our farm animals with thirst?"

[4]So Moses cried to the Lord, "What can I do with these people? They are almost ready to kill me with stones."

[5]The Lord said to Moses, "Go ahead of the people of Israel. And take some of the elders of Israel with you. Carry with you the walking stick that you used to strike the Nile River. Now go! [6]I will stand in front of you on a rock at Mount Sinai. Hit that rock with the stick, and water will come out of it. Then the people can drink." Moses did these things as the elders of Israel watched.

Let's Pray

I love you, Lord. You are my strength.
The Lord is my rock, my protection, my
Savior.
My God is my rock.
I can run to him for safety.
He is my shield and my saving strength,
my high tower.
I will call to the Lord.
He is worthy of praise.

—Psalm 18:1–3

Going Deeper

Read It! Jesus is our living water. Read about it in John 7:37–39.

Do It! On a hot summer day, open up a lemonade stand as a family. But instead of asking for money, share your lemonade for free.

Did You Know?
In the book of Numbers, we learn that Moses performed another "water miracle" and angered God. Read Numbers 20:1–13 to find out why God was so angry.

God Gives the Law

Exodus 19:16–19; 20:1–4, 7–17

Moses led the Israelites toward the promised land. For hundreds of years they had been under the rule of the king of Egypt. But now God was calling them to be his people, and he wanted them to follow his rules. These rules were called the Ten Commandments.

It was the morning of the third day. There
was thunder and lightning with a thick
cloud on the mountain. And there was a
very loud blast from a trumpet. All the
people in the camp were frightened. [17]Then
Moses led the people out of the camp to
meet God. They stood at the foot of the
mountain. [18]Mount Sinai was covered with
smoke. This happened because the Lord
came down on it in fire. The smoke rose
from the mountain like smoke from a
furnace. And the whole mountain shook
wildly. [19]The sound from the trumpet
became louder. Then Moses spoke, and the
voice of God answered him. . . .

[20:1]Then God spoke all these words: [2]"I
am the Lord your God. I brought you out of
the land of Egypt where you were slaves.

[3]"You must not have any other gods
except me.

[4]"You must not make for yourselves any
idols. . . .

[7]"You must not use the name of the Lord
your God thoughtlessly. The Lord will punish
anyone who is guilty and misuses his name.

[8]"Remember to keep the Sabbath as a
holy day. [9]You may work and get everything
done during six days each week. [10]But the
seventh day is a day of rest to honor the
Lord your God. On that day no one may do
any work. . . .

[11]"The reason is that in six days the Lord
made everything. He made the sky, earth,
sea and everything in them. And on the seventh day, he rested. So the Lord blessed the
Sabbath day and made it holy.

[12]"Honor your father and your mother.
Then you will live a long time in the land. The
Lord your God is going to give you this land.

[13]"You must not murder anyone.

[14]"You must not be guilty of adultery.

[15]"You must not steal.

[16]"You must not tell lies about your
neighbor in court.

[17]"You must not want to take your neighbor's house. You must not want his wife or his
men or women slaves. You must not want his
ox or his donkey. You must not want to take
anything that belongs to your neighbor."

Let's Pray

My God, I want to do what you want.
Your teachings are in my heart.
—Psalm 40:8

Quote of the Day:
Children, obey your parents the way the Lord wants. This is the right thing to do.
—Ephesians 6:1

GOING DEEPER

READ IT! Jesus said that all the laws of the Old Testament could be summed up in just two commandments. Find out what they are in Matthew 22:37–40.

DO IT! Make a poster of the Ten Commandments to help you remember to obey them.

Heavenly Father, hear my prayer:
Night and day I'm in your care;
Look upon me from above,
Bless the home I dearly love;
Bless the friends with whom I play,
Make us kinder day by day.

—Unknown

A Place to Worship

Exodus 25:1–22

The Israelites needed a place to worship God, but they were still traveling in the wilderness. So God told the Israelites to build a Holy Tent, a place of worship they could take along with them. Only the most beautiful and expensive materials were used to create this movable house of God. Inside it was kept the Holy Box of Agreement, which contained the tablets of the Ten Commandments.

The Lord said to Moses, 2"Tell the Israelites
to bring me gifts. Receive for me the gifts
each man wants to give. 3These are the
gifts that you should receive from them:
gold, silver, bronze, 4blue, purple and red
thread, and fine linen. Receive cloth made
of goat hair. 5Receive the male sheep skins
that are dyed red. Receive fine leather, acacia wood 6and olive oil to burn in the lamps.
And receive spices for sweet-smelling
incense and the special olive oil poured on
a person's head to make him a priest. 7Also
accept onyx stones and other jewels to be
put on the holy vest and the chest covering.

8"The people must build a holy place for
me. Then I can live among them. 9Build
this Holy Tent and everything in it by the
plan I will show you.

10"Use acacia wood and build a Holy Box.
It must be 45 inches long, 27 inches wide
and 27 inches high. 11Cover the Holy Box
inside and out with pure gold. And put a
gold strip all around it. 12Make four gold
rings for the Holy Box. Attach the gold
rings to its four feet, two rings on each
side. 13Then make poles from acacia wood
and cover them with gold. 14Put the poles
through the rings on the sides of the Box.
Use these poles to carry the Holy Box.
15These poles must always stay in the rings
of the Holy Box. Do not take the poles out.
16Then put the two flat stones in the Holy
Box. I will give you these stones on which
the commands are written.

17"Then make a lid of pure gold for the
Holy Box. This lid is the mercy seat. Make it
45 inches long and 27 inches wide. 18Then
hammer gold to make two creatures with
wings. Put one on each end of the lid. 19Put
one creature with wings on one end of the
lid. And put the other creature with wings
on the other end. Attach the creatures with
wings to the lid so that they will all be one
piece. 20The creatures' wings should be
spread out over the lid. The creatures are to
face each other across the lid. 21Put this lid
on top of the Holy Box. Also put in this Holy
Box the agreement which I will make with
you. 22I will meet with you there, above the
lid between the two creatures with wings.
These are on the Box of the Agreement.
There I will give you all my commands for
the Israelites."

Did You Know?
The Holy Box of Agreement is also called the ark of the covenant. Later, a jar of manna and Aaron's staff were also put inside (Hebrews 9:4).

Let's Pray

Lord, just as you gave the Israelites a Holy Tent, you have given us your Holy Spirit. Thank you that, no matter where I go, your Presence is always with me. In Jesus' name, amen.

Going Deeper

READ IT! When Jesus came, he took away the need for a specific place to worship. See what Jesus said in John 4:21–24 about how we should worship.

DO IT! As a family, do something special for your church. Help put up a bulletin board, plant flowers, or tidy up the pews.

The Golden Calf

Exodus 32:1–7, 15–16, 19, 25–26, 35

Do you ever forget to talk to God before you go to sleep at night? Are there times when you complain about going to church? When we forget to put God first in our lives, when we forget the blessings he gives us every day, other things become like gods to us. In this story, that's exactly what happened to the children of Israel—they bowed down to other gods!

The people saw that a long time had passed.
And Moses had not come down from the
mountain. So they gathered around Aaron.
They said to him, "Moses led us out of Egypt.
But we don't know what has happened to
him. So make us gods who will lead us."
2 Aaron said to the people, "Take off the gold
earrings that your wives, sons and daughters
are wearing. Bring them to me." 3 So all the
people took their gold earrings and brought
them to Aaron. 4 Aaron took the gold from the
people. Then he melted it and made a statue
of a calf. He finished it with a tool. Then the
people said, "Israel! These are your gods who
brought you out of the land of Egypt!"
5 Aaron saw all this, and he built an
altar before the calf. Then he made an
announcement. He said, "Tomorrow there
will be a special feast to honor the Lord."
6 The people got up early the next morning.
They offered whole burnt offerings and
fellowship offerings. First the people sat
down to eat and drink. . . .
7 And the Lord said to Moses, "Go down
from this mountain. Your people, the people you brought out of the land of Egypt,
have done a terrible sin." . . .
15 Then Moses went down the mountain. In
his hands he had the two stone tablets with
the agreement on them. . . . 16 God himself
had made the stones. And God himself had
written the commands on the stones. . . .
19 When Moses came close to the camp,
he saw the gold calf and the dancing.
He became very angry. He threw down
the stone tablets which he was carrying. He broke them at the bottom of the
mountain. . . .
25 Moses saw that the people were acting
wildly. He saw that Aaron had let them get
out of control. Their enemies would laugh
at them. 26 So Moses stood at the entrance to
the camp. He said, "Let anyone who wants
to follow the Lord come to me." And all the
people from the family of Levi gathered
around Moses. . . .
35 So the Lord caused terrible things to
happen to the people. He did this because of
what they did with the calf Aaron had made.

Let's Pray

Take away my sin, and I will be clean.
  Wash me, and I will be whiter than
    snow. . . .
Turn your face from my sins.
  Wipe out all my guilt.
Create in me a pure heart, God.
  Make my spirit right again.

—Psalm 51:7, 9–10

Going Deeper

Read It! The New Testament also warns us to stay away from idols. Read 1 John 5:21.

Do It! Even good things can become idols if you put them before God. What kinds of things could become idols for you and take you away from God? Could it be friends or computers or ball games?

Don't forget to take time for God. Turn off the television, the computer, and the music. Spend some time praying and singing praises to your Lord.

Quote of the Day:
As long as you want anything very much, especially more than you want God, it is an idol.
—A. B. Simpson

Snakes in the Desert

Numbers 21:4–9

Many years after the golden calf, when Moses was 120 years old, the people were tired of wandering around in the desert. Once again they grumbled at God. Instead of being grateful for the food God gave them, they complained—and they made God very angry!

The Israelites left Mount Hor and went on the road toward the Gulf of Aqaba. They did this to go around the country of Edom. But the people became impatient on the way.
5They grumbled at God and Moses. They said, "Why did you bring us out of Egypt? We will die in this desert! There is no bread! There is no water! And we hate this terrible food!"
6So the Lord sent them poisonous snakes. They bit the people, and many of the Israelites died.
7The people came to Moses and said, "We sinned when we grumbled at you and the Lord. Pray that the Lord will take away these snakes." So Moses prayed for the people.
8The Lord said to Moses, "Make a bronze snake. And put it on a pole. If anyone is bitten, he should look at it. Then he will live."
9So Moses made a bronze snake. And he put it on a pole. Then when a snake bit anyone, he looked at the bronze snake and lived.

Let's Pray

Protect me, God,
because I trust in you.
I said to the Lord, "You are my Lord.
Every good thing I have comes from
you."

—Psalm 16:1–2

God, please help me to trust you, both in good times and in bad. In Jesus' name, amen.

Going Deeper

READ IT! Just as the snake was lifted up to save the Israelites, Jesus was lifted up to save us. Read about it in John 3:14–15.

DO IT! Say a prayer for someone who needs God's healing touch today.

Special Words: *The caduceus, is a symbol that shows two snakes curled around a staff. This symbol is often worn by doctors and other medical workers.*

Did You Know?
The Israelites saved the bronze snake and hundreds of years later made it an idol! It was destroyed by King Hezekiah in 715 BC (2 Kings 18:4).

Moses Sees the Promised Land

Deuteronomy 32:48–52; 34:1, 4–7

Some mistakes we make have big consequences. Because Moses disobeyed God, he would never be allowed to enter the promised land. But the Lord showed mercy to Moses. God took him high up on a mountain so he could see the land God had promised to give the Israelites, his chosen people.

The Lord spoke to Moses again that same day. He said, 49"Go up the Abarim Mountains. Go to Mount Nebo in the country of Moab. It is across from Jericho. Look at the land of Canaan. I am giving it to the Israelites to own. 50You will die on that mountain that you climb. This is how your brother Aaron died on Mount Hor. 51You both sinned against me at the waters of Meribah Kadesh. That is in the Desert of Zin. You did not honor me as holy there among the Israelites. 52So now you will only look at the land from far away. You will not enter the land I am giving the people of Israel." . . .

34:1Then Moses climbed up Mount Nebo. He went from the plains of Moab to the top of Mount Pisgah. It is across from Jericho. From there the Lord showed him all the land. He could see from Gilead to Dan. . . . 4Then the Lord said to Moses, "This is the land I promised to Abraham, Isaac and Jacob. I said to them, 'I will give this land to your descendants.' I have let you look at it, Moses. But you will not cross over there."

5Then Moses, the servant of the Lord, died there in Moab. It was as the Lord had said. 6The Lord buried Moses in Moab in the valley opposite Beth Peor. But even today no one knows where his grave is. 7Moses was 120 years old when he died. His eyes were not weak. And he was still strong.

Let's Pray

Praise God because he is great!
He is like a rock. What he does is perfect.
He is always fair.
He is a faithful God who does no wrong.

—Deuteronomy 32:3–4

I praise you, Almighty God! No one is greater than you! In Jesus' name, amen.

Going Deeper

Read It! Heaven is our promised land. And Jesus has gone to prepare a place for us there. Read about it in John 14:1–3.

Do It! Luke 12:40 tells us that we won't know exactly when Jesus is coming back, so we need to be ready for his return at any time. How would you live if you knew Jesus was coming back today?

Special Words: Mount Nebo is the highest peak of Mount Pisgah. This is where Moses viewed the promised land. It is eight miles east of the mouth of the Jordan River, near the Dead Sea.[13]

Rahab Believes

Joshua 2:1, 3–9, 12–14

After Moses died, Joshua sent spies ahead of the Israelites to scout out Canaan. One woman, Rahab, risked her life to keep them safe. She was a nobody in the city of Jericho, but she had faith in the one true God—and she and her family would be saved because of it!

Joshua son of Nun secretly sent out two spies from Acacia. Joshua said to them, "Go and look at the land. Look closely at the city of Jericho."

So the men went to Jericho. They went to the house of a prostitute and stayed there. This woman's name was Rahab. . . .

3So the king of Jericho sent this message to Rahab: "Bring out the men who came to you and entered your house. They have come to spy out our whole land."

4Now the woman had hidden the two men. She said, "They did come here. But I didn't know where they came from. 5In the evening, when it was time to close the city gate, they left. I don't know where they went. Go quickly. Maybe you can catch them." 6(But the woman had taken the men up to the roof. She had hidden them there under stalks of flax. She had spread the flax out there to dry.) 7So the king's men went out looking for the spies from Israel. . . .

8The spies were ready to sleep for the night. So Rahab went to the roof and talked to them. 9She said, "I know the Lord has given this land to your people. You frighten us very much. Everyone living in this land is terribly afraid of you. . . . 12So now, make me a promise before the Lord. Promise that you will show kindness to my family just as I showed you kindness. Give me some proof that you will do this. 13Promise me you will allow my family to live. Save my father, mother, brothers, sisters and all of their families from death."

14The men agreed. They said, "We will trade our lives for your lives. Don't tell anyone what we are doing. When the Lord gives us our land, we will be kind to you. You may trust us."

Let's Pray

When I am afraid,
I will trust you.

—Psalm 56:3

Going Deeper

Read It! Rahab is listed as one of the heroes of faith in the New Testament. Read about her in Hebrews 11:31.

Do It! Movie night! Watch *The Hiding Place* or *The Diary of Anne Frank* and talk about the bravery of those who helped the Jews. What would you have done? (Parents, note that these movies deal with serious themes that may not be appropriate for young children.)

Did You Know? Archaeologists discovered that Jericho had an inner and outer wall. Houses—like Rahab's—were built between them.[14]

Miracle at the Jordan

Joshua 3:5–8, 14–17

For forty years, the Israelites wandered in the wilderness. This wandering was God's punishment to them for worshiping the golden calf idol. In today's story, their wanderings are over at last. They are about to go into the promised land. But first they must cross the Jordan River.

Then Joshua told the people, "Make yourselves holy for the Lord. Tomorrow the Lord will do amazing things among you."

[6]Joshua said to the priests, "Take the Box of the Agreement. Cross over the river ahead of the people." So the priests lifted the Holy Box and carried it ahead of the people.

[7]Then the Lord said to Joshua, "Today I will begin to make you a great man to all the Israelites. So the people will know I am with you just as I was with Moses. [8]The priests will carry the Box of the Agreement. Tell them this: 'Go to the edge of the Jordan River and stand in the water.'" . . .

[14]So the priests carried the Box of the Agreement. And the people left the place where they had camped. Then they started across the Jordan River. [15]During harvest the Jordan is flooded. So the river was at its fullest. The priests who were carrying the Holy Box came to the edge of the river. And they stepped into the water. [16]Just at that moment, the water stopped flowing. It stood up in a heap a great distance away at Adam. This is a town near Zarethan. The water flowing down to the Sea of Arabah (the Dead Sea) was completely cut off. So the people crossed the river near Jericho. [17]The ground there became dry. The priests carried the Box of the Agreement with the Lord to the middle of the river and stopped. They waited there while all the people of Israel walked across. They crossed the Jordan River on dry land.

Let's Pray

O may this bounteous God
  through all our life be near us,
With ever joyful hearts
  and blessèd peace to cheer us;
And keep us in His grace,
  and guide us when perplexed;
And free us from all ills,
  in this world and the next!

—Martin Rinkart

Going Deeper

Read It! God created the Jordan River, so he can control it. In the New Testament, Jesus showed that he is God's Son by controlling the wind and waves. Read about it in Mark 4:35–41.

Do It! The first thing God commanded the Israelites to do before beginning their march around Jericho was, "Make yourselves holy (verse 6)." What can you do to make yourself holy today?

Victory at Jericho

Joshua 6:8–12, 14–16, 20

Remember how, when you were little, you'd build a tower of blocks, then knock them to the ground? In this story, the Israelites prepared to attack the mighty city of Jericho. God had a plan, but it was unlike any other battle plan ever fought! Would the Israelites follow it?

So Joshua finished speaking to the people.
Then the seven priests began marching
before the Lord. They carried the seven
trumpets and blew them as they marched.
The priests carrying the Box of the
Agreement with the Lord followed them.
9The soldiers with weapons marched in
front of the priests. And armed men walked
behind the Holy Box. They were blowing
their trumpets. 10But Joshua had told the
people not to give a war cry. He said, "Don't
shout. Don't say a word until the day I tell
you. Then shout!" 11So Joshua had the Holy
Box of the Lord carried around the city one
time. Then they went back to camp for the
night.

12Early the next morning Joshua got up.
And the priests carried the Holy Box of the
Lord again. . . . 14So on the second day they
marched around the city one time. Then
they went back to camp. They did this every
day for six days.

15On the seventh day they got up at dawn.
They marched around the city seven times.
They marched just as they had on the days
before. But on that day they marched around
the city seven times. 16The seventh time
around the priests blew their trumpets.
Then Joshua gave the command: "Now,
shout! The Lord has given you this city!" . . .

20When the priests blew the trumpets, the
people shouted. At the sound of the trumpets and the people's shout, the walls fell.
And everyone ran straight into the city. So
the Israelites defeated that city.

Let's Pray

Praise the Lord! . . .
Praise him with trumpet blasts.
  Praise him with harps and lyres.
Praise him with tambourines and dancing.
  Praise him with stringed instruments
    and flutes.
Praise him with loud cymbals.
  Praise him with crashing cymbals.
Let everything that breathes praise the
    Lord.
Praise the Lord!

—Psalm 150:1, 3–6

Going Deeper

Read It! When Jericho fell, Joshua kept Rahab and her family safe just as the spies had promised (Joshua 6:22–25). However, Joshua did curse anyone who tried to rebuild the city. This curse was later fulfilled in 1 Kings 16:34.

Do It! Build a tower of blocks and act out the story of the march around Jericho.

Did You Know? Joshua *means "The Lord is salvation."*[15]

Whom Will You Serve?

Joshua 24:1–5, 13–15

You have to make choices every day—what to have for lunch, what to do, what to read. Some choices are more important than others. One of the most important choices you will ever make is whether or not to serve God. Choosing God will not only make a difference in this life but for all of eternity. Joshua and the Israelites had to make this choice. What did they choose?

Then all the tribes of Israel met together at Shechem. Joshua called them all together there. Then he called the elders, heads of families, judges and officers of Israel. These men stood before God.

2Then Joshua spoke to all the people.
He said, "Here's what the Lord, the God of Israel, says to you: 'A long time ago your ancestors lived on the other side of the Euphrates River. I am talking about men like Terah, the father of Abraham and Nahor.
They worshiped other gods. 3But I, the
Lord, took your ancestor Abraham out of the land on the other side of the river. I led him through the land of Canaan. And I gave him many children. I gave him his son Isaac.
4And I gave Isaac two sons named Jacob and Esau. I gave the land around the mountains of Edom to Esau. But Jacob and his sons went
down to Egypt. 5Then I sent Moses and Aaron
to Egypt. I caused many terrible things to happen to the Egyptians. Then I brought you people out. . . .

13"It was I, the Lord, who gave you that land. I gave you land where you did not have to work. I gave you cities that you did not have to build. And now you live in that land and in those cities. You eat from vineyards and olive trees. But you did not have to plant them.'"

14Then Joshua spoke to the people. He said, "Now you have heard the Lord's words. So you must respect the Lord and serve him fully and sincerely. Throw away the false gods that your people worshiped. That happened on the other side of the Euphrates River and in Egypt. Now you
must serve the Lord. 15But maybe you don't
want to serve the Lord. You must choose for yourselves today. You must decide whom you will serve. You may serve the gods that your people worshiped when they lived on the other side of the Euphrates River. Or you may serve the gods of the Amorites who lived in this land. As for me and my family, we will serve the Lord."

Let's Pray

Tell the greatness of the Lord with me.
Let us praise his name together.

—Psalm 34:3

Lord, there is none greater than you. I praise your name this day and every day! In Jesus' name, amen.

Quote of the Day:
"You must worship the Lord your God. Serve only him!"
—Jesus, in Matthew 4:10

Going Deeper

Read It! Jesus asked his disciples to choose also. Would they follow Jesus, or would they leave him? Find out in John 6:60–69.

Do It! Make your own reminder of your choice to serve God. Make a sign from paper, poster board, or even wood. Write on it, "As for me and my family, we will serve the Lord" (Joshua 24:15).

Deborah the Prophetess

Judges 4:1–10, 23

After Joshua's death, the Israelites were led by judges. Most of these judges were military heroes and other wise men. But one of them was a prophetess—a woman—who helped deliver her people from foreign armies.

The people of Israel again did what the Lord said was wrong. [2]So he let Jabin, a king of Canaan, defeat Israel. Jabin ruled in the city of Hazor. Sisera was the commander of Jabin's army. Sisera lived in Harosheth Haggoyim. [3]He had 900 iron chariots and was very cruel to the people of Israel for 20 years. So they cried to the Lord for help.

[4]There was a prophetess named Deborah. She was the wife of Lappidoth. She was judge of Israel at that time. [5]Deborah would sit under the Palm Tree of Deborah. This was between the cities of Ramah and Bethel, in the mountains of Ephraim. And the people of Israel would come to her to settle their arguments.

[6]Deborah sent a message to a man named Barak. . . . Deborah said to Barak, "The Lord, the God of Israel, commands you: 'Go and gather 10,000 men of Naphtali and Zebulun. Lead them to Mount Tabor. [7]I will make Sisera, the commander of Jabin's army, come to you. Sisera, his chariots and his army will meet you at the Kishon River. I will help you to defeat Sisera there.'"

[8]Then Barak said to Deborah, "I will go if you will go with me. But if you will not go with me, I won't go."

[9]"Of course I will go with you," Deborah answered. "But you will not get credit for the victory. The Lord will let a woman defeat Sisera." So Deborah went with Barak to Kedesh. [10]At Kedesh, Barak called the people of Zebulun and Naphtali together. From them, he gathered 10,000 men to follow him. Deborah went with Barak also. . . .

[23]On that day God defeated Jabin king of Canaan in the sight of Israel.

Let's Pray

Thank you, God, for creating holy heroes, men and women with the strength and wisdom to do your will. Help me, God, to be a holy hero too. In Jesus' name, amen.

Going Deeper

DO IT! Just as Deborah encouraged the warriors, send an encouraging note to a soldier in your church or community.

Did You Know?

Although Joshua had conquered the Canaanites, they were not completely driven out, as God had commanded (Deuteronomy 7:2–4). This may have been because the Canaanites had learned how to use iron and make weapons and chariots.[16]

Gideon

Judges 6:12–16; 7:1, 19–22

The people of Israel did what God said was wrong. So God allowed them to be conquered by the people of Midian. The Midianites were cruel, attacking the Israelites and stealing their food. In today's story, a young man named Gideon was hiding while he threshed his wheat. Suddenly, an angel of the Lord appeared to him—with some very surprising news!

The angel of the Lord appeared to Gideon and said, "The Lord is with you, mighty warrior!"

[13]Then Gideon said, "Pardon me, sir. If the Lord is with us, why are we having so many troubles? Our ancestors told us he did miracles. They told us the Lord brought them out of Egypt. But now he has left us. He has allowed the Midianites to defeat us."

[14]The Lord turned to Gideon and said, "You have the strength to save the people of Israel. Go and save them from the Midianites. I am the one who is sending you."

[15]But Gideon answered, "Pardon me, Lord. How can I save Israel? My family group is the weakest in Manasseh. And I am the least important member of my family."

[16]The Lord answered him, "I will be with you. It will seem as if you are fighting only one man." . . .

[7:1]Early in the morning Jerub-Baal and all his men set up their camp at the spring of Harod. (Jerub-Baal is also called Gideon.) The Midianites were camped north of them. The Midianites were camped in the valley at the bottom of the hill called Moreh. . . .

[19]So Gideon and the 100 men with him came to the edge of the enemy camp. They came just after the enemy had changed guards. It was during the middle watch of the night. Then Gideon and his men blew their trumpets and smashed their jars.
[20]All three groups of Gideon's men blew their trumpets and smashed their jars. They held the torches in their left hands and the trumpets in their right hands. Then they shouted, "A sword for the Lord and for Gideon!" [21]Each of Gideon's men stayed in his place around the camp. But inside the camp, the men of Midian began shouting and running away.

[22]When Gideon's 300 men blew their trumpets, the Lord caused all the men of Midian to fight each other with their swords! The enemy army ran away.

Let's Pray

We have troubles all around us, but we are not defeated. We do not know what to do, but we do not give up. We are persecuted, but God does not leave us.

—2 Corinthians 4:8–9

Lord, no matter what troubles come my way, I know you are with me and will see me through them. I love and trust you. In Jesus' name, amen.

Did You Know?
Gideon twice tested the angel of the Lord to see if he was really God's angel—once in Judges 6:17–22, and again in Judges 6:36–40.

Going Deeper

Read It! Gideon's army started with some thirty-two thousand men. But the Lord said that was too many—God wanted the Israelites to know that *he* was fighting for them. Read how Gideon's three hundred warriors were chosen in Judges 7:2–8.

Do It! Make your own sword from a piece of sturdy cardboard. Then act out Gideon and his warriors shouting, "A sword for the Lord and for Gideon!" (Judges 7:20).

Samson and Delilah

Judges 16:23–25, 28–30

Did you ever tell a secret to a friend—and then find out that he or she couldn't be trusted to keep it? Samson was a man with superhuman strength, but he had a weakness for a beautiful but greedy woman named Delilah. When wicked men wanted to capture Samson, they offered to pay her well to find out the secret of Samson's strength. She nagged and pestered Samson until he gave in and told her the source of his strength: his long hair. Then one day, as Samson slept, Delilah quietly called in one of the Philistines to shave Samson's head. When Samson awoke, his strength was gone. The Philistines quickly captured him and gouged out his eyes. But God gave Samson one more chance to be a hero.

The kings of the Philistines gathered to
celebrate. They were going to offer a great
sacrifice to their god Dagon. They said,
"Our god has given us Samson our enemy."
24When they saw him, they praised their
god. They said,

"This man destroyed our country.
He killed many of us!
But our god helped us
capture our enemy."

25The people were having a good time at
the celebration. They said, "Bring Samson
out to perform for us." So they brought
Samson from the prison. He performed for
them. They made him stand between the
pillars of the temple of Dagon. . . .

28Then Samson prayed to the Lord. He
said, "Lord God, remember me. God,
please give me strength one more time.
Let me pay these Philistines back for putting out my two eyes!" 29Then Samson held
the two center pillars of the temple. These
two pillars supported the whole temple. He
braced himself between the two pillars. His
right hand was on one, and his left hand was
on the other. 30Samson said, "Let me die
with these Philistines!" Then he pushed as
hard as he could. And the temple fell on the
kings and all the people in it. So Samson
killed more of the Philistines when he died
than when he was alive.

Let's Pray

The Lord is my light and the one who saves me.
I fear no one.
The Lord protects my life.
I am afraid of no one.

—Psalm 27:1

Going Deeper

Read It! Before Samson was born, the angel of the Lord told Samson's mother that he would be a Nazarite. Find out what that means in Numbers 6:2–8.

Do It! Make dinner together as a family. As you work and eat, talk about Samson and his decisions. What were Samson's weaknesses? What are yours? How can you and your family members help one another do what is right?

Ruth and Boaz

Ruth 2:1–3, 5–12; 4:13, 16–17

The story of Ruth is a beautiful example of love. When Ruth's first husband died, Ruth traveled back to the homeland of her mother-in-law, Naomi. There, Ruth worked hard to take care of herself and Naomi. She adopted Naomi's people and their belief in God as her own. Ruth even became part of the family tree of Jesus. But first she had to meet her new husband.

Now there was a rich man living in
Bethlehem whose name was Boaz. Boaz
was one of Naomi's close relatives from
Elimelech's family.
[2]One day Ruth, the woman from Moab,
said to Naomi, "Let me go to the fields.
Maybe someone will be kind and let me
gather the grain he leaves in his field."
Naomi said, "Go, my daughter."
[3]So Ruth went to the fields. She followed
the workers who were cutting the grain.
And she gathered the grain that they had
left. It just so happened that the field belonged to Boaz. He was a close relative from
Elimelech's family. . . .
[5]Then Boaz spoke to his servant who was in
charge of the workers. He asked, "Whose girl
is that?"
[6]The servant answered, "She is the
Moabite woman who came with Naomi from
the country of Moab. [7]She said, 'Please let
me follow the workers and gather the grain
that they leave on the ground.' She came
and has remained here. From morning until just now, she has stopped only a few moments to rest in the shelter."
[8]Then Boaz said to Ruth, "Listen, my
daughter. Stay here in my field to gather
grain for yourself. Do not go to any other
person's field. Continue following behind
my women workers. [9]Watch to see which
fields they go to and follow them. I have
warned the young men not to bother you.
When you are thirsty, you may go and
drink. Take water from the water jugs that
the servants have filled."
[10]Then Ruth bowed low with her face to the
ground. She said to Boaz, "I am a stranger.
Why have you been so kind to notice me?"
[11]Boaz answered her, "I know about all
the help you have given to Naomi, your
mother-in-law. You helped her even after
your husband died. You left your father and
mother and your own country. You came to
this nation where you did not know anyone. [12]The Lord will reward you for all you
have done. You will be paid in full by the
Lord, the God of Israel. You have come to
him as a little bird finds shelter under the
wings of its mother." . . .
[4:13]So Boaz took Ruth and married her.
The Lord let her become pregnant, and she
gave birth to a son. . . .
[16]Naomi took the boy, held him in her
arms and cared for him. [17]The neighbors
gave the boy his name. These women said,
"This boy was born for Naomi." The neighbors named him Obed. Obed was Jesse's
father. And Jesse was the father of David.

Let's Pray

He took me to a safe place.
Because he delights in me, he saved me.
—Psalm 18:19

No matter what troubles come my way, God, I trust that you will find a way to rescue me—because you delight in me. In Jesus' name, amen.

Going Deeper

Read It! Find out what it means to be a child of God. Read about it in Romans 8:14–17.

Do It! As a child of God, you will inherit heaven. What do you think your heavenly inheritance will be like?

Hannah and Samuel

1 Samuel 1:9–20

Have you ever prayed very hard for something, only to be disappointed when God didn't answer your prayer the way you wanted? In today's story, Hannah wanted a baby. She had so much love to share and didn't understand why God wouldn't send her a child. One day Hannah went to the temple to pour out her unhappiness to God, and someone was watching!

Eli the priest was sitting on a chair near the
entrance to the Lord's Holy Tent. 10Hannah
was very sad. She cried much and prayed to
the Lord. 11She made a promise. She said,
"Lord of heaven's armies, see how bad I
feel. Remember me! Don't forget me. If
you will give me a son, I will give him back
to you all his life." . . .
12While Hannah kept praying, Eli watched
her mouth. 13She was praying in her heart.
Her lips moved, but her voice was not
heard. So Eli thought she was drunk. 14He
said to her, "Stop getting drunk! Throw
away your wine!"
15Hannah answered, "No, master, I have
not drunk any wine or beer. I am a woman
who is deeply troubled. I was telling the Lord
about all my problems. 16Don't think of me as
an evil woman. I have been praying because
of my many troubles and much sadness."
17Eli answered, "Go in peace. May the God
of Israel give you what you asked of him."
18Hannah said, "I want to be pleasing to
you always." Then she left and ate something. She was not sad anymore.
19Early the next morning Elkanah's family got up and worshiped the Lord. Then
they went back home to Ramah. . . . 20So
Hannah became pregnant, and in time she
gave birth to a son. She named him Samuel.
She said, "His name is Samuel because I
asked the Lord for him."

Let's Pray

Thank you, Lord, for always listening to my prayers. Help me to trust you and to remember that it is for my own good that sometimes you say yes, sometimes you say no, and sometimes you say not yet. In Jesus' name, amen.

Going Deeper

READ IT! Jesus prayed in the Garden of Gethsemane, but God said no to his prayer. Read Jesus' prayer in Luke 22:41–42.

DO IT! At dinner tonight, take turns praying for one another.

Quote of the Day:
Only the prayer which comes from our heart can get to God's heart.
—Charles Spurgeon

A Voice in the Night

1 Samuel 3:1–19

When Samuel was still just a small boy, Hannah kept her promise to God. She brought Samuel to live at the temple and help the high priest, Eli. Eli took good care of Samuel, and Samuel loved Eli like his own father. In today's story, Samuel was awakened by a voice that he thought was Eli's. But Eli helped Samuel understand that someone much greater was calling to him.

The boy Samuel served the Lord under
Eli. In those days the Lord did not speak
directly to people very often. There were
very few visions.
2Eli's eyes were so weak he was almost
blind. One night he was lying in bed.
3Samuel was also in bed in the Lord's Holy
Tent. The Box of the Agreement was in the
Holy Tent. God's lamp was still burning.
4Then the Lord called Samuel. Samuel
answered, "I am here!" 5He ran to Eli and
said, "I am here. You called me."
But Eli said, "I didn't call you. Go back to
bed." So Samuel went back to bed.
6The Lord called again, "Samuel!"
Samuel again went to Eli and said, "I am
here. You called me."
Again Eli said, "I didn't call you. Go back
to bed."
7Samuel did not yet know the Lord. The
Lord had not spoken directly to him yet.
8The Lord called Samuel for the third
time. Samuel got up and went to Eli. He
said, "I am here. You called me."
Then Eli realized the Lord was calling the
boy. 9So he told Samuel, "Go to bed. If he
calls you again, say, 'Speak, Lord. I am your
servant, and I am listening.'" So Samuel
went and lay down in bed.
10The Lord came and stood there. He
called as he had before. He said, "Samuel,
Samuel!"
Samuel said, "Speak, Lord. I am your
servant, and I am listening."
11The Lord said to Samuel, "See, I am
going to do something in Israel. It will
shock those who hear about it. 12At that time
I will do to Eli and his family everything I
promised. I will not stop until I have finished. 13I told Eli I would punish his family forever. I will do it because Eli knew his
sons were evil. They spoke against me, but
he did not control them. 14So here is what I
promised Eli's family: 'Your guilt will never
be removed by sacrifice or offering.'"
15Samuel lay down until morning. Then
he opened the doors of the Tent of the Lord.
He was afraid to tell Eli about the vision.
16But Eli said to him, "Samuel, my son!"
Samuel answered, "I am here."
17Eli asked, "What did the Lord say to you?
Don't hide it from me." . . . 18So Samuel told
Eli everything. He did not hide anything
from him. Then Eli said, "He is the Lord.
Let him do what he thinks is best."
19The Lord was with Samuel as he grew
up. He did not let any of Samuel's messages
fail to come true.

Special Words:
"God's lamp" (verse 3) was kept burning throughout the night in the temple as a sign of God's presence (Leviticus 24:2–3). It was put out just before sunrise.

Let's Pray

Dear God, I am listening for your voice. How can I serve you today? In Jesus' name, amen.

Going Deeper

READ IT! Jesus said that unless we become like little children, we will not enter heaven. Check it out in Matthew 19:13–15.

DO IT! This week invite God to speak to you just as Samuel did. Say, "Speak, Lord. I am your servant, and I am listening." God speaks to us in many ways—through the Bible, through other people, and through our hearts. What is God saying to you this week?

I hear no voice, I feel no touch,
I see no glory bright;
But yet I know that God is near,
In darkness as in light.
He watches ever by my side,
And hears my whispered prayer:
The Father for his little child
Both night and day does care.

—Anonymous

North and south and east and west,
May your holy name be blessed;
Everywhere beneath the sun,
As in heaven, your will be done.

—William Canton (adapted)

Samuel Anoints a King

1 Samuel 8:7; 9:15–17; 10:1

Give us a king!" the elders of Israel demanded. All the other nations around them had a king, and the Israelites wanted to be like them. Samuel didn't want to do this. He knew that the people belonged to God alone. But when Samuel took the people's request to the Lord, he was surprised by God's answer.

The Lord told Samuel, "Listen to whatever the people say to you. They have not rejected you. They have rejected me from being their king." . . .

9:15The day before Saul came, the Lord
had told Samuel: 16"About this time to-
morrow I will send you a man. He will be from Benjamin. You must appoint him as leader over my people Israel. He will save my people from the Philistines. I have seen the suffering of my people. I have listened to their cry."

17When Samuel first saw Saul, the Lord
spoke to Samuel. He said, "This is the man I told you about. He will rule my people." . . .

10:1Samuel took a jar of olive oil. He
poured the oil on Saul's head. He kissed Saul and said, "The Lord has appointed you to be leader of his people Israel. You will rule over the people of the Lord. You will save them from their enemies all around. This will be the sign that the Lord has appointed you as leader of his people.

Let's Pray

My king and my God, I pray to you.
Lord, every morning you hear my voice.
Every morning, I tell you what I need.
And I wait for your answer.

—Psalm 5:2–3

Dear Lord, help me to keep you as the King of my life. In Jesus' name, amen.

Going Deeper

Read It! Pilate asked Jesus if he was king of the Jews. Read Jesus' answer in Matthew 27:11.

Do It! It's important to pray for our leaders. Pray that they will follow God's will and make wise decisions. This week say a prayer for our president and other government leaders.

Special Words: *The word* Christ *comes from the Greek word* Christos *and means "anointed one."* Messiah *is the Hebrew word for "anointed one."*[17]

David and Goliath

1 Samuel 17:4, 24, 26, 31–32, 48–50

David was only a young shepherd boy when the prophet Samuel secretly anointed him as Israel's future king (1 Samuel 16:13). However, God's Spirit was strong in him. When David was sent to bring supplies to his brothers, who were fighting in King Saul's army against the Philistines, he heard the challenge of the Philistines' champion, Goliath. David volunteered to fight the giant. He armed himself with only a sling and five smooth stones—the same weapons he used to defend his father's sheep.

The Philistines had a champion fighter
named Goliath. He was from Gath. He was
about nine feet four inches tall. He came
out of the Philistine camp. . . . 24When the
Israelites saw Goliath, they were very much
afraid and ran away.

26David asked the men who stood near
him, . . . "Goliath is a Philistine. He is
not circumcised. Why does he think he
can speak against the armies of the living
God?" . . .

31Some men heard what David said and
told Saul. Then Saul ordered David to be
sent to him.

32David said to Saul, "Don't let anyone
be discouraged. I, your servant, will go and
fight this Philistine!" . . .

48As Goliath came near to attack him,
David ran quickly to meet him. 49He took
a stone from his pouch. He put it into
his sling and slung it. The stone hit the
Philistine on his forehead and sank into it.
Goliath fell facedown on the ground. 50So
David defeated the Philistine with only a
sling and a stone.

Let's Pray

Lord, give me the courage of David to stand up against evil. In Jesus' name, amen!

Going Deeper

Read It! Who was often called the "Son of David"? Find out in Matthew 21:9.

Do It! Be kind to one another today, and spread that kindness everywhere you go. Is there a bully on the playground? Make a point to be kind to the children that person is picking on—and even be kind to the bully!

Did You Know?
Goliath was probably a descendant of a tribe of giants known as the Anakites, or descendants of Anak (Numbers 13:33).[18]

Abigail

1 Samuel 25:1–6, 8–20, 23–25, 32–33, 36–39

In today's story, David was on the run from King Saul. He and his men had protected the flocks of Nabal while they camped nearby. They had hoped to be rewarded with food. But instead Nabal insulted them and refused to give them anything. Wise Abigail hurried to make things right—but would she be in time to keep David from making a terrible mistake?

Then David moved to the Desert of Maon. 2A man in Maon who had land at Carmel was very rich. He had 3,000 sheep and 1,000 goats. He was cutting the wool off his sheep at Carmel. 3His name was Nabal, and he was a descendant of Caleb. His wife was named Abigail. She was a wise and beautiful woman. But Nabal was cruel and mean.

4David was in the desert. He heard that Nabal was cutting the wool from his sheep. 5So he sent ten young men. He told them, "Go to Nabal at Carmel. Greet him for me. 6Say to Nabal, 'May you and your family have good health! And may all who belong to you have good health. . . . 8Be kind to my young men. Please give them anything you can find for them. Please do this for your son David.'"

9When the men arrived, they gave the message to Nabal. But Nabal insulted them. 10He answered them, "Who is David? Who is this son of Jesse? . . . 11I have bread and water. And I have meat that I killed for my servants who cut the wool. But I won't give it to men I don't know."

12David's men went back and told him all Nabal had said. 13Then David said to them, "Put on your swords!" So they put on their swords, and David put on his also. About 400 men went with David. But 200 men stayed with the supplies.

14One of Nabal's servants spoke to Abigail, Nabal's wife. He said, "David sent messengers from the desert to greet our master. But Nabal insulted them. 15These men were very good to us. They did nothing wrong to us. . . . 16Night and day they protected us. They were like a wall around us while we were with them caring for the sheep. 17Now think about it, and decide what you can do. Terrible trouble is coming to our master and all his family. Nabal is such a wicked man that no one can even talk to him."

18Abigail hurried. She took 200 loaves of bread, 2 leather bags full of wine and 5 cooked sheep. She took about a bushel of cooked grain, 100 cakes of raisins and 200 cakes of pressed figs. She put all these on donkeys. 19Then she told her servants, "Go on. I'll follow you." But she did not tell her husband.

20Abigail rode her donkey and came down into the mountain ravine. There she met David and his men coming down toward her. . . .

23When Abigail saw David, she quickly got off her donkey. She bowed facedown on the ground before David. 24She lay at David's feet. She said, "My master, let the blame be on me! Please let me talk to you! Listen to what I say. 25My master, don't pay attention to this worthless man Nabal. He is the same as his name. His name means 'fool,' and he

is truly foolish. But I, your servant, didn't
see the men you sent." . . .
32 David answered Abigail, "Praise the
Lord, the God of Israel. He sent you to meet
me. 33 May you be blessed for your wisdom.
You have kept me from killing or punishing
people today." . . .
36 When Abigail went back to Nabal, he was
in the house. He was eating like a king. He
was very drunk and in a good mood. So she
told him nothing until the next morning.
37 In the morning he was not drunk. Then
his wife told him everything. His heart
failed him, and he became like a stone.
38 About ten days later the Lord struck Nabal
and caused him to die.
39 When David heard that Nabal was dead,
he said, "Praise the Lord! Nabal insulted
me, but the Lord has supported me! He has
kept me from doing wrong. And the Lord
caused Nabal to die because he did wrong."
Then David sent a message to Abigail. He
asked her to become his wife.

Let's Pray!

Lord, when I face a bad situation, please give me the wisdom to make it better—just as Abigail did. In Jesus' name, amen.

Going Deeper

Read It! Abigail and David had one son. Find out his name in 1 Chronicles 3:1.

Do It! Abigail brought David cakes of pressed raisins and figs. Have a snack of raisins and fig cookies today as you think about the story of Abigail.

David Spares Saul

1 Samuel 26:2–3, 5, 7–12

King Saul believed that David was a threat to his kingdom. Saul's heart hardened toward God, and soon Saul was looking for ways to destroy David. Knowing his life was in danger, David fled King Saul's court, but he never lost his respect for Saul, who was God's anointed king. In this story, spies told King Saul where to find David, and Saul's men went to capture him. But God had other plans.

So Saul went down to the Desert of Ziph. His
3,000 chosen men of Israel went with him.
They looked for David in the Desert of Ziph.
3 Saul made his camp on the hill of Hakilah,
beside the road opposite Jeshimon. But
David stayed in the desert. He heard Saul
had followed him. . . .
5 Then David went to the place where Saul
had camped. He saw where Saul and Abner
son of Ner were sleeping. Abner was the
commander of Saul's army. Saul was sleeping in the middle of the camp with all the
army around him. . . .
7 So that night David and Abishai went
into Saul's camp. Saul was asleep in the
middle of the camp. His spear was stuck in
the ground near his head. Abner and the
army were sleeping around Saul. 8 Abishai
said to David, "Today God has let you defeat
your enemy! Let me pin Saul to the ground
with the spear. I'll only do it once! I won't
hit him twice."
9 But David said to Abishai, "Don't kill
Saul! No one can harm the Lord's appointed king and still be innocent! 10 As
surely as the Lord lives, the Lord himself
will punish Saul. Maybe Saul will die natu-
rally. Or maybe he will go into battle and
be killed. 11 But may the Lord keep me from
harming his appointed king! Now pick up
the spear and water jug that are near Saul's
head. Then let's go."
12 So David took the spear and water jug
that were near Saul's head. They left, and no
one saw them. No one knew about it or woke
up. The Lord had made them stay asleep.

Let's Pray

Thank you, God, for your kindness toward me even when I don't deserve it. Help me to be kind to others. In Jesus' name, amen.

Going Deeper

READ IT! In the New Testament, Jesus told us how he wants us to treat our enemies. Read about it in Luke 6:27–36.

DO IT! Love your enemies! Is there someone at school who just isn't very nice? Make a point to be truly kind to that person and pray for him or her every day.

Quote for the Day:
Kindness is the noblest weapon to conquer with.
—Thomas Fuller

David and the Holy Box

2 Samuel 6:1–2, 6–7, 9–15, 17–19

After the death of Saul (1 Samuel 31:1–6), David was made king. One of his first acts as king was to drive the Philistines from the land and capture Jerusalem—something Saul had been unable to do. David made Jerusalem his capital, and he quickly ordered that the Holy Box of God be brought back to the city. In all the excitement, one man made a terrible mistake, and King David was reminded that he must honor God, whose glory is greater than that of any earthly king.

David again gathered all the chosen men
of Israel. There were 30,000 of them.
2 Then David and all his people went to
Baalah in Judah. They took the Holy Box of
God from Baalah in Judah and moved it to
Jerusalem. . . .
6 When David's men came to the threshing
floor of Nacon, the oxen stumbled. The Holy
Box of God began to fall off the cart. So Uzzah
reached out and took hold of it. 7 The Lord
was angry with Uzzah and killed him. Uzzah
had not honored God when he touched the
Holy Box. So Uzzah died there beside it. . . .
9 David was afraid of the Lord that day.
He said, "How can the Holy Box of the Lord
come to me now?" 10 So David would not
move the Holy Box of the Lord to be with
him in Jerusalem. Instead, he took it to the
house of Obed-Edom, a man from Gath.
11 The Holy Box of the Lord stayed in Obed-
Edom's house for three months. And the
Lord blessed Obed-Edom and all his family.
12 The people told David, "The Lord has
blessed the family of Obed-Edom. And all
his things are blessed. This is because the
Holy Box of God is there." So David went
and brought it up from Obed-Edom's house
to Jerusalem with joy. 13 When the men carrying the Holy Box of the Lord had walked
six steps, David sacrificed a bull and a fat
calf. 14 Then David danced with all his might
before the Lord. He had on a holy linen vest.
15 David and all the Israelites shouted with
joy. They blew the trumpets as they brought
the Holy Box of the Lord to the city. . . .
17 David put up a tent for the Holy Box.
Then the Israelites put it in its place inside the tent. David offered whole burnt
offerings and fellowship offerings before
the Lord. 18 When David finished offering
the whole burnt offerings and the fellowship offerings, he blessed the people in
the name of the Lord of heaven's armies.
19 David gave a loaf of bread, a cake of dates
and a cake of raisins to everyone. He gave
them to all the Israelites, both men and
women. Then all the people went home.

Let's Pray

Praise the Lord, you angels.
Praise the Lord's glory and power.
Praise the Lord for the glory of his name.
Worship the Lord because he is holy.

—Psalm 29:1–2

Lord, I praise you! In Jesus' name, amen.

Did You Know?
Only Levites were allowed to carry the Holy Box of the Lord. Obed-Edom was a Levite, so God's Holy Box could be safely kept in his home.

Going Deeper

Read It! Did you know that an unborn baby leapt for joy? Read about it in Luke 1:41–45.

Do It! Take a nature walk together as a family. Collect interesting rocks, twigs, leaves, and flowers, and praise God for his beautiful creation.

David Blesses Mephibosheth

2 Samuel 9:1–11, 13

David and Jonathan were the best of friends even though Jonathan was the son of David's enemy, King Saul. One time Jonathan saved David's life. After David became king, he did not forget their friendship. Even though Jonathan was gone, David wanted to honor him. In today's reading, we find out how he did it.

David asked, "Is there anyone still left in Saul's family? I want to show kindness to this person for Jonathan's sake!"

[2]Now there was a servant named Ziba from Saul's family. So David's servants called Ziba to him. King David said to him, "Are you Ziba?"

He answered, "Yes, I am Ziba, your servant."

[3]The king asked, "Is there anyone left in Saul's family? I want to show God's kindness to this person."

Ziba answered the king, "Jonathan has a son still living. He is crippled in both feet."

[4]The king asked Ziba, "Where is this son?"

Ziba answered, "He is at the house of Makir son of Ammiel in Lo Debar."

[5]Then King David had servants bring Jonathan's son. . . . [6]Mephibosheth, Jonathan's son, came before David and bowed facedown on the floor.

David said, "Mephibosheth!"

Mephibosheth said, "I am your servant."

[7]David said to him, "Don't be afraid. I will be kind to you for your father Jonathan's sake. I will give you back all the land of your grandfather Saul. And you will always be able to eat at my table."

[8]Mephibosheth bowed to David again. Mephibosheth said, "You are being very kind to me, your servant!" . . .

[9]Then King David called Saul's servant Ziba. David said to him, "I have given your master's grandson everything that belonged to Saul and his family. [10]You, your sons and your servants will farm the land for Mephibosheth. You will harvest the crops. Then your master's grandson will have food to eat. But Mephibosheth, your master's grandson, will always be able to eat at my table."

(Now Ziba had 15 sons and 20 servants.) [11]Ziba said to King David, "I am your servant. I will do everything my master, the king, commands me."

So Mephibosheth ate at David's table as if he were one of the king's sons. . . . [13]Mephibosheth was crippled in both feet. He lived in Jerusalem and always ate at the king's table.

Let's Pray!

What a Friend we have in Jesus,
All our sins and griefs to bear!
What a privilege to carry
Everything to God in prayer!

—Joseph Scriven

God, thank you for the best friend of all—Jesus, your Son. In his name I pray, amen.

Quote of the Day:
Two people are better than one. They get more done by working together. If one person falls, The other can help him up.
—Ecclesiastes 4:9–10

Going Deeper

READ IT! Jonathan once saved David's life. Read about it in 1 Samuel 20.

DO IT! Do something extra special for your best friend today—just because!

Solomon, a Wise King

1 Kings 3:16–20, 22, 24–28

After David died, his son Solomon became king. God appeared to Solomon in a dream and told him to ask for anything he wanted and it would be given to him. Solomon asked for wisdom to rule God's people in the right way. God was so pleased that he not only gave Solomon wisdom but also riches, honor, and a long life (1 Kings 3:5–14). It is good that King Solomon asked for wisdom, because in today's story he would need it to sort out a tricky problem.

One day two women who were prostitutes
came to Solomon. They stood before him.
17One of the women said, "My master,
this woman and I live in the same house.
I gave birth to a baby while she was there
with me. 18Three days later this woman also
gave birth to a baby. No one else was in the
house with us. There were only the two of
us. 19One night this woman rolled over on
her baby, and it died. 20So during the night
she took my son from my bed while I was
asleep. She carried him to her bed. Then
she put the dead baby in my bed."...
22But the other woman said, "No! The
living baby is my son. The dead baby is
yours!"... So the two women argued before
the king....
24Then King Solomon sent his servants
to get a sword. When they brought it to
him, 25he said, "Cut the living baby into two
pieces. Give each woman half of the baby."
26The real mother of the living child was
full of love for her son. She said to the king,
"Please, my master, don't kill him! Give
the baby to her!"
But the other woman said, "Neither of us
will have him. Cut him into two pieces!"
27Then King Solomon said, "Give the
baby to the first woman. Don't kill him.
She is the real mother."
28When the people of Israel heard about
King Solomon's decision, they respected
him very much. They saw he had wisdom
from God to make the right decisions.

Let's Pray

Wisdom begins with respect for the Lord.
Those who obey his orders have good
understanding.

—Psalm 111:10

Lord, please bless me with wisdom so I may serve you better. In Jesus' name, amen.

Going Deeper

READ IT! How can you get wisdom? Find out in James 1:5.

DO IT! To help you be wise, read a verse from Proverbs every day.

Did You Know?
King Solomon wrote three thousand proverbs and more than a thousand songs. He also taught about plants, "animals, birds, crawling things and fish" (1 Kings 4:32–33).

Elijah Hides from the King

1 Kings 16:29–17:6

Have you ever done something you knew was right—but gotten in trouble with those who wanted you to go along with the crowd? In today's story, God's prophet Elijah brought a message to the wicked king Ahab. That message angered both Ahab and Queen Jezebel (a woman who had already killed many of God's prophets). Fleeing for his life, Elijah cried out to God for help. God provided a safe place for Elijah to hide—and a most unusual way of getting food to him!

So Ahab son of Omri became king of Israel. This was during Asa's thirty-eighth year as king of Judah. Ahab ruled Israel in the town of Samaria for 22 years. [30]Ahab did many things that the Lord said were wrong. He did more evil than any of the kings before him. [31]He sinned in the same ways that Jeroboam son of Nebat had sinned. But he did even worse things. He married Jezebel daughter of Ethbaal. (Ethbaal was king of the city of Sidon.) Then Ahab began to serve Baal and worship him. [32]He built a temple in Samaria for worshiping Baal. And he put an altar there for Baal. [33]Ahab also made an idol for worshiping Asherah. He did more things to make the Lord, the God of Israel, angry than all the other kings before him.

[34]During the time of Ahab, Hiel from Bethel rebuilt the town of Jericho. It cost Hiel the life of Abiram, his oldest son, to begin work on the city. And it cost the life of Segub, his youngest son, to build the city gates. The Lord had said, through Joshua, that this would happen. (Joshua was the son of Nun.)

[17:1]Now Elijah was a prophet from the town of Tishbe in Gilead. Elijah said to King Ahab, "I serve the Lord, the God of Israel. As surely as the Lord lives, I tell you the truth. No rain or dew will fall during the next few years unless I command it."

[2]Then the Lord spoke his word to Elijah: [3]"Leave this place. Go east and hide near Kerith Ravine. It is east of the Jordan River. [4]You may drink from the brook. And I have commanded ravens to bring you food there." [5]So Elijah did what the Lord told him to do. He went to Kerith Ravine, east of the Jordan, and lived there. [6]The birds brought Elijah bread and meat every morning and every evening. And he drank water from the brook.

Let's Pray

Lord, just as you provided for Elijah in his time of need, I know that I can trust you to provide for me too. Thank you for your faithfulness. In Jesus' name, amen.

Special Words: Elijah *means "The Lord is my God."*[19]

Did You Know?
Ahab was the most wicked of all the Israelite kings. His wife, Jezebel, was even more wicked than he! She built a temple for Baal and killed God's prophets.[20]

Going Deeper

Read It! God tells us not to worry about food. Read about it in Matthew 6:25–27.

Do It! Are there things that you are worried about? Say a prayer about them right now, asking God to take care of them. Then thank him for doing so!

Elijah and the Widow

1 Kings 17:10–24

After the immediate danger of the king's anger had passed, Elijah made his way from Cherith to Zarephath. There he met a widow and her young son who were suffering terribly because of the drought. Elijah asked the widow for just a little food and water, but would she share the last of her food with a stranger?

So Elijah went to Zarephath. When he reached the town gate, he saw a widow there. She was gathering wood for a fire. Elijah asked her, "Would you bring me a little water in a cup? I would like to have a drink." 11As she was going to get his water, Elijah said, "Please bring me a piece of bread, too."

12The woman answered, "As surely as the Lord your God lives, I tell you the truth. I have no bread. I have only a handful of flour in a jar. And I have only a little olive oil in a jug. I came here to gather some wood. I will take it home and cook our last meal. My son and I will eat it and then die from hunger."

13Elijah said to her, "Don't worry. Go home and cook your food as you have said. But first make a small loaf of bread from the flour you have. Bring it to me. Then cook something for yourself and your son. 14The Lord, the God of Israel, says, 'That jar of flour will never become empty. The jug will always have oil in it. This will continue until the day the Lord sends rain to the land.'"

15So the woman went home. And she did what Elijah told her to do. So Elijah, the woman and her son had enough food every day. 16The jar of flour and the jug of oil were never empty. This happened just as the Lord, through Elijah, said it would.

17Some time later the son of the woman who owned the house became sick. He grew worse and worse. Finally he stopped breathing. 18So the woman said to Elijah, "You are a man of God. What have you done to me? Did you come here to remind me of my sin? Did you come here to kill my son?"

19Elijah said to her, "Give me your son." So Elijah took the boy from her and carried him upstairs. Elijah laid the boy on the bed in the room where he was staying. 20Then he prayed to the Lord. He said, "Lord my God, this widow is letting me stay in her house. Why have you done this terrible thing to her? Why have you caused her son to die?" . . . 21Elijah prayed to the Lord, "Lord my God, let this boy live again!"

22The Lord answered Elijah's prayer. The boy began breathing again, and he was alive. 23Elijah carried the boy downstairs. He gave the boy to his mother and said, "See! Your son is alive!"

24The woman said to Elijah, "Now I know you really are a man from God. I know that the Lord truly speaks through you!"

Let's Pray

God, sometimes I am just like the widow—I am quick to doubt you when something bad happens, even though you have taken care of me time and time again. Help my faith be like that jug of oil—and never run out. In Jesus' name, amen.

Quote of the Day:
Man may dismiss compassion from his heart, but God never will.
—William Cowper

GOING DEEPER

READ IT! The New Testament writer James was writing about Elijah when he said, "When a good man prays, great things happen" (James 5:16). Read about Elijah's prayer in James 5:17–18.

DO IT! Is there a single mom or a widow in your church or neighborhood who could use a little extra help? Take her some cookies, offer to wash her car, or take out the trash for her.

Elijah and the Prophets of Baal

1 Kings 18:25–26, 29–30, 33–39

When a terrible drought came, King Ahab became very angry and blamed Elijah. (Actually, the drought was Ahab's fault. God was punishing him for worshiping idols.) To prove God's power once and for all, Elijah challenged the priests of Baal (a false god) to a showdown: two altars, two offerings, and whichever deity responded by sending fire for the sacrifice would be the true God.

Then Elijah said to the prophets of Baal, ". . . Choose a bull and prepare it. Pray to your god, but don't start the fire."

26So they took the bull that was given to them and prepared it. They prayed to Baal from morning until noon. They shouted, "Baal, answer us!" But there was no sound. No one answered. They danced around the altar they had built. . . .

29The afternoon passed, and the prophets continued to act wildly. They continued until it was time for the evening sacrifice. But no voice was heard. Baal did not answer. No one paid attention.

30Then Elijah said to all the people, "Now come to me." . . .

33Elijah put the wood on the altar. He cut the bull into pieces and laid them on the wood. Then he said, "Fill four jars with water. Put the water on the meat and on the wood."

34Then Elijah said, "Do it again." And they did it again.

Then he said, "Do it a third time." And they did it the third time.
35So the water ran off of the altar and filled the ditch.

36It was time for the evening sacrifice. So the prophet Elijah went near the altar. He prayed, "Lord, you are the God of Abraham, Isaac and Israel. I ask you now to prove that you are the God of Israel. And prove that I am your servant. Show these people that you commanded me to do all these things.
37Lord, answer my prayer. Show these people that you, Lord, are God. Then the people will know that you are bringing them back to you."

38Then fire from the Lord came down. It burned the sacrifice, the wood, the stones and the ground around the altar. It also dried up the water in the ditch.
39When all the people saw this, they fell down to the ground. They cried, "The Lord is God! The Lord is God!"

Let's Pray

God, thank you for showing yourself to me. Help me to live so that my words and actions show you to others. In Jesus' name, amen.

Going Deeper

READ IT! God doesn't want us to pray the same words over and over again. Read about it in Matthew 6:7.

DO IT! "Offer it up!" Have you ever heard this expression? In the Old Testament, God's people offered up sacrifices of animals. Today, we offer up sacrifices of praise. As a family, sing together and make music to praise the Lord!

The Chariot of Fire

2 Kings 2:5–12

For twenty-five years the prophet Elijah wandered the northern kingdom of Israel, trying to keep it from being totally destroyed. He advised kings, worked miracles, and urged the people to love the one true God and to turn away from idols, but Elijah was nearing the end of his life. At God's command, Elijah anointed Elisha to take his place as God's prophet. Then God took Elijah home to heaven in a most amazing way!

A group of the prophets at Jericho came to Elisha. They said, "Do you know that the Lord will take your master away from you today?"

Elisha answered, "Yes, I know. But don't talk about it."

6Elijah said to Elisha, "Stay here. The Lord has sent me to the Jordan River."

Elisha answered, "As the Lord lives, and as you live, I won't leave you."

So the two of them went on. 7Fifty men from a group of the prophets came. They stood far from where Elijah and Elisha were by the Jordan. 8Elijah took off his coat. Then he rolled it up and hit the water. The water divided to the right and to the left. Then Elijah and Elisha crossed over on dry ground.

9After they had crossed over, Elijah said to Elisha, "What can I do for you before I am taken from you?"

Elisha said, "Leave me a double share of your spirit."

10Elijah said, "You have asked a hard thing. But if you see me when I am taken from you, it will be yours. If you don't, it won't happen."

11Elijah and Elisha were still walking and talking. Then a chariot and horses of fire appeared. The chariot and horses of fire separated Elijah from Elisha. Then Elijah went up to heaven in a whirlwind. 12Elisha saw it and shouted, "My father! My father! The chariots of Israel and their horsemen!" Elisha did not see him anymore. Elisha grabbed his own clothes and tore them to show how sad he was.

Let's Pray!

Day by day, dear Lord,
Of thee three things I pray:
To see thee more clearly,
To love thee more dearly,
To follow thee more nearly,
Day by day.

—Richard of Chichester

Going Deeper

Read It! Satan wanted Jesus to worship him instead of God. Read what Jesus said to the devil in Matthew 4:8–10.

Do It! Sit together outside or around a table, and take turns telling one another what you are thankful for.

Did You Know?
Enoch (Genesis 5:24) and Elijah are two examples of God's friends who were taken straight to heaven without having to die.

Naaman Is Healed

2 Kings 5:1–16

Although Elijah and Elisha were both holy men of God, they were very different. Elijah was a fiery prophet. Like John the Baptist, he had a zeal for the Lord and wanted every idol to be completely destroyed. Elisha was more like a gentle wind. He worked in people's hearts through kindness. The miracles of Elisha are recorded in 2 Kings 2 and 4–7.

Naaman was commander of the army of the king of Aram. He was a great man to his master. He had much honor because the Lord had used him to give victory to Aram. He was a mighty and brave man. But he had a harmful skin disease.

2The Arameans had gone out to steal from the Israelites. And they had taken a little girl as a captive from Israel. This little girl served Naaman's wife. 3She said to her mistress, "I wish that my master would meet the prophet who lives in Samaria. He would heal Naaman of his disease."

4Naaman went to the king. He told him what the girl from Israel had said. 5The king of Aram said, "Go now. And I will send a letter to the king of Israel." . . . 6He brought the letter to the king of Israel. It read, "I am sending my servant Naaman to you. I'm sending him so you can heal him of his skin disease."

7The king of Israel read the letter. Then he tore his clothes to show how upset he was. He said, "I'm not God! I can't kill and make alive again! Why does this man send someone with a harmful skin disease for me to heal? You can see that the king of Aram is trying to start trouble with me!"

8Elisha, the man of God, heard that the king of Israel had torn his clothes. So he sent a message to the king. It said, "Why have you become so upset that you tore your clothes? Let Naaman come to me. Then he will know there is a prophet in Israel!" 9So Naaman went with his horses and chariots to Elisha's house. And he stood outside the door.

10Elisha sent a messenger to Naaman. The messenger said, "Go and wash in the Jordan River seven times. Then your skin will be healed, and you will be clean."

11Naaman became angry and left. He said, "I thought Elisha would surely come out and stand before me. I thought he would call on the name of the Lord his God. I thought he would wave his hand over the place and heal the disease! 12Abana and Pharpar, the rivers of Damascus, are better than all the waters of Israel! Why can't I wash in them and become clean?" So Naaman went away very angry.

13But Naaman's servants came near and talked to him. They said, "My father, if the prophet had told you to do some great thing, wouldn't you have done it? Doesn't it make more sense just to do it? After all, he only told you, 'Wash, and you will be clean.'" 14So Naaman went down and dipped in the Jordan seven times. He did just as Elisha had said. Then Naaman's skin became new again. It was like the skin of a little boy. And Naaman was clean!

15Naaman and all his group came back to Elisha. He stood before Elisha and said,

"Look. I now know there is no God in all the earth except in Israel! Now please accept a gift from me."

16 But Elisha said, "I serve the Lord. As surely as the Lord lives, I won't accept anything." Naaman urged him to take the gift, but he refused.

SPECIAL WORDS: *Naaman's "harmful skin disease" was leprosy. Leprosy could not be cured in Bible times.*

LET'S PRAY

Thank you, Lord, for all you have done for me! In Jesus' name, amen.

GOING DEEPER

READ IT! Jesus once healed ten lepers all at once—but only one of them thanked him. Read about it in Luke 17:11–19.

DO IT! Naaman may never have been healed if that little servant girl hadn't suggested that her master go and see God's servant Elisha. Even though you are young, never be afraid to point people to God.

Hezekiah Prays

2 Kings 19:15–19, 35–36

Have you ever been around a bully, someone bigger and meaner than you could ever be, someone who always tries to push the smaller, weaker kids around? In today's story, we meet a bully, the king of Assyria, who wanted to overthrow King Hezekiah, a good and godly king. But God had different plans. "Don't be afraid of what you've heard," the Lord told Hezekiah through his prophet Isaiah. God himself would take care of this bully!

[Hezekiah] prayed to the Lord: "Lord, God
of Israel, your throne is between the gold
creatures with wings! Only you are God of
all the kingdoms of the earth. You made
the heavens and the earth. [16]Hear, Lord,
and listen. Open your eyes, Lord, and see.
Listen to the word Sennacherib has said
to insult the living God. [17]It is true, Lord.
The kings of Assyria have destroyed these
countries and their lands. [18]These kings
have thrown the gods of these nations into
the fire. But they were only wood and rock
statues that men made. So the kings have
destroyed them. [19]Now, Lord our God, save
us from the king's power. Then all the kingdoms
of the earth will know that you, Lord,
are the only God." . . .

[35]That night the angel of the Lord went
out. He killed 185,000 men in the Assyrian
camp. The people got up early the next
morning. And they saw all the dead bodies!
[36]So Sennacherib king of Assyria left.
He went back to Nineveh and stayed there.

Let's Pray

Father, I thank you for sending Jesus to save me. Help me share with others the message of his love and sacrifice. In Jesus' name, amen.

Going Deeper

Read It! Today our battle is against the evil one, Satan. But God gives us some special armor to help us in the fight. Read about it in Ephesians 6:10–17.

Do It! Make cookies for the preachers and other workers in your church to thank them for all they do.

Did You Know?
King Hezekiah helped rebuild the wall of Jerusalem. Modern archaeologist Professor Nahum Avigad found a 200-foot section of the wall. It was 23 feet thick and over 10 feet tall.[21]

Good King Josiah

2 Kings 23:1–4, 21–25

Can you think of a time when someone else made a big mistake and you had to fix it? Josiah was only eight years old when he became king of Judah. At sixteen, he came to know the God of David, and at twenty, he began a long line of changes to bring the people back to worshiping the one true God. Sadly, the people's hearts were slow to turn away from their false idols.

Then the king [Josiah] gathered all the elders of Judah and Jerusalem together. [2]He went up to the Temple of the Lord. All the men from Judah and Jerusalem went with him. The priests, prophets and all the people—from the least important to the most important—went with him. He read to them all the words of the Book of the Agreement. That book was found in the Temple of the Lord. [3]The king stood by the pillar. He made an agreement in the presence of the Lord. He agreed to follow the Lord and obey his commands, rules and laws with his whole being. He agreed to do what was written in this book. Then all the people promised to obey the agreement.

[4]The king gave a command to Hilkiah the high priest. He also gave it to the priests of the next rank and the gatekeepers. He told them to bring out of the Temple of the Lord everything made for Baal, Asherah and all the stars of heaven. Then Josiah burned them outside Jerusalem in the fields of the Kidron Valley. And he carried the ashes to Bethel. . . .

[21]The king gave a command to all the people. He said, "Celebrate the Passover to the Lord your God. Do it as it is written in this Book of the Agreement." [22]No Passover like this one had been celebrated since the judges led Israel. Nor had one like it happened while there were kings of Israel and kings of Judah. [23]This Passover was celebrated to the Lord in Jerusalem. It was the eighteenth year of King Josiah's rule.

[24]Josiah destroyed the mediums, fortune-tellers, house gods and idols. He destroyed all the hated gods seen in the land of Judah and Jerusalem. He did this to obey the words of the teachings. They were written in the book Hilkiah the priest had found in the Temple of the Lord.

[25]There was no king like Josiah before or after him. He obeyed the Lord with all his heart, soul and strength. He followed all the Teachings of Moses.

Let's Pray

Dear God, there are many evil and sinful things in our world today. Please use me to show others that you are the one true God. In Jesus' name, amen.

Going Deeper

Read It! What kind of religion does God accept? Find out by reading James 1:27.

Do It! As a family, plan a random act of kindness for someone. You could pay for the food of the car behind you in the drive-through, fill up someone else's parking meter, or serve food at a shelter. Afterward, talk about how you felt as you were helping these people.

All for You, dear God.
Everything I do,
Or think,
Or say,
The whole day long.
Help me to be good.

—Unknown

King Joash Repairs the Temple

2 Chronicles 24:1–2, 4–14

For six years the land of Judah was ruled by the evil queen Athaliah, who, like her wicked mother, Jezebel, worshiped Baal and dishonored the God of Israel. She rose to power by killing the royal children of King Jehu; only the baby Joash was saved. At the age of seven, Joash became king. He began his forty-year reign by tearing down the altars to the false gods and repairing the temple.

Joash was seven years old when he became
king. And he ruled 40 years in Jerusalem. . . .
2Joash did what the Lord said was right as long
as Jehoiada the priest was alive. . . .

4Joash decided to repair the Temple of
the Lord. 5He called the priests and the
Levites together. He said to them, "Go to
the towns of Judah. Gather the money all
the Israelites have to pay every year. Use it
to repair the Temple of your God. Do this
now." But the Levites did not hurry.

6So King Joash called Jehoiada the leading priest. Joash said to him, "Why haven't
you made the Levites bring in the tax
money from Judah and Jerusalem? Moses
the Lord's servant and the people of Israel
used that money for the Holy Tent."

7In the past the sons of wicked Athaliah
had broken into the Temple of God. They
had used its holy things for worshiping the
Baal idols.

8King Joash commanded that a box
for contributions be made. It was to be
put outside, at the gate of the Temple of
the Lord. 9Then the Levites made an announcement in Judah and Jerusalem. They
told the people to bring the tax money to
the Lord. Moses the servant of God had
made the Israelites give it while they were
in the desert. 10All the officers and people
were happy to give their money. They put
it in the box until the box was full. 11Then
the Levites would take the box to the king's
officers. They would see that it was full of
money. Then the king's royal assistant and
the leading priest's officer would come and
take out the money. Then they would take
the box back to its place. They did this often
and gathered much money. 12King Joash
and Jehoiada gave the money to the people
who worked on the Temple of the Lord. And
they hired stoneworkers and carpenters to
repair the Temple of the Lord. They also
hired people to work with iron and bronze
to repair the Temple.

13The people worked hard. And the work
to repair the Temple went well. They rebuilt
the Temple of God to be as it was before. And
they made it stronger. 14When the workers finished, they brought the money that
was left to King Joash and Jehoiada. They
used that money to make things for the
Temple of the Lord. They made things for
the service in the Temple and for the burnt
offerings. They also made bowls and other
things from gold and silver. Burnt offerings were given every day in the Temple of
the Lord while Jehoiada was alive.

Did You Know?
Jehoiada was the chief priest of the Lord. His wife, Jehosheba, rescued Joash from wicked Queen Athaliah. They hid him in the temple for six years until he was old enough to rule (2 Kings 11:1–3).

Let's Pray

Lord, help me remember that I am never too young to serve you faithfully. Please give me wisdom to know what I ought to do and the courage and strength to do it. In Jesus' name, amen.

Going Deeper

Read It! You are never too young to serve God. Read what Paul said about young people serving God in 1 Timothy 4:12.

Do It! Do you think it was hard for Joash to be king when he was only seven? What would you do if you were king or queen today?

King Uzziah Angers God

2 Chronicles 26:1–8, 15–20

Have you ever watched a child learning to ride a bike with his mom or dad holding on to the back? If the child gets going a little too fast, his parents have to let go, and then the bike topples! Sometimes we get a little too sure of our own abilities, and we have to learn the hard way to slow down and stay safe! King Uzziah, who ruled Judah for fifty-two years, had to learn that same lesson. As long as he followed God, Judah prospered and raised a huge army that defeated the Philistines, Arabs, and Ammonites. But sadly, King Uzziah became too proud of his own power, and God had to teach him a lesson!

Then all the people of Judah chose Uzziah to be king. He became king in place of Amaziah, his father. Uzziah was 16 years old. 2He rebuilt the town of Elath and made it part of Judah again. He did this after Amaziah died.

3Uzziah was 16 years old when he became king. And he ruled 52 years in Jerusalem. . . . 4He did what the Lord said was right. He obeyed God just as his father Amaziah had done. 5Uzziah obeyed God while Zechariah was alive. Zechariah taught Uzziah how to respect and obey God. As long as Uzziah obeyed the Lord, God gave him success.

6Uzziah fought a war against the Philistine people. . . . 7God helped Uzziah fight the Philistines, the Arabs living in Gur Baal and the Meunites. 8The Ammonites made payments Uzziah demanded. Uzziah was very powerful. So his name became famous all the way to the border of Egypt. . . .

15In Jerusalem Uzziah made devices that were invented by clever men. These devices were put on the towers and corners of the city walls. They were used to shoot arrows and large rocks. So Uzziah became famous in faraway places. He had much help until he became powerful.

16But when Uzziah became strong, his pride caused him to be destroyed. He was unfaithful to the Lord his God. He went into the Temple of the Lord to burn incense on the altar for incense. 17Azariah and 80 other brave priests who served the Lord followed Uzziah into the Temple. 18They told Uzziah he was wrong. They said to him, "You don't have the right to burn incense to the Lord. Only the priests, Aaron's descendants, should burn the incense. They have been made holy for the Lord to do this special duty. Leave this holy place. You have been unfaithful to God. The Lord God will not honor you for this."

19Uzziah was standing beside the altar for incense in the Temple of the Lord. He had in his hand a pan for burning incense. He was very angry with the priests. As he was standing in front of the priests, a harmful skin disease broke out on his forehead. 20Azariah the leading priest and all the other priests looked at him. They could see the harmful skin disease on his forehead. So they hurried him out of the Temple. Uzziah rushed out, because the Lord had punished him.

Let's Pray

Thank you, Lord, for godly people who are not afraid to tell the truth. Bless your church with many such people—and help me to be one of them. In Jesus' name, amen.

Going Deeper

Read It! It's important to follow only leaders who truly follow God. Read Matthew 15:14 to see what Jesus said about following leaders who don't follow God.

Do It! Do you know someone who won't come to church because of something hurtful that someone else said? Say a prayer for that person. Invite him or her to go to church and sit with you and your family!

Rebuilding the Temple

Ezra 3:1–13

In today's story, the Israelites had been in captivity in Babylon for many years. When King Cyrus became ruler over Babylon, he proclaimed throughout his kingdom that the Israelites would be allowed to go back to Jerusalem. They could rebuild the temple!

By the seventh month, the Israelites were settled in their hometowns. They met together in Jerusalem. [2]Then Jeshua son of Jozadak and his fellow priests joined Zerubbabel son of Shealtiel. They began to build the altar of the God of Israel. That's where they offered burnt offerings just as it is written in the Teachings of Moses. Moses was the man of God. [3]They were afraid of the people living around them. But they still built the altar where it had been before. They offered burnt offerings on it to the Lord morning and evening. [4]Then, to obey what was written, they celebrated the Feast of Shelters. They offered the right number of sacrifices for each day of the festival. [5]After the Feast of Shelters, they had regular sacrifices every day. They had sacrifices for the New Moon and all the festivals commanded by the Lord. Also there were special offerings brought as gifts to the Lord. [6]On the first day of the seventh month they began to bring burnt offerings to the Lord. But the foundation of the Lord's Temple had not yet been laid.

[7]Then they gave money to the stoneworkers and carpenters. They also gave food, wine and oil to the cities of Sidon and Tyre. This was so they would float cedar logs from Lebanon to the seacoast town of Joppa. Cyrus king of Persia had given permission for this.

[8]It was in the second year after their arrival at the Temple of God in Jerusalem. In the second month Zerubbabel and Jeshua began the work. So did the rest of their fellow priests and Levites. And all who had returned from captivity to Jerusalem began to work. They chose Levites 20 years old and older to be in charge of the building of the Temple of the Lord. [9]These men were in charge of the work of building the Temple of God: Jeshua and his sons and brothers; Kadmiel and his sons who were the descendants of Hodaviah; and the sons of Henadad and their sons and brothers. They were all Levites.

[10]The builders finished laying the foundation of the Temple of the Lord. Then the priests, dressed in their robes, got trumpets. And the Levites, the sons of Asaph, had cymbals. They all took their places. They praised the Lord just as David king of Israel had said to do. [11]With praise and thanksgiving, they sang to the Lord:

"He is good;
his love for Israel continues forever."
And then all the people shouted loudly, "Praise the Lord! The foundation of his Temple has been laid."
12But many of the older priests, Levites and family leaders cried aloud. They had seen the first Temple. Now they saw the foundation of this Temple. But most of the other people were shouting with joy.
13The people made so much noise no one could tell the difference between the joyful shouting and the sad crying. It could be heard far away.

Let's Pray!

Thank you, Lord, for our church. Help us to always treat it with the respect your house deserves. In Jesus' name, amen.

Going Deeper

Read It! Jesus said that if the temple were destroyed, he would raise it up again in three days. What temple was he talking about? Find out in John 2:21.

Do It! Your body is the temple of the Holy Spirit (1 Corinthians 6:19). Use your body to worship God today. Sing praises and jump for joy, because Jesus is alive!

Esther

Esther 5:3–4; 7:1–7, 9–10

The story of Esther is a tale of great bravery. Esther was a young Jewish girl. Her parents were gone, so her uncle, Mordecai, took care of her. But when the great Persian king Xerxes saw how beautiful Esther was, he took her to be his queen. Mordecai warned Esther not to tell anyone that she was Jewish. But soon after, Mordecai's life and the lives of every Jew in the kingdom were put in danger when he refused to bow down to the king's closest adviser, Haman. Esther knew she must go to the king for help. But to go to him uninvited could mean her own death! Only if he held out the golden scepter would she be safe. What would happen if Esther risked her life to save her people?

The king asked, "What is it, Queen Esther?
What do you want to ask me? I will give you
as much as half of my kingdom."
[4]Esther answered, "My king, if it pleases
you, come today with Haman to a banquet. I
have prepared it for you." . . .
[7:1]So the king and Haman went in to eat
with Queen Esther. [2]They were drinking
wine. And the king said to Esther on this
second day also, "What are you asking for? I
will give it to you. What is it you want? I will
give you as much as half of my kingdom."
[3]Then Queen Esther answered, "My king,
I hope you are pleased with me. If it pleases
you, let me live. This is what I ask. And let
my people live, too. This is what I want. [4]I
ask this because my people and I have been
sold to be destroyed. We are to be killed and
completely wiped out. If we had been sold
as male and female slaves, I would have
kept quiet. That would not be enough of a
problem to bother the king."
[5]Then King Xerxes asked Queen Esther,
"Who is he? Where is he? Who has done
such a thing?"
[6]Esther said, "A man who is against us!
Our enemy is this wicked Haman!"
Then Haman was filled with terror before
the king and queen. [7]The king was very
angry. He got up, left his wine and went out
into the palace garden. But Haman stayed
inside to beg Queen Esther to save his life.
He could see that the king had already
decided to kill him. . . .
[9]The king said, "Hang Haman on it!" [10]So
they hanged Haman on the platform he had
prepared for Mordecai. Then the king was
not so angry anymore.

Let's Pray

When people look at me, dear Lord, please let them see Jesus shining through. In his name, amen.

Going Deeper

Read It! Esther *interceded*—or pleaded with the king—to save her people. Someone intercedes to save us too. Find out who in Romans 8:34.

Do It! Part of the Purim celebration—which honors Esther—is giving gifts to the poor. As a family, help someone in need this week.

Did You Know?
The Jews celebrate Purim each year to remember how Queen Esther helped save her people. It is celebrated with costumes, gifts, and treats.

Job

Job 1:1, 3; 2:1–4, 6–10; 42:10, 12

When we hear the name Job, we think of someone who has suffered greatly. But when Job's story began, we find that he was a man who had many blessings—great wealth, a large family, and many friends. But one day God allowed Job's faith to be tested. Everything was taken away from him. God believed that Job would trust him no matter what. But would Job be able to keep his faith when everyone around him told him not to?

A man named Job lived in the land of Uz. He was an honest man and innocent of any wrong. He honored God and stayed away from evil. [2]Job had seven sons and three daughters. [3]He owned 7,000 sheep, 3,000 camels, 500 pairs of oxen and 500 female donkeys. And he had a large number of servants. He was the greatest man among all the people of the East. . . .

[2:1]On another day the angels came to show themselves before the Lord. And Satan also came with them. . . .

[3]Then the Lord said to Satan, "Have you noticed my servant Job? No one else on earth is like him. He is an honest man, innocent of any wrong. He honors God and stays away from evil." . . .

[4]Satan answered. . . .

[6]The Lord said to Satan, "All right, then. Job is in your power. But you must let him live."

[7]So Satan left the Lord's presence. And he put painful sores all over Job's body. They went from the top of his head to the soles of his feet. [8]Then Job took a piece of broken pottery. And he used it to scrape himself. He sat in ashes to show how upset he was.

[9]Job's wife said to him, "Are you still trying to stay innocent? You should just curse God and die!"

[10]Job answered, "You are talking like a foolish woman. Should we take only good things from God and not trouble?" In all this Job did not sin in what he said. . . .

[42:10]After Job had prayed for his friends, God gave him success again. God gave Job twice as much as he had owned before. . . .

[12]The Lord blessed the last part of Job's life even more than the first part. Job had 14,000 sheep and 6,000 camels. He had 1,000 pairs of oxen and 1,000 female donkeys.

Let's Pray

Father, even when bad things happen, you can bring good out of them. Thank you for doing that for me. In Jesus' name, amen.

Going Deeper

READ IT! Read Romans 8:28. How does this verse fit with Job's story?

DO IT! Don't be like Job's friends. Instead of making someone feel worse, use your words to make someone feel better today.

The Shepherd Psalm

Psalm 23

As a boy, long before he played his harp for King Saul, David spent hours roaming the countryside, watching over his father's sheep. In this psalm, David the shepherd combined his love for God with his love for God's creatures to create this most familiar and comforting of all David's songs.

The Lord is my shepherd.
I have everything I need.
2He gives me rest in green pastures.
He leads me to calm water.
3He gives me new strength.
For the good of his name,
he leads me on paths that are right.
4Even if I walk
through a very dark valley,
I will not be afraid
because you are with me.
Your rod and your walking stick
comfort me.
5You prepare a meal for me
in front of my enemies.
You pour oil on my head.
You give me more than I can hold.
6Surely your goodness and love will be with
me
all my life.
And I will live in the house of the Lord
forever.

Let's Pray

Now I lay me down to sleep,
I pray the Lord my soul to keep.
God, be with me through the night,
and wake me with the morning light.
Amen.

—Traditional Bedtime Prayer

Going Deeper

READ IT! Jesus called himself the Good Shepherd. Read about how Jesus takes care of you—his sheep—in John 10:7–18.

DO IT! Memorize Psalm 23.

Quote of the Day: *"I am the good shepherd. The good shepherd gives his life for the sheep."* *—Jesus, in John 10:11*

We Worship You, Lord

Psalm 32

It is such a blessing to be forgiven of our sins. Carrying around unforgiven sins is like hauling around heavy, dirty bags of garbage. They weigh us down and make us tired. They make us feel dirty inside. But when we ask for forgiveness, Jesus takes our sins away and washes us clean!

Happy is the person
whose sins are
forgiven,
whose wrongs are pardoned.
2Happy is the person
whom the Lord does not consider
guilty.
In that person there is nothing false.
3When I kept things to myself,
I felt weak deep inside me.
I moaned all day long.
4Day and night
you punished me.
My strength was gone
as in the summer heat. *Selah*
5Then I confessed my sins to you.
I didn't hide my guilt.
I said, "I will confess my sins to the Lord."
And you forgave my guilt. *Selah*
6For this reason, all who obey you
should pray to you while they still can.
When troubles rise like a flood,
they will not reach them.
7You are my hiding place.
You protect me from my troubles.
You fill me with songs of salvation. *Selah*
8The Lord says, "I will make you wise. I
will show you where to go.
I will guide you and watch over you.
9So don't be like a horse or donkey.
They don't understand.
They must be led with bits and reins,
or they will not come near you."
10Wicked people have many troubles.
But the Lord's love surrounds those who
trust him.
11Good people, rejoice and be happy in the
Lord.
All you whose hearts are right, sing.

Let's Pray

You are my hiding place, O Lord. You protect me from my troubles, and you fill my heart with songs when I am afraid. I will always trust in you! In Jesus' name, amen.

Special Words: Selah *is a Hebrew word meaning "pause."*

Did You Know?
David wrote this psalm as a prayer of repentance after he sinned. Repentance *means turning away from sin and turning back to God.*[23]

GOING DEEPER

READ IT! In the book of Acts, Peter preached to the people, and they became very sorry for their sins. What did Peter tell them to do so they would be right with God? Read about it in Acts 2:38.

DO IT! *Repentance* is a big word, but it's not hard to do. When you mess up, tell God you are sorry—and then try not to make that same mistake again!

Praise the Lord!

Psalm 148:1–13

This is one of the five "Hallelujah Psalms," which are Psalms 146–150. They tell of the greatness of the Lord. Let all the angels, the sun and moon and stars, and all the heavens shout, "Hallelujah!"

Praise the Lord!
Praise the Lord from the heavens.
Praise him high above the earth.
2Praise him, all you angels.
Praise him, all you armies of heaven.
3Praise him, sun and moon.
Praise him, all you shining stars.
4Praise him, highest heavens
and you waters above the sky.
5Let them praise the Lord
because they were created by his command.
6He set them in place forever and ever.
He made a law that will never end.
7Praise the Lord from the earth.
Praise him, you large sea animals and all the oceans.
8Praise him, lightning and hail, snow and clouds,
and stormy winds that obey him.
9Praise him, mountains and all hills,
fruit trees and all cedar trees.
10Praise him, you wild animals and all cattle,
small crawling animals and birds.
11Praise him, you kings of the earth and all nations,
princes and all rulers of the earth.
12Praise him, you young men and women,
old people and children.
13Praise the Lord.
He alone is great.
He is greater than heaven and earth.

Let's Pray!
Today, Father, I lift up my praise to you! In Jesus' name, amen!

Going Deeper

Read It! Read more of God's praises in Revelation 5:13 and Revelation 15:3–4.

Do It! What's your favorite way to praise the Lord? Do you like to sing, dance, draw, or pray? Make up your own special way to praise God today, and share it with your family.

Did You Know?
The word Hallelujah *is a form of the word* Alleluia, *which means "Praise the Lord."*[24]

Solomon's Wisdom

Proverbs 3:1–6

The book of Proverbs was written by King Solomon. Both he and his father, King David, were great friends of God, and their writings form the large part of the Bible that is called "Wisdom Literature." The book of Proverbs is filled with wonderful advice and examples for how to live a good, Christian life. Today's reading is just a sample of that wisdom.

My child, do not forget my teaching.
Keep my commands in mind.
2Then you will live a long time.
And your life will be successful.
3Don't ever stop being kind and truthful.
Let kindness and truth show in all you do.
Write them down in your mind as if on a tablet.
4Then you will be respected
and pleasing to both God and men.
5Trust the Lord with all your heart.
Don't depend on your own understanding.
6Remember the Lord in everything you do.
And he will give you success.

LET'S PRAY!

God in heaven hear my prayer,
Keep me in thy loving care.
Be my guide in all I do,
Bless all those who love me too.
Amen.

—Traditional

DID YOU KNOW?
*When they are at prayer, some Jewish men literally bind the Scriptures to themselves, using use phylacteries (*tefellin *in Hebrew). These are small, leather boxes tied to the forehead and arm. Inside, there are strips of paper with verses written on them.*[25]

Going Deeper

READ IT! When you become a child of God, he blesses you with the fruit of the Spirit. Find out what those fruits are in Galatians 5:22–23.

DO IT! Luke 6:43–45 tells us that we are known by our "fruit"—whether we do good things or bad things. What "good fruit" can you give to others today?

A Good Wife

Proverbs 31:10–12, 20–22, 27–31

This chapter of Proverbs describes the godly woman and tells us how much she is worth—"more than rubies"! Let's read to see what kind of woman is pleasing to God.

It is hard to find an excellent wife.
She is worth more than rubies.
11 Her husband trusts her completely.
With her, he has everything he needs.
12 She does him good and not harm
for as long as she lives. . . .
20 She welcomes the poor.
She helps the needy.
21 She does not worry about her family
when it snows.
They all have fine clothes to keep them
warm.
22 She makes coverings for her bed.
Her clothes are made of linen and other
expensive material. . . .
27 She watches over her family.
And she is always busy.
28 Her children bless her.
Her husband also praises her.
29 He says, "There are many excellent
wives,
but you are better than all of them."
30 Charm can fool you, and beauty can trick
you.
But a woman who respects the Lord
should be praised.
31 Give her the reward she has earned.
She should be openly praised for what
she has done.

Let's Pray!

Thank you, God, for the gift of mothers and wives. I especially thank you for my mother, my grandmothers, and all the other godly women who love and care for me. In Jesus' name, amen.

Going Deeper

Read It! Read God's description of a beautiful woman in 1 Peter 3:3–4.

Do It! Tonight at dinner, talk about what real beauty is. For starters, is it on the inside or outside?

Quote of the Day:
How goodness heightens beauty!
—Hannah More

Sing to the Lord a new song.
Sing to the Lord, all the earth.
Sing to the Lord and praise his name.
Every day tell how he saves us.
Tell the nations of his glory.
Tell all peoples the miracles he does.

The Lord is great; he should be praised.
He should be honored more than all the gods.
All the gods of the nations are only idols.
But the Lord made the skies.
The Lord has glory and majesty.
He has power and beauty in his Temple.

Praise the Lord, all nations on earth.
Praise the Lord's glory and power.
Praise the glory of the Lord's name.

Bring an offering and come into his Temple courtyards.
Worship the Lord because he is holy.
The whole earth should tremble before the Lord.
Tell the nations, "The Lord is king."
The earth is set, and it cannot be moved.
He will judge the people fairly.
Let the skies rejoice and the earth be glad.
Let the sea and everything in it shout.
Let the fields and everything in them show their joy.
Then all the trees of the forest will sing for joy.
They will sing before the Lord because he is coming.
He is coming to judge the world.
He will judge the world with fairness
and the nations with truth.

—Psalm 96

A Time for Everything

Ecclesiastes 3:1–8, 14

The book of Ecclesiastes may have been written by King Solomon, the son of David. In today's reading, he reminds us that our lives will have good times and bad times—but the bad times will not last forever. The good that God does in your heart will last forever.

There is a right time for everything.
Everything on earth has its special season.
2There is a time to be born
and a time to die.
There is a time to plant
and a time to pull up plants.
3There is a time to kill
and a time to heal.
There is a time to destroy
and a time to build.
4There is a time to cry
and a time to laugh.
There is a time to be sad
and a time to dance.
5There is a time to throw away stones
and a time to gather them.
There is a time to hug
and a time not to hug.
6There is a time to look for something
and a time to stop looking for it.
There is a time to keep things
and a time to throw things away.
7There is a time to tear apart
and a time to sew together.
There is a time to be silent
and a time to speak.
8There is a time to love
and a time to hate.
There is a time for war
and a time for peace. . . .
14I know anything God does will continue
forever.

LET'S PRAY!

O Lord, I know that there will be good times and bad times. But I also know that you have a plan for my life. Help me to look to you always. In Jesus' name, amen.

GOING DEEPER

READ IT! What does God say in the New Testament about how you use your time? Find out in Colossians 4:5.

DO IT! Serving God and others is the best use of time, but it doesn't have to take a lot of time. Say something kind to every person you meet—it's a quick and easy way to serve that you can do every day!

DID YOU KNOW? Ecclesiastes *comes from the Greek word meaning "teacher."*

Isaiah's Vision

Isaiah 6:1–8

Have you ever wondered what heaven is like? The prophet Isaiah is called the "messianic prophet" because he so often spoke of the coming of Christ. He is quoted more often in the New Testament than any other prophet. In this passage, God blessed Isaiah with a beautiful vision of heaven. Let's read about it!

In the year that King Uzziah died, I saw the
Lord. He was sitting on a very high throne.
His long robe filled the Temple. 2Burning
heavenly creatures stood above him. Each
creature had six wings. They used two wings
to cover their faces. They used two wings to
cover their feet. And they used two wings
for flying. 3Each creature was calling to the
others:

"Holy, holy, holy is the Lord of heaven's
armies.
His glory fills the whole earth."

4Their voices caused the frame around
the door to shake. The Temple filled with
smoke.

5I said, "Oh, no! I will be destroyed. I am
not pure. And I live among people who are
not pure. But I have seen the King, the Lord
of heaven's armies."

6On the altar there was a fire. One of the
burning heavenly creatures used a pair of
tongs to take a hot coal from the fire. Then
he flew to me with the hot coal in his hand.
7The creature touched my mouth with the
hot coal. Then he said, "Look. Your guilt
is taken away because this hot coal has
touched your lips. Your sin is taken away."

8Then I heard the Lord's voice. He said,
"Whom can I send? Who will go for us?"

So I said, "Here I am. Send me!"

Let's Pray!

Dear God, thank you for being holy and good. I want to serve you. Here I am—send me! In Jesus' name, amen.

Going Deeper

READ IT! The apostle John also had a vision of heaven and of Jesus. Read his description in Revelation 1:12–18.

DO IT! When Isaiah heard God ask, "Who can I send?" Isaiah said, "Send me!" What would you say?

Special Words: *The "heavenly creatures" described in verse 2 are called seraphim. They are the highest order of angels, those closest to God.*

Jeremiah

Jeremiah 1:4–10, 13–15

One hundred years after Isaiah, God raised up a prophet named Jeremiah. He sent Jeremiah to the Israelites with a message: stop worshiping idols and worship the one true God! But did they listen? No! In today's story, God spoke to Jeremiah again, and he showed him how he will punish the Israelites. They would be conquered by the Babylonians!

The Lord spoke these words to me:
5"Before I made you in your mother's
womb, I chose you.
Before you were born, I set you apart for
a special work.
I appointed you as a prophet to the
nations."
6Then I said, "But Lord God, I don't know
how to speak. I am only a boy."
7But the Lord said to me, "Don't say, 'I
am only a boy.' You must go everywhere
that I send you. You must say everything I
tell you to say. 8Don't be afraid of anyone,
because I am with you. I will protect you,"
says the Lord.
9Then the Lord reached out with his
hand and touched my mouth. He said to
me, "See, I am putting my words in your
mouth. 10Today I have put you in charge of
nations and kingdoms. You will pull up and
tear down, destroy and overthrow. You will
build up and plant." . . .
13The Lord spoke his word to me again:
"Jeremiah, what do you see?"
I answered the Lord and said, "I see a pot
of boiling water. It is tipping over from the
north!"
14The Lord said to me, "Disaster will
come from the north. It will happen to all
the people who live in this country. 15In a
short time I will call all of the people in the
northern kingdoms," said the Lord.
"Those kings will come and set up their
thrones
near the entrance of the gates of
Jerusalem.
They will attack the city walls around
Jerusalem.
They will attack all the cities in Judah."

Let's Pray!

Thank you, Lord, for the gifts you have given me to share with the world. Help me to be brave and wise about knowing when to use them. In Jesus' name, amen!

Going Deeper

READ IT! God knew you before you were even born. Read Psalm 139 to see how precious you are to God.

DO IT! Make a stained glass window using crayons and wax paper. Ask your parents to look up the directions online. Be sure to have your parents help you!

Jerusalem Captured

Jeremiah 52:4–9, 11–16

The Israelites were stunned when Nebuchadnezzar captured the temple. They never imagined God would allow such a thing! But because they had worshiped idols, God let his people spend seventy years of exile in Babylon. This is the story of how it happened.

Then Nebuchadnezzar king of Babylon
marched against Jerusalem with his whole
army. They made a camp around the city.
Then they built devices all around the city
walls to attack it. This happened during
Zedekiah's ninth year, tenth month and
tenth day as king. 5The city was under attack
until Zedekiah's eleventh year as king.

6By the ninth day of the fourth month,
the hunger was terrible in the city. There
was no food for the people to eat. 7Then
the city wall was broken through. And the
whole army ran away at night. They went
through the gate between the two walls by
the king's garden. The Babylonians were
still surrounding the city. Zedekiah and his
men ran toward the Jordan Valley.

8But the Babylonian army chased King
Zedekiah. They caught up with him in the
plains of Jericho. All of his army was scattered from him. 9So they captured Zedekiah
and took him to the king of Babylon at
Riblah. Riblah is in the land of Hamath.
There he passed sentence on Zedekiah. . . .
And the king kept Zedekiah in prison there
until the day he died.

12Nebuzaradan was the commander of the
king's special guards. This servant of the
king of Babylon came to Jerusalem. This
was on the tenth day of the fifth month. This
was in Nebuchadnezzar's nineteenth year
as king of Babylon. 13Nebuzaradan set fire to
the Temple of the Lord and the palace. He
also set fire to all the houses of Jerusalem.
Every important building was burned.
14The whole Babylonian army broke down
the walls around Jerusalem. That army was
led by the commander of the king's special
guards. 15Nebuzaradan, the commander of
the guards, took captive some of the poorest
people. And he took those who were left in
Jerusalem. He took captive those who had
surrendered to the king of Babylon. And he
took away the skilled craftsmen who were
left in Jerusalem. 16But Nebuzaradan left
behind the rest of the poorest people of the
land. They were to take care of the vineyards
and fields.

Let's Pray!

Lord, when we have not any light,
And mothers are asleep;
Then through the stillness of the night,
Thy little children keep.

When shadows haunt the quiet room,
Help us to understand
That Thou art with us through the gloom,
To hold us by the hand.

—Annie Matheson

Did You Know?
This period of Israel's history—when many of their people were taken into captivity in Babylon—is known as the Exile. *It lasted seventy years.*

Going Deeper

READ IT! Read about the Babylonian destruction of the temple in Jerusalem in 2 Kings 24:18–25:21.

DO IT! Ask your parents to help you look online for drawings of what the temple of God looked like.

Ezekiel's Challenge

Ezekiel 3:16–21

The prophet Ezekiel was taken into captivity in Babylon several years before the fall of Jerusalem. He may have been a student of Jeremiah. In today's passage, God came to Ezekiel with a special message. God wanted Ezekiel to warn his people to stop their sinning. Let's read his warning!

After seven days the Lord spoke his word to
me again. He said, [17]"Human being, I have
made you a watchman for Israel. Any time
you hear a word from my mouth, warn them
for me. [18]When I say to an evil person, 'You
will surely die,' you must warn him. If you
don't speak out to warn the evil person to
leave his evil way, he will die in his sin. But
I will hold you responsible for his death.
[19]You must warn the evil person. Then if he
does not turn from his wickedness or his
evil ways, he will die because of his sin. But
you will have saved yourself.
[20]"Again, a person who does right may
turn away from his goodness. He may do
evil. If I caused him to sin, he will die.
Because you have not warned him, he will
die because of his sin. And the good he did
will not be remembered. But I will hold you
responsible for his death. [21]But if you do
warn that good person not to sin, he may
not sin. Then he will surely live. This is
because he was warned. And you will save
yourself."

LET'S PRAY!

Lord, I trust in you.
Let me never be disgraced.
Save me because you do what is right.
Listen to me.
Save me quickly.
Be my rock of protection,
a strong city to save me.
You are my rock and my protection.
For the good of your name, lead me and guide me.
Set me free from the trap they set for me.
You are my protection.
I give you my life.
Save me, Lord, God of truth.

—Psalm 31:1–5

GOING DEEPER

READ IT! Just as God sent Ezekiel with a message for his people, Jesus sends you with a message for others! Read about it in Matthew 28:19–20.

DO IT! Pray for missionaries all over the world who are sharing God's Word with those who do not know him.

DID YOU KNOW?
Several images from the book of Ezekiel appear again in Revelation: four living creatures (Ezekiel 1), the scroll (Ezekiel 3), Gog and Magog (Ezekiel 38), New Jerusalem (Ezekiel 40–48), and the river of the water of life (Ezekiel 47).[26]

Shadrach, Meshach, and Abednego

Daniel 3:8–12, 19–23, 26–28

This story reminds us that God protects the faithful. Even when bad things happen, we can trust God to take care of us. Our souls, which last forever, are safe in his hands.

Then some Babylonians came up to
the king. They began speaking against
the men of Judah. 9They said to King
Nebuchadnezzar, "Our king, live forever!
10Our king, you gave a command. You said
that everyone would hear the horns, lyres,
zithers, harps, pipes and all the other mu-
sical instruments. Then they would have
to bow down and worship the gold statue.
11Anyone who wouldn't do this was to be
thrown into a blazing furnace. 12Our king,
there are some men of Judah who did not
pay attention to your order. You made them
important officers in the area of Babylon.
Their names are Shadrach, Meshach and
Abednego. They do not serve your gods.
And they do not worship the gold statue you
have set up." . . .

19Then Nebuchadnezzar was furious
with Shadrach, Meshach and Abednego.
He ordered the furnace to be heated seven
times hotter than usual. 20Then he commanded some of the strongest soldiers in
his army to tie up Shadrach, Meshach and
Abednego. The king told the soldiers to
throw them into the blazing furnace.

21So Shadrach, Meshach and Abednego
were tied up and thrown into the blazing furnace. They were still wearing their
robes, trousers, turbans and other clothes.
22The king was very angry when he gave
the command. And the furnace was made
very hot. The fire was so hot that the
flames killed the strong soldiers who took
Shadrach, Meshach and Abednego there.
23Firmly tied, Shadrach, Meshach and
Abednego fell into the blazing furnace. . . .

26Then Nebuchadnezzar went to the
opening of the blazing furnace. He shouted,
"Shadrach, Meshach and Abednego, come
out! Servants of the Most High God, come
here!"

So Shadrach, Meshach and Abednego
came out of the fire. 27When they came out,
the princes, assistant governors, governors
and royal advisers crowded around them.
They saw that the fire had not harmed their
bodies. Their hair was not burned. Their
robes were not burned. And they didn't
even smell like smoke.

28Then Nebuchadnezzar said, "Praise the
God of Shadrach, Meshach and Abednego.
Their God has sent his angel and saved his
servants from the fire! These three men
trusted their God. They refused to obey
my command. And they were willing to die
rather than serve or worship any god other
than their own."

Let's Pray!

Sing praises to the Lord. *Selah*
Sing to the one who rides through the
skies, which are from long ago.
He speaks with a thundering voice.
Announce that God is powerful.

—Psalm 68:32–35

GOING DEEPER

READ IT! Another angel helped Jesus escape a dangerous situation when he was only a baby. Read about it in Matthew 2:13–15.

DO IT! As you grow up, you will have to choose between following God and following others. Decide now that you will choose to follow God. Then, when you are faced with a tough choice, it will be easier to do the right thing!

The Hand of God

Daniel 5:1–2, 4–9, 17, 25–29

On the night of the fall of Babylon, King Belshazzar held a great feast. The prophet Daniel, who had been King Nebuchadnezzar's adviser for many years, was now an old man. But his zeal for the Lord was still strong. The hand of the Lord was upon Daniel; in this story, that hand had a message for everyone!

King Belshazzar gave a big banquet for 1,000 royal guests. And he drank wine with them. [2]As Belshazzar was drinking his wine, he gave an order to his servants. He told them to bring the gold and silver cups that his ancestor Nebuchadnezzar had taken from the Temple in Jerusalem. King Belshazzar wanted his royal guests to drink from those cups. He also wanted his wives and his slave women to drink from them. . . . [4]As they were drinking, they praised their gods. Those gods were made from gold, silver, bronze, iron, wood and stone.

[5]Then suddenly a person's hand appeared. The fingers wrote words on the plaster on the wall. This was near the lampstand in the royal palace. The king watched the hand as it wrote.

[6]King Belshazzar was very frightened. His face turned white, and his knees knocked together. He could not stand up because his legs were too weak. [7]The king called for the magicians and wise men to be brought to him. He said to the wise men of Babylon, "I will give a reward to anyone who can read this writing and explain it. I will give him purple clothes fit for a king. I will put a gold chain around his neck. And I will make him the third highest ruler in the kingdom."

[8]So all the king's wise men came in. But they could not read the writing. And they could not tell the king what it meant. [9]King Belshazzar became even more afraid. His face became even whiter. His royal guests were confused. . . .

[17]Then Daniel answered the king, ". . . I will read the writing on the wall for you. And I will explain to you what it means. . . .

[25]"These are the words that were written on the wall: 'Mene, mene, tekel, parsin.'

[26]"This is what these words mean: Mene: God has counted the days until your kingdom will end. [27]Tekel: You have been weighed on the scales and found not good enough. [28]Parsin: Your kingdom is being divided. It will be given to the Medes and the Persians."

[29]Then Belshazzar gave an order for Daniel to be dressed in purple clothes. A gold chain was put around his neck. And he was announced to be the third highest ruler in the kingdom.

DID YOU KNOW? When Babylon fell to Persia and Darius the Mede became king, Daniel was made one of three governors.

Special Words:
The expression "the writing is on the wall" comes from this story. It means that the outcome of an event or situation is easy to see.

Let's Pray!
Lord, you are so great, and I am so small. Please be with me. In Jesus' name, amen.

Going Deeper
Read It! Jesus warned about another fall of Jerusalem. Read about it in Matthew 23:37–38.
Do It! Write your grandparents letters this week, and tell them how much you love them.

Daniel in the Lions' Den

Daniel 6:13–23

Do you ever feel lonely because of your faith? Daniel did. Even after seventy years in Babylon, he was still an outsider when King Darius made Daniel one of three governors. Darius's men were jealous of Daniel and plotted to get rid of him. But Daniel was so honest that they could not accuse him of anything. So they used his faith in God against him and tricked King Darius into making a law that would trap Daniel. That law said that whoever prayed to anyone but the king had to spend the night in a den of lions! What would Daniel do?

Then those men spoke to the king. They said, "Daniel is one of the captives from Judah. And he is not paying attention to the law you wrote. Daniel still prays to his God three times every day." [14]The king became very upset when he heard this. He decided he had to save Daniel. He worked until sunset trying to think of a way to save him.

[15]Then those men went as a group to the king. They said, "Remember, our king, the law of the Medes and Persians. It says that no law or command given by the king can be changed."

[16]So King Darius gave the order. They brought Daniel and threw him into the lions' den. The king said to Daniel, "May the God you serve all the time save you!" [17]A big stone was brought. It was put over the opening of the lions' den. Then the king used his signet ring to put his special seal on the rock. . . . [18]Then King Darius went back to his palace. He did not eat that night. He did not have any entertainment brought to entertain him. And he could not sleep.

[19]The next morning King Darius got up at dawn. He hurried to the lions' den. [20]As he came near the den, he was worried. He called out to Daniel. He said, "Daniel, servant of the living God! Has your God that you always worship been able to save you from the lions?"

[21]Daniel answered, "My king, live forever! [22]My God sent his angel to close the lions' mouths. They have not hurt me, because my God knows I am innocent. I never did anything wrong to you, my king."

[23]King Darius was very happy. He told his servants to lift Daniel out of the lions' den. So they lifted him out and did not find any injury on him. This was because Daniel had trusted in his God.

Let's Pray!

The Lord is powerful.
He gives power and victory to his chosen one.

—Psalm 28:8

Going Deeper

Read It! Daniel went into his room to pray. See what Jesus said about that in Matthew 6:5–6.

Do It! Get some crayons and draw a picture of Daniel in the lions' den.

Hosea and Gomer

Hosea 1:2–10

Hosea was from the northern kingdom of Israel. He lived around the time of the fall of the northern capital, Samaria (about 721 BC).[27] Worshiping idols was common among the people, and the national god was a golden calf! God used Hosea's wife to teach us all a lesson about his divine love—a love that does not stop even when we turn away from our heavenly Father. And a love that is always waiting for his people to come back to him and be his children.

The Lord said to him, "Go, and marry a
woman who will be unfaithful to you. She
will give you children whose fathers are
other men. Do this because people in this
country have acted like an unfaithful wife
toward the Lord." 3So Hosea married Gomer
daughter of Diblaim. Gomer became pregnant and gave birth to Hosea's son.
4The Lord said to Hosea, "Name him
Jezreel. This is because soon I will punish
the family of Jehu for the people they killed
at Jezreel. Then I will put an end to the
kingdom of Israel. 5And I will also break
the power of Israel's army in the Valley of
Jezreel."
6Gomer became pregnant again and gave
birth to a daughter. The Lord said to Hosea,
"Name her Lo-Ruhamah. This is because I
will not pity Israel anymore. I will no longer forgive them. 7But I will show pity to the
people of Judah. I will save them. I will not
use bows or swords, horses or horsemen,
or weapons of war to save them. I, the Lord
their God, will save them."
8After Gomer had finished nursing Lo-
Ruhamah, she became pregnant again. And
she gave birth to another son. 9The Lord
said, "Name him Lo-Ammi because you are
not my people. And I am not your God.
10"But the people of Israel will become
like the grains of sand of the sea. You cannot measure or count them. Now it is said to
Israel, 'You are not my people.' But later they
will be called 'children of the living God.'"

Let's Pray!

My whole being, praise the Lord.
All my being, praise his holy name.
My whole being, praise the Lord.
Do not forget all his kindnesses.
The Lord forgives me for all my sins.
He heals all my diseases.
He saves my life from the grave.
He loads me with love and mercy.
He satisfies me with good things.
He makes me young again, like the
eagle.

—Psalm 103:1–5

Going Deeper

Read It! God is faithful to us, and he asks that we be faithful to him. Read about God's faithfulness in 2 Thessalonians 3:3.

Do It! Time and again God's people were unfaithful to him, just as we are sometimes unfaithful to him. Today as a family, offer a prayer of thanksgiving for God's love, which never fails.

Jonah

Jonah 1:1–7, 10–12, 15–17

God had a job for Jonah: to go to Nineveh and tell the people there to change their sinful ways. But Jonah didn't want to go to Nineveh. Jonah thought the people of Nineveh were so sinful that God should just destroy them all. So Jonah tried to run away from God. Would his plan work?

The Lord spoke his word to Jonah son of Amittai: 2"Get up, go to the great city of Nineveh and preach against it. I see the evil things they do."

3But Jonah got up to run away from the Lord. He went to the city of Joppa. There he found a ship that was going to the city of Tarshish. Jonah paid for the trip and went aboard. He wanted to go to Tarshish to run away from the Lord.

4But the Lord sent a great wind on the sea. This wind made the sea very rough. So the ship was in danger of breaking apart. 5The sailors were afraid. Each man cried to his own god. The men began throwing the cargo into the sea. This would make the ship lighter so it would not sink.

But Jonah had gone down into the ship to lie down. He fell fast asleep. 6The captain of the ship came and said, "Why are you sleeping? Get up! Pray to your god! Maybe your god will pay attention to us. Maybe he will save us!"

7Then the men said to each other, "Let's throw lots to see who caused these troubles to happen to us."

So the men threw lots. The lot showed that the trouble had happened because of Jonah. . . .

10Then the men were very afraid. They asked Jonah, "What terrible thing did you do?" They knew Jonah was running away from the Lord because Jonah had told them.

11The wind and the waves of the sea were becoming much stronger. So the men said to Jonah, "What should we do to you to make the sea calm down?"

12Jonah said to them, "Pick me up, and throw me into the sea. Then it will calm down. I know it is my fault that this great storm has come on you." . . .

15Then the men picked up Jonah and threw him into the sea. So the sea became calm. 16Then they began to fear the Lord very much. They offered a sacrifice to the Lord. They also made promises to him.

17And the Lord caused a very big fish to swallow Jonah. Jonah was in the stomach of the fish three days and three nights.

Let's Pray!

In their misery they cried out to the Lord.
  And he saved them from their troubles.
He made the storm be still.
  He calmed the waves.

—Psalm 107:28–29

Thank you, God, for saving me. In Jesus' name, amen.

Going Deeper

READ IT! Read the rest of Jonah's adventure in Jonah 2–4.

DO IT! Family movie night! Watch *Jonah: A VeggieTales movie*.

Zechariah's Chariots

Zechariah 6:1–15

In today's story, God gave the prophet Zechariah a powerful vision. The four chariots represent the angelic hosts God sends to the four ends of the earth. The chariot with the black horses brings the Lord's anger to the land of Babylon for keeping his people so long in captivity and for their idolatry.

I looked up again. I saw four chariots coming from between two mountains. They were mountains of bronze. 2Red horses pulled the first chariot. Black horses pulled the second chariot. 3White horses pulled the third chariot. And strong, spotted horses pulled the fourth chariot. 4I spoke to the angel who was talking with me. I asked, "What are these, sir?"

5He said, "These are going to the four directions on earth. They have just come from the presence of the Lord of the whole world. 6The chariot pulled by the black horses will go north. The white horses will go west. And the spotted horses will go south."

7The powerful horses were trying to go through all the earth. So he said, "Go through all the earth." And they did.

8Then he called to me, "Look. The horses that went north have calmed the Lord's anger that came from there to punish."

9The Lord spoke his word to me. He said: 10"Heldai, Tobijah and Jedaiah were captives in Babylon. Get silver and gold from them. Go that same day to the house of Josiah son of Zephaniah. 11Make the silver and gold into a crown. And put it on the head of Joshua son of Jehozadak. Joshua is the high priest. 12Tell him this is what the Lord of heaven's armies says: 'There is a man whose name is the Branch. He will branch out from where he is. He will build the Temple of the Lord. 13One man will build the Temple of the Lord. And the other will receive the honor of a king. One man will sit on his throne and rule. And the other will be a priest on his throne. And these two men will work together in peace.' 14The crown will be kept in the Temple of the Lord. It will remind Heldai, Tobijah, Jedaiah and Josiah son of Zephaniah of God's king. 15People living far away will come and build the Temple of the Lord. Then you will know the Lord of heaven's armies has sent me to you. This will happen if you completely obey the Lord your God."

Let's Pray!

Rejoice, people of Jerusalem.
  Shout for joy, people of Jerusalem.
Your king is coming to you.
  He does what is right, and he saves.
  He is gentle and riding on a donkey.
  He is on the colt of a donkey.

—Zechariah 9:9

Going Deeper

READ IT! Read Revelation 7:1–8. How is it like Ezekiel 6:8–14?

DO IT! Make fancy paper crowns to celebrate the Prince of Peace!

Did You Know?
Zechariah prophesied eight different things about Christ, from his dying for our sins (3:8–9) to his betrayal for thirty pieces of silver (11:12–13).[28]

Stories from the New Testament

The Angel Visits Mary

Luke 1:26–38

Mary was only a young teenager, engaged to be married, when the angel Gabriel came to tell her she was about to become the mother of the holy Son of God. This news would forever change Mary's life. What would she say to God's own messenger?

During Elizabeth's sixth month of preg-
nancy, God sent the angel Gabriel to a virgin who lived in Nazareth, a town in Galilee.
She was engaged to marry a man named
Joseph from the family of David. Her name
was Mary. 28The angel came to her and said,
"Greetings! The Lord has blessed you and
is with you."

29But Mary was very confused by what the
angel said. Mary wondered, "What does
this mean?"

30The angel said to her, "Don't be afraid,
Mary, because God is pleased with you.
31Listen! You will become pregnant. You
will give birth to a son, and you will name
him Jesus. 32He will be great, and people
will call him the Son of the Most High. The
Lord God will give him the throne of King
David, his ancestor. 33He will rule over the
people of Jacob forever. His kingdom will
never end."

34Mary said to the angel, "How will this
happen? I am a virgin!"

35The angel said to Mary, "The Holy Spirit
will come upon you, and the power of the
Most High will cover you. The baby will
be holy. He will be called the Son of God.
36Now listen! Elizabeth, your relative, is
very old. But she is also pregnant with a
son. Everyone thought she could not have
a baby, but she has been pregnant for six
months. 37God can do everything!"

38Mary said, "I am the servant girl of the
Lord. Let this happen to me as you say!"
Then the angel went away.

LET'S PRAY!

Jesus, Friend of little children,
Be a friend to me;
Take my hand and ever keep me
Close to Thee.
Teach me how to grow in goodness,
Daily as I grow;
Thou hast been a child, and surely
Thou dost know.
Never leave, nor forsake me;
Ever be my Friend;
For I need Thee, from life's dawning
To its end.

—Walter J. Mathams

Did You Know?
It is believed that Luke—who wrote this book—was told this story by Mary herself.[29]

Going Deeper

Read It! Hundreds of years before Jesus was born, Isaiah prophesied about how the Son of God would be born. Read about it in Isaiah 7:14.

Do It! The angel brought Mary some wonderful news. With whom can you share the wonderful news of Jesus?

Little drops of water,
little grains of sand,
make the mighty ocean
and the pleasant land.

And the little moments,
humble though they be,
make the mighty ages
of eternity.

Little deeds of kindness,
little words of love,
make our pleasant earth below,
like the heaven above.

So our little errors
lead the soul away,
from the paths of virtue
far in sin to stray.

Little seeds of mercy
sown by youthful hands,
grow to bless the nations
far in heathen lands.

Glory then forever
be to God on high,
beautiful and loving,
to eternity.

—Julia Carney

Mary Visits Elizabeth

Luke 1:39–56

When the angel Gabriel visited Mary, he told her that her relative Elizabeth was also pregnant—even though she was old. This was wonderful news! At long last, Elizabeth and Zechariah were going to have a baby. And something miraculous happened when Elizabeth saw Mary!

Mary got up and went quickly to a town
in the mountains of Judea. 40She went to
Zechariah's house and greeted Elizabeth.
41When Elizabeth heard Mary's greeting,
the unborn baby inside Elizabeth jumped.
Then Elizabeth was filled with the Holy
Spirit. 42She cried out in a loud voice,
"God has blessed you more than any other
woman. And God has blessed the baby
which you will give birth to. 43You are the
mother of my Lord, and you have come to
me! Why has something so good happened
to me? 44When I heard your voice, the
baby inside me jumped with joy. 45You are
blessed because you believed what the Lord
said to you would really happen."

46Then Mary said,
"My soul praises the Lord;
47my heart is happy because God is my
Savior.
48I am not important, but God has shown
his care for me, his servant girl.
From now on, all people will say that I
am blessed,
49because the Powerful One has done
great things for me.
His name is holy.
50God will always give mercy
to those who worship him.
51God's arm is strong.
He scatters the people who are proud
and think great things about
themselves.
52God brings down rulers from their
thrones,
and he raises up the humble.
53God fills the hungry with good things,
but he sends the rich away with
nothing.
54God has helped his people Israel who
serve him.
He gave them his mercy.
55God has done what he promised to our
ancestors,
to Abraham and to his children
forever."

56Mary stayed with Elizabeth for about
three months and then returned home.

Let's Pray!

I will praise you, Lord, with all my heart.
I will tell all the miracles you have done.
I will be happy because of you.
God Most High, I will sing praises to
your name.

—Psalm 9:1–2

Did You Know?
Zechariah questioned the angel who came to tell him that Elizabeth would have a baby. Because of that, Zechariah was not able to speak again until after the birth the baby, John the Baptist. (Luke 1:5–25, 57–64).

Going Deeper

Read It! God is a God of miracles. Elizabeth wasn't the only woman in the Bible to have a child in her old age. Read the story of Sarah in Genesis 18 and 21.

Do It! Sit down with your parents and look through your baby pictures. How have you grown and changed?

Joseph Sees an Angel

Matthew 1:18–25

Joseph, a young carpenter, was engaged to Mary. He must have been very surprised and hurt when he heard that Mary was going to have a child! Joseph thought he would quietly call off the wedding, but then an angel of the Lord appeared to him in a dream. God had a different plan, but would Joseph follow God's plan?

The mother of Jesus Christ was Mary. And this is how the birth of Jesus came about. Mary was engaged to marry Joseph. But before they married, she learned that she was going to have a baby. She was pregnant by the power of the Holy Spirit. [19]Mary's husband, Joseph, was a good man. He did not want to disgrace her in public, so he planned to divorce her secretly.

[20]While Joseph thought about this, an angel of the Lord came to him in a dream. The angel said, "Joseph, descendant of David, don't be afraid to take Mary as your wife. The baby in her is from the Holy Spirit. [21]She will give birth to a son. You will name the son Jesus. Give him that name because he will save his people from their sins."

[22]All this happened to make clear the full meaning of what the Lord had said through the prophet: [23]"The virgin will be pregnant. She will have a son, and they will name him Immanuel." This name means "God is with us."

[24]When Joseph woke up, he did what the Lord's angel had told him to do. Joseph married Mary. . . . [25]And Joseph named the son Jesus.

LET'S PRAY!

Lord, please help me obey your Word even when it is hard—just as Joseph obeyed you. In Jesus' name, amen.

GOING DEEPER

READ IT! God spoke to people in their dreams several times in the Bible. To whom did he speak in Genesis 28:10–16?

DO IT! You can be an angel in someone's life today. Do something kind for someone who could use a little cheering up.

Quote of the Day:
The Bible tells us very little about Joseph. We know that he was a carpenter and that he had at least seven children (Matthew 13:55–56). He must have been a wonderful man, for God to choose him as Jesus' earthly father![30]

The Birth of Jesus

Luke 2:1–20

O little town of Bethlehem, how still we see thee lie." Each year at Christmas, we celebrate the birth of Jesus—God's own Son, who made angels sing, stars shine, and shepherds leave their sheep.

At that time, Augustus Caesar sent an order to all people in the countries that were under Roman rule. The order said that they must list their names in a register. [2]This was the first registration taken while Quirinius was governor of Syria. [3]And everyone went to their own towns to be registered.

[4]So Joseph left Nazareth, a town in Galilee. He went to the town of Bethlehem in Judea. This town was known as the town of David. Joseph went there because he was from the family of David. [5]Joseph registered with Mary because she was engaged to marry him. (Mary was now pregnant.) [6]While Joseph and Mary were in Bethlehem, the time came for her to have the baby. [7]She gave birth to her first son. There were no rooms left in the inn. So she wrapped the baby with cloths and laid him in a box where animals are fed.

[8]That night, some shepherds were in the fields nearby watching their sheep. [9]An angel of the Lord stood before them. The glory of the Lord was shining around them, and suddenly they became very frightened. [10]The angel said to them, "Don't be afraid, because I am bringing you some good news. It will be a joy to all the people. [11]Today your Savior was born in David's town. He is Christ, the Lord. [12]This is how you will know him: You will find a baby wrapped in cloths and lying in a feeding box."

[13]Then a very large group of angels from heaven joined the first angel. All the angels were praising God, saying:

[14]"Give glory to God in heaven,
and on earth let there be peace to the
people who please God."

[15]Then the angels left the shepherds and went back to heaven. The shepherds said to each other, "Let us go to Bethlehem and see this thing that has happened. We will see this thing the Lord told us about."

[16]So the shepherds went quickly and found Mary and Joseph. [17]And the shepherds saw the baby lying in a feeding box. Then they told what the angels had said about this child. [18]Everyone was amazed when they heard what the shepherds said to them. [19]Mary hid these things in her heart; she continued to think about them. [20]Then the shepherds went back to their sheep, praising God and thanking him for everything that they had seen and heard. It was just as the angel had told them.

Let's Pray!

Dear Jesus, thank you for being born into our world as one of us. Help us to be like the shepherds and hurry to worship you. In Jesus' name, amen.

Quote of the Day:
Away in a manger
No crib for His bed,
The little Lord Jesus
Laid down His sweet head.
The stars in the bright sky
Looked down where He lay,
The little Lord Jesus
Asleep on the hay.
—Martin Luther

Going Deeper

Read It! The Old Testament prophet Micah told of Jesus' birth in Bethlehem. Read his prophecy in Micah 5:2.

Do It! Make Christmas cookies—even if it's July!

Simeon and Anna

Luke 2:22–38

In Jesus' time, parents took their babies to the temple to present them to the Lord when they were forty days old. When Mary and Joseph brought baby Jesus to the temple forty days after his birth, Simeon and Anna were there, as they had been every day for decades—and they had still more amazing news for Mary and Joseph about their baby boy.

The time came for Mary and Joseph to do
what the law of Moses taught about being
made pure. They took Jesus to Jerusalem to
present him to the Lord. 23It is written in
the law of the Lord: "Give every firstborn
male to the Lord." 24Mary and Joseph also
went to offer a sacrifice, as the law of the
Lord says: "You must sacrifice two doves or
two young pigeons."

25A man named Simeon lived in
Jerusalem. He was a good man and very
religious. He was waiting for the time when
God would help Israel. The Holy Spirit was
in him. 26The Holy Spirit told Simeon that
he would not die before he saw the Christ
promised by the Lord. 27The Spirit led
Simeon to the Temple. Mary and Joseph
brought the baby Jesus to the Temple to
do what the law said they must do. 28Then
Simeon took the baby in his arms and
thanked God:

29"Now, Lord, you can let me, your servant,
die in peace as you said.
30I have seen your Salvation with my own
eyes.
31You prepared him before all people.
32He is a light for the non-Jewish people
to see.
He will bring honor to your people, the
Israelites."

33Jesus' father and mother were amazed at
what Simeon had said about him. 34Then
Simeon blessed them and said to Mary,
"Many in Israel will fall and many will rise
because of this child. He will be a sign from
God that many people will not accept. 35The
things they think in secret will be made
known. And the things that will happen will
make your heart sad, too."

36Anna, a prophetess, was there at
the Temple. She was from the family of
Phanuel in the tribe of Asher. Anna was
very old. She had once been married for
seven years. 37Then her husband died and
she lived alone. She was now 84 years old.
Anna never left the Temple. She worshiped
God by going without food and praying
day and night. 38She was standing there at
that time, thanking God. She talked about
Jesus to all who were waiting for God to free
Jerusalem.

LET'S PRAY!

God bless all those that I love;
God bless all those that love me;
God bless all those that love those that I love,
And all those who love those that love me.

—From an old New England Sampler

Did You Know?

We know that Mary and Joseph must have not have had much money. How? Because the law of Moses said that forty days after a woman gave birth, she should offer a sacrifice of a lamb and a dove. But if she was poor, she could offer two doves instead (Leviticus 12:2–8).

Going Deeper

READ IT! Simeon called Jesus "a light for the non-Jewish people to see" (verse 32). Which apostle did Jesus send to share his message with the non-Jewish, or Gentile, people? Find out in Acts 22:1–21.

DO IT! Give part of your allowance this week to help a missionary who is taking God's Word to those who don't know him. And remember—God loves a cheerful giver!

The Wise Men

Matthew 2:1–12

Sometime between the age of forty days and two years old, Jesus had some very special visitors. Wise men, called magi, traveled from far away to see the newborn King and to bring him gifts. But King Herod was not happy to hear about another king.

Jesus was born in the town of Bethlehem
in Judea during the time when Herod was
king. After Jesus was born, some wise men
from the east came to Jerusalem. 2They
asked, "Where is the baby who was born to
be the king of the Jews? We saw his star in
the east. We came to worship him."
3When King Herod heard about this new
king of the Jews, he was troubled. And all
the people in Jerusalem were worried too.
4Herod called a meeting of all the leading
priests and teachers of the law. He asked
them where the Christ would be born.
5They answered, "In the town of Bethlehem
in Judea. The prophet wrote about this in
the Scriptures:

6'But you, Bethlehem, in the land of Judah,
you are important among the rulers of
Judah.
A ruler will come from you.
He will be like a shepherd for my
people, the Israelites.'" *Micah 5:2*

7Then Herod had a secret meeting with
the wise men from the east. He learned
from them the exact time they first saw
the star. 8Then Herod sent the wise men to
Bethlehem. He said to them, "Go and look
carefully to find the child. When you find
him, come tell me. Then I can go worship
him too."
9The wise men heard the king and then
left. They saw the same star they had seen
in the east. It went before them until it
stopped above the place where the child
was. 10When the wise men saw the star,
they were filled with joy. 11They went to the
house where the child was and saw him
with his mother, Mary. They bowed down
and worshiped the child. They opened
the gifts they brought for him. They gave
him treasures of gold, frankincense, and
myrrh. 12But God warned the wise men in
a dream not to go back to Herod. So they
went home to their own country by a different way.

Let's Pray!

Dear God, just as the Magi brought gifts to Jesus, I bring you the gift of my service. Please use me so that others may come to know you. In Jesus' name, amen.

Quote of the Day:
What can I give Him,
Poor as I am?
If I were a shepherd,
I would bring a lamb;
If I were a wise man,
I would do my part;
Yet what can I give Him?
Give my heart.
—Christina Rossetti

Special Words:
Myrrh is a natural tree resin. It had healing properties and was also used as a painkiller.

Going Deeper

Read It! Myrrh was given to Jesus at the beginning of his life. It was also given to him at the end of his life. Read about it in Mark 15:23.

Do It! As a family, act out the story of the wise men coming to see Jesus.

Flight into Egypt

Matthew 2:13–23

King Herod was ruler over Judea at the time of Jesus' birth. He was not pleased to hear that there was another king in his kingdom. He was even angrier to discover that the wise men had escaped without telling him who that king was. So Herod sent out a terrible order, but God had a plan to save his Son.

After [the wise men] left, an angel of the
Lord came to Joseph in a dream. The angel
said, "Get up! Take the child and his mother
and escape to Egypt. Herod will start looking for the child to kill him. Stay in Egypt
until I tell you to return."

14So Joseph got up and left for Egypt during the night with the child and his mother.
15Joseph stayed in Egypt until Herod died.
This was to make clear the full meaning of what the Lord had said through the
prophet. The Lord said, "I called my son
out of Egypt."

16When Herod saw that the wise men
had tricked him, he was very angry. So
he gave an order to kill all the baby boys
in Bethlehem and in all the area around
Bethlehem who were two years old or
younger. This was in keeping with the
time he learned from the wise men. 17So
what God had said through the prophet
Jeremiah came true:

18"A sound was heard in Ramah.
It was painful crying and much
sadness.
Rachel cries for her children,
and she cannot be comforted,
because her children are dead."

Jeremiah 31:15

19After Herod died, an angel of the Lord
came to Joseph in a dream. This happened
while Joseph was in Egypt. 20The angel said,
"Get up! Take the child and his mother and
go to Israel. The people who were trying to
kill the child are now dead."

21So Joseph took the child and his mother
and went to Israel. 22But he heard that
Archelaus was now king in Judea. Archelaus
became king when his father Herod died.
So Joseph was afraid to go there. After
being warned in a dream, he went to the
area of Galilee. 23He went to a town called
Nazareth and lived there. And so what God
had said through the prophets came true:
"He will be called a Nazarene."

LET'S PRAY!

Lord, keep us safe tonight,
Secure from all fears.
May angels guard us while we sleep
'Til morning light appears.

—John Leland

Going Deeper

Read It! Jesus is King of all kings! Read about it in 1 Timothy 6:14–15.

Do It! God created families to take care of one another. What can you do to help take care of each person in your family this week?

Did You Know?

"When Israel was a child, I loved him. And I called my son out of Egypt" (Hosea 11:1). These words from the prophet Hosea remind us that God had control over the life story of his Son long before he was born in that stable. Wicked kings, wise men from the East, dreams and visions—everything worked together perfectly as part of God's plan to help Mary, Joseph, and baby Jesus escape.

Joseph and Mary Look for Jesus

Luke 2:39–52

After King Herod died, Mary, Joseph, and Jesus left Egypt and returned to Nazareth. As Jesus grew up, he probably helped Joseph in his carpenter's shop and played with children in the village. We know that he had brothers and sisters. But the Bible says very little about Jesus' childhood, except for one event that happened when he was twelve and his parents took him to the temple in Jerusalem.

Joseph and Mary finished doing everything that the law of the Lord commanded. Then they went home to Nazareth, their own town in Galilee. 40The little child began to grow up. He became stronger and wiser, and God's blessings were with him.

41Every year Jesus' parents went to Jerusalem for the Passover Feast. 42When Jesus was 12 years old, they went to the feast as they always did. 43When the feast days were over, they went home. The boy Jesus stayed behind in Jerusalem, but his parents did not know it. 44Joseph and Mary traveled for a whole day. They thought that Jesus was with them in the group. Then they began to look for him among their family and friends, 45but they did not find him. So they went back to Jerusalem to look for him there. 46After three days they found him. Jesus was sitting in the Temple with the religious teachers, listening to them and asking them questions. 47All who heard him were amazed at his understanding and wise answers. 48When Jesus' parents saw him, they were amazed. His mother said to him, "Son, why did you do this to us? Your father and I were very worried about you. We have been looking for you."

49Jesus asked, "Why did you have to look for me? You should have known that I must be where my Father's work is!" 50But they did not understand the meaning of what he said.

51Jesus went with them to Nazareth and obeyed them. His mother was still thinking about all that had happened. 52Jesus continued to learn more and more and to grow physically. People liked him, and he pleased God.

LET'S PRAY!

Lord, even when I feel lost, I am never far from your love. Thank you for being near. And thank you, too, for those who care enough to teach me about you. In Jesus' name, amen!

Quote of the Day:
Happy is the person who doesn't listen to the wicked. He doesn't go where sinners go. He doesn't do what bad people do. He loves the Lord's teachings. He thinks about those teachings day and night. —Psalm 1:1–2

Going Deeper

Read It! In the Old Testament, one child actually lived in the tabernacle of God. Find out who he was in 1 Samuel 1:19–28.

Do It! Do you ever have trouble obeying Mom and Dad the first time they ask? Create a jar labeled "Make Mom and Dad Smile!" Have them drop a coin in it each time you make a good choice and obey the first time. When you have saved up enough coins, go out together for a treat so you can all smile!

John the Baptist

Matthew 3:1–12

John the Baptist was the son of Elizabeth and Zechariah. He had jumped for joy at the sound of Mary's voice even before he was born! John the Baptist grew up to be a great prophet of God. His job was to "prepare the way" (Luke 3:4) for people to receive the message of Jesus. Let's read about what John had to say to the people.

About that time John the Baptist came and
began preaching in the desert area of Judea.
2John said, "Change your hearts and lives
because the kingdom of heaven is coming
soon." 3John the Baptist is the one Isaiah
the prophet was talking about. Isaiah said:

"This is a voice of a man
who calls out in the desert:
'Prepare the way for the Lord.
Make the road straight for him.'"

Isaiah 40:3

4John's clothes were made from camel's
hair. He wore a leather belt around his
waist. For food, he ate locusts and wild
honey. 5Many people went to hear John
preach. They came from Jerusalem and all
Judea and all the area around the Jordan
River. 6They told of the sins they had done,
and John baptized them in the Jordan River.
7Many of the Pharisees and Sadducees
came to the place where John was baptizing
people. When John saw them, he said:
"You are snakes! Who warned you to run
away from God's anger that is coming?
8You must do the things that show that you
have really changed your hearts and lives.
9And don't think that you can say to yourselves,
'Abraham is our father.' I tell you
that God could make children for Abraham
from these rocks. 10The ax is now ready to
cut down the trees. Every tree that does not
produce good fruit will be cut down and
thrown into the fire.
11"I baptize you with water to show that
your hearts and lives have changed. But
there is one coming later who is greater than
I am. I am not good enough to carry his sandals.
He will baptize you with the Holy Spirit
and with fire. 12He will come ready to clean
the grain. He will separate the good grain
from the chaff. He will put the good part of
the grain into his barn. And he will burn the
chaff with a fire that cannot be put out."

Let's Pray!

Lord, change my heart! Make it a little bit more like Jesus' every day. In his name I pray, amen

Quote of the Day:

*Hear me, Father, this I pray,
Forgive the sins I've done this day.
Wash my heart, clean and new;
Fill it with great love for you.
Teach me to do all that's right,
To serve others with all my might.
Keep me close to you this day,
Hear me, Father, this I pray.*

—Tama Fortner

Going Deeper

Read It! Another prophet of God wore clothes similar to John's. Find out who in 2 Kings 1:8.

Do It! John's message focused on repentance—that is, on asking God to forgive your sins and to help you not to sin anymore. Is there anything you need to repent of? If so, do it right away!

John Baptizes Jesus

Matthew 3:13–17

"I baptize you with water," John told his followers, "but there is one coming later who can do more than I can. . . . He will baptize you with the Holy Spirit and with fire" (Luke 3:16). But before Jesus began his ministry, he wanted John to do something for him.

At that time Jesus came from Galilee to the Jordan River. He came to John and wanted John to baptize him. [14]But John tried to stop him. John said, "Why do you come to me to be baptized? I should be baptized by you!"

[15]Jesus answered, "Let it be this way for now. We should do all things that are right." So John agreed to baptize Jesus.

[16]Jesus was baptized and came up out of the water. Heaven opened, and he saw God's Spirit coming down on him like a dove. [17]And a voice spoke from heaven. The voice said, "This is my Son and I love him. I am very pleased with him."

LET'S PRAY!

Dear Lord, John the Baptist obeyed you even when he didn't understand why. Please help me be able to obey you without asking why. In Jesus' name, amen.

GOING DEEPER

READ IT! John baptized people to show that their hearts had changed (Matthew 3:11). Why did Jesus say we should be baptized? Read about it in Matthew 28:19.

DO IT! Talk with your parents or preacher about what baptism means.

DID YOU KNOW?
Jesus' public life and ministry began with his baptism by John in the Jordan River.

Temptation in the Desert

Matthew 4:1–11

I dare you!" Have you ever said this to another kid when you wanted him to do something that you both knew he shouldn't? In today's story, Jesus had been fasting in the wilderness for forty days. That's when Satan decided to tempt him—when he knew that Jesus was hungry and tired. Satan dared Jesus to do things they both knew he shouldn't. How would Jesus be able to stand up to his enemy?

Then the Spirit led Jesus into the desert to be
tempted by the devil. 2Jesus ate nothing for
40 days and nights. After this, he was very
hungry. 3The devil came to Jesus to tempt
him. The devil said, "If you are the Son of
God, tell these rocks to become bread."
4Jesus answered, "It is written in the
Scriptures, 'A person does not live only by
eating bread. But a person lives by everything the Lord says.'"
5Then the devil led Jesus to the holy city
of Jerusalem. He put Jesus on a very high
place of the Temple. 6The devil said, "If you
are the Son of God, jump off. It is written in
the Scriptures,

'He has put his angels in charge of you.
They will catch you with their hands.
And you will not hit your foot on a
rock.'" *Psalm 91:11–12*

7Jesus answered him, "It also says in
the Scriptures, 'Do not test the Lord your
God.'"
8Then the devil led Jesus to the top of a
very high mountain. He showed Jesus all
the kingdoms of the world and all the great
things that are in those kingdoms. 9The
devil said, "If you will bow down and worship me, I will give you all these things."
10Jesus said to the devil, "Go away from
me, Satan! It is written in the Scriptures,
'You must worship the Lord your God.
Serve only him!'"
11So the devil left Jesus. And then some
angels came to Jesus and helped him.

Let's Pray!

Pray the Lord's Prayer (Matthew 4:9–13). Take a moment to think about the words "Do not cause us to be tested; but save us from the Evil One."

Did You Know? Only three people in the Bible ever fasted for forty days—Jesus, Moses, and Elijah. Moses fasted for forty days on Mount Sinai when God gave him the Ten Commandments (Exodus 34:28). Elijah also fasted for forty days after facing down the prophets of Baal (1 Kings 19:7–9).

Going Deeper

Read It! Angels also came and comforted Elijah. Read about it in 1 Kings 19:1–9.

Do It! It can be difficult for people to do the right thing when they are hungry. Gather up canned goods for your church's pantry or for a Christian homeless center to help take care of those who are hungry.

Jesus Calls His Disciples

Matthew 4:17–22

When Jesus began his ministry, he picked twelve men to be his apostles—those who would help him teach others. They were Peter, Andrew, James, John, Philip, Thomas, Matthew, Bartholomew, James the Less, Simon, Thaddeus, and Judas. He began with two brothers. Let's find out who they are.

Jesus began to preach, saying, "Change
your hearts and lives, because the kingdom
of heaven is coming soon."
18 Jesus was walking by Lake Galilee. He
saw two brothers, Simon (called Peter)
and Simon's brother Andrew. The brothers were fishermen, and they were fishing
in the lake with a net. 19 Jesus said, "Come
follow me. I will make you fishermen for
men." 20 At once Simon and Andrew left
their nets and followed him.
21 Jesus continued walking by Lake
Galilee. He saw two other brothers, James
and John, the sons of Zebedee. They were
in a boat with their father Zebedee, preparing their nets to catch fish. Jesus told
them to come with him. 22 At once they left
the boat and their father, and they followed
Jesus.

Let's Pray!

I always pray to the God of our Lord Jesus Christ—to the glorious Father. I pray that he will give you a spirit that will make you wise in the knowledge of God—the knowledge that he has shown you. I pray that you will have greater understanding in your heart. Then you will know the hope that God has chosen to give us. I pray that you will know that the blessings God has promised his holy people are rich and glorious. And you will know that God's power is very great for us who believe.

—Ephesians 1:17–19

Going Deeper

Read It! When Judas betrayed Jesus, they needed to find a new apostle. Find out who he was in Acts 1:26.

Do It! It must have taken a lot of courage for Simon and Andrew to leave everything they knew and follow Jesus. At dinner tonight, talk about what you would do if Jesus called you.

Sermon on the Mount

Matthew 5:3–12

As word spread about Jesus' miracles and his wisdom, crowds of people began to follow him. One day Jesus climbed up on small mount to teach the people how to live as God wanted them to. These teachings are known as the Sermon on the Mount. Today's reading is a small part of the sermon, called the "Beatitudes." The Beatitudes are a map for how to live a good, Christian life.

"Those people who know they have great
spiritual needs are happy.
The kingdom of heaven belongs to them.
4 Those who are sad now are happy.
God will comfort them.
5 Those who are humble are happy.
The earth will belong to them.
6 Those who want to do right more than
anything else are happy.
God will fully satisfy them.
7 Those who give mercy to others are happy.
Mercy will be given to them.
8 Those who are pure in their thinking are
happy.
They will be with God.
9 Those who work to bring peace are happy.
God will call them his sons.
10 Those who are treated badly for doing
good are happy.
The kingdom of heaven belongs to them.

11 "People will say bad things about you
and hurt you. They will lie and say all kinds
of evil things about you because you follow
me. But when they do these things to you,
you are happy. 12 Rejoice and be glad. You
have a great reward waiting for you in
heaven. People did the same evil things to
the prophets who lived before you."

Let's Pray!

A light shines in the dark for honest
people.
It shines for those who are good and
kind and merciful.
It is good to be kind and generous.
Whoever is fair in his business
will never be defeated.
A good person will be remembered from
now on.
He won't be afraid of bad news.
He is safe because he trusts the Lord.

—Psalm 112:4–7

Father, thank you for your grace. Help me to always trust you and obey your Word.

Quote of the Day:
The kingdom of heaven
is of the childlike,
of those who are easy to please,
who love and give pleasure.
—Robert Louis Stevenson

Going Deeper

Read It! Jesus gave his disciples a new commandment. Find out what it is in John 13:34–35.

Do It! Is there someone who says "all kinds of evil things about you because you follow" Jesus? Say an extra prayer for that person—and try to find something kind that you can do for him or her.

A Light on a Hill

Matthew 5:13–22

Today's reading is also a part of the Sermon on the Mount. In these verses, Jesus explained that he wants his followers to do everything out of love for God. He doesn't want us to just pretend to be good so other people will think well of us. "Be a light for other people," Jesus reminded us. "Live so that they will see the good things you do. Live so that they will praise your Father in heaven" (Matthew 5:16). This light is the love of God, which warms our hearts and helps us care even for those people who are hardest to love.

"You are the salt of the earth. But if the salt
loses its salty taste, it cannot be made salty
again. It is good for nothing. It must be
thrown out for people to walk on.
14"You are the light that gives light to the
world. A city that is built on a hill cannot be
hidden. 15And people don't hide a light under a bowl. They put the light on a lampstand.
Then the light shines for all the people in
the house. 16In the same way, you should be
a light for other people. Live so that they will
see the good things you do. Live so that they
will praise your Father in heaven.
17"Don't think that I have come to destroy
the law of Moses or the teaching of the
prophets. I have not come to destroy their
teachings but to do what they said. 18I tell
you the truth. Nothing will disappear from
the law until heaven and earth are gone.
The law will not lose even the smallest letter or the smallest part of a letter until all
has happened. 19Whoever refuses to obey
any command and teaches other people
not to obey that command will be the least
important in the kingdom of heaven. But
whoever obeys the law and teaches other
people to obey the law will be great in the
kingdom of heaven. 20I tell you that you
must do better than the teachers of the law
and the Pharisees. If you are not better
than they are, you will not enter the kingdom of heaven.
21"You have heard that it was said to our
people long ago, 'You must not murder
anyone. Anyone who murders another will
be judged.' 22But I tell you, if you are angry
with your brother, you will be judged. And
if you say bad things to your brother, you
will be judged by the Jewish council. And if
you call your brother a fool, then you will be
in danger of the fire of hell."

LET'S PRAY!

God, make my life a little light
Within the world to glow,
A little flame that burneth bright,
Wherever I may go.

God, make my life a little flower,
That giveth joy to all,
Content to bloom in native bower
Although its place be small.

God, make my life a little song
That comforteth the sad;
That helpeth others to be strong,
And makes the singer glad.

God, make my life a little staff,
Whereon the weak may rest,
That so what health and strength I have
May serve my neighbors best.

God, make my life a little hymn
Of tenderness and praise;
Of faith, that never waxeth dim,
In all His wondrous ways.

—Mathilda Betham-Edwards

Did You Know?
Just as our bodies need water and oxygen to survive, they also need salt!

Going Deeper

Read It! Did you know that one woman was turned into a pillar of salt for disobeying God's angels? Find out who she was in Genesis 19:23–26.

Do It! Can you name all the apostles? (Remember, there are fourteen, including the apostle to the Gentiles and the one who replaced Judas.)

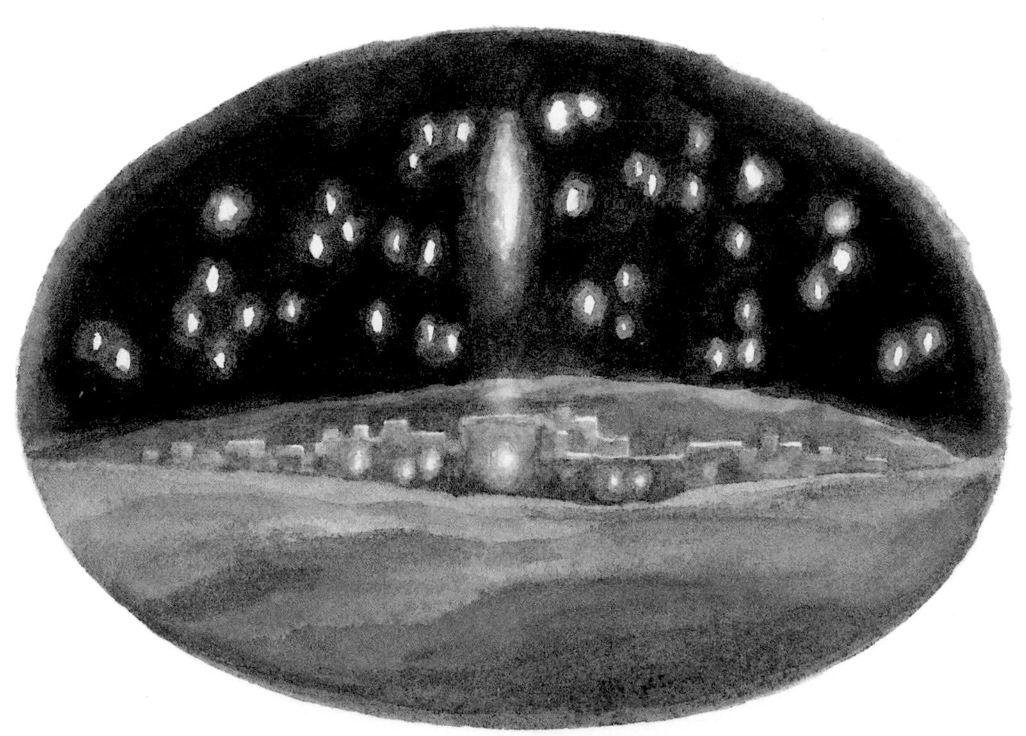

Wedding at Cana

John 2:1–11

There was a beautiful bride and a happy groom. Their families had prepared a great wedding feast that would last for many days. They invited Jesus; his mother, Mary; and his disciples. For days, everyone had a wonderful time, eating and laughing. Suddenly, the man in charge of the feast looked very worried. When Mary heard what the problem was, she knew just what to do.

Two days later there was a wedding in the
town of Cana in Galilee. Jesus' mother was
there. 2Jesus and his followers were also
invited to the wedding. 3When all the wine
was gone, Jesus' mother said to him, "They
have no more wine."

4Jesus answered, "Dear woman, why
come to me? My time has not yet come."

5His mother said to the servants, "Do
whatever he tells you to do."

6In that place there were six stone water
jars. The Jews used jars like these in their
washing ceremony. Each jar held about 20
or 30 gallons.

7Jesus said to the servants, "Fill the jars
with water." So they filled the jars to the top.

8Then he said to them, "Now take some
out and give it to the master of the feast."

So the servants took the water to the
master. 9When he tasted it, the water had
become wine. He did not know where the
wine came from. But the servants who
brought the water knew. The master of
the wedding called the bridegroom 10and
said to him, "People always serve the best
wine first. Later, after the guests have been
drinking a lot, they serve the cheaper wine.
But you have saved the best wine till now."

11So in Cana of Galilee, Jesus did his first
miracle. There he showed his glory, and his
followers believed in him.

Let's Pray!

Lord, Mary trusted you to solve the problem. When I face problems, help me trust you too. In Jesus' name, amen.

Quote of the Day:
All good gifts around us
Are sent from heaven above.
Then thank the Lord,
O thank the Lord,
For all his love.
—Matthias Claudius
(translated by Jane
Montgomery Campbell)

Going Deeper

READ IT! The very first wedding was in the garden of Eden. Read what the Bible says about marriage in Genesis 2:24.

DO IT! Look through your parents' wedding album, and ask them to tell you about their wedding day.

When I wake up in the morning,
thank you, God, for being there.
When I come to school each day,
thank you, God, for being there.
When I am playing with my friends,
thank you, God, for being there.
And when I go to bed at night,
thank you, God, for being there.

—Unknown

Father, we thank thee for the night,
And for the lovely morning light;
For rest and food and loving care,
And all that makes the day so fair.

Help us to do the things we should,
To be to others kind and good;
In all we do, in work, or play,
To grow more loving ev'ry day.

—Rebecca J. Weston

Jesus Clears the Temple

John 2:13–25

One of God's Ten Commandments is to "remember to keep the Sabbath as a holy day" (Exodus 20:8). We keep the Sabbath by going to church each week—dressing neatly, praying, singing, and worshiping with the rest of God's people. In today's story, Jesus saw some people who were not keeping God's temple holy. They were dishonoring God in his own house! What would Jesus do about that?

It was almost time for the Jewish Passover Feast. So Jesus went to Jerusalem. [14]In the Temple he found men selling cattle, sheep, and doves. He saw others sitting at tables, exchanging money. [15]Jesus made a whip out of cords. Then he forced all these men, with the sheep and cattle, to leave the Temple. He turned over the tables and scattered the money of the men who were exchanging it. [16]Then he said to those who were selling pigeons, "Take these things out of here! Don't make my Father's house a place for buying and selling!"

[17]When this happened the followers remembered what was written in the Scriptures: "My strong love for your Temple completely controls me."

[18]The Jews said to Jesus, "Show us a miracle for a sign. Prove that you have the right to do these things."

[19]Jesus answered, "Destroy this temple, and I will build it again in three days."

[20]The Jews answered, "Men worked 46 years to build this Temple! Do you really believe you can build it again in three days?"

[21](But the temple Jesus meant was his own body. [22]After Jesus was raised from death, his followers remembered that Jesus had said this. Then they believed the Scripture and the words Jesus said.)

[23]Jesus was in Jerusalem for the Passover Feast. Many people believed in him because they saw the miracles he did. [24]But Jesus did not trust himself to them because he knew them all. [25]He did not need anyone to tell him about people. Jesus knew what was in a person's mind.

LET'S PRAY!

The Lord's teachings are perfect.
  They give new strength.
The Lord's rules can be trusted.
  They make plain people wise. . . .
It is good to respect the Lord.
  That respect will last forever.
The Lord's judgments are true.
  They are completely right.

—Psalm 19:7, 9

DID YOU KNOW?
Jesus actually cleaned out the temple twice! This time, at the beginning of his ministry, and then again in Matthew 21:12–15, near the end of his ministry.

God, thank you for the Sabbath day—that special time to worship you. But help me to keep each day holy and to worship you always in my heart. In Jesus' name, amen.

Did You Know?
The temple of Jesus' time had four different courts—one each for priests, male Israelites, women, and Gentiles. The whole area of the temple was surrounded by a massive wall that was one thousand feet long on each side. It covered an area of twenty-five football fields![31]

Going Deeper

Read It! When Jesus first cleaned out the temple, he said, "Don't make my Father's house a place for buying and selling!" (verse 16). Some three years later, Jesus cleaned out the temple again. What did he say the people had turned it into this time? Find out in Matthew 21:13.

Do It! We should worship God every day—not just Sunday! What will you do to worship God today?

A Nighttime Visit

John 3:1–13

Many people began to follow Jesus and to believe that he was the Son of God—the Messiah, or Savior, whom God had promised to send. But not everyone believed. Almost from the very beginning of his ministry, Jesus had powerful enemies among the Jewish leaders. And yet, he also had a handful of "secret believers." These men were afraid of the Jewish leaders, so they wouldn't publicly follow Jesus, but they admired him and his teachings. Today's story is about one such man. And he had some questions for Jesus—in the middle of the night!

There was a man named Nicodemus who was
one of the Pharisees. He was an important
Jewish leader. 2One night Nicodemus came
to Jesus. He said, "Teacher, we know that you
are a teacher sent from God. No one can do
the miracles you do, unless God is with him."
3Jesus answered, "I tell you the truth.
Unless you are born again, you cannot be in
God's kingdom."
4Nicodemus said, "But if a man is already
old, how can he be born again? He cannot
enter his mother's body again. So how can
he be born a second time?"
5But Jesus answered, "I tell you the truth.
Unless one is born from water and the
Spirit, he cannot enter God's kingdom.
6A person's body is born from his human
parents. But a person's spiritual life is born
from the Spirit. 7Don't be surprised when I
tell you, 'You must all be born again.' 8The
wind blows where it wants to go. You hear
the wind blow. But you don't know where
the wind comes from or where it is going. It
is the same with every person who is born
from the Spirit."
9Nicodemus asked, "How can all this be
possible?"
10Jesus said, "You are an important teacher
in Israel. But you still don't understand
these things? 11I tell you the truth. We talk
about what we know. We tell about what we
have seen. But you don't accept what we tell
you. 12I have told you about things here on
earth, but you do not believe me. So surely
you will not believe me if I tell you about the
things of heaven! 13The only one who has
ever gone up to heaven is the One who came
down from heaven—the Son of Man."

Let's Pray!

Lord, it was Nicodemus who first heard the famous words "God loved the world so much that he gave his only Son. . . . So that whoever believes in him may not be lost, but have eternal life" (John 3:16). Jesus, I believe in you! Thank you for loving me. In his name, amen.

Going Deeper

Read It! God doesn't want anyone to be left out of heaven. That's why he sent Jesus—to give everyone a chance to be saved. Read about it in 2 Peter 3:9.

Do It! John 3:16 is one of the most beautiful verses in the Bible. Memorize it together as a family.

Quote of the Day:
"I am the way. And I am the truth and the life. The only way to the Father is through me."
—Jesus, in John 14:6

The Woman at the Well

John 4:1–14

In the summertime, as the sun rises high in the sky, people often try to stay cool by going inside or seeking out a shady spot. When it's very hot, we tend to slow down, drink lots of water, and cover up to prevent sunburn. But in today's story a Samaritan woman chose the very hottest part of the day to lug her water pitcher down to the town's well. This woman had made many mistakes and lived a shameful life. Most likely, she was trying to avoid seeing the other people of the town, who might be unkind to her. But then she met Jesus, and she couldn't wait to tell everyone what had happened!

The Pharisees heard that Jesus was making
and baptizing more followers than John.
2(But really Jesus himself did not baptize
people. His followers did the baptizing.)
Jesus knew that the Pharisees had heard
about him. 3So he left Judea and went back
to Galilee. 4On the way he had to go through
the country of Samaria.

5In Samaria Jesus came to the town called
Sychar. This town is near the field that
Jacob gave to his son Joseph. 6Jacob's well
was there. Jesus was tired from his long
trip. So he sat down beside the well. It was
about noon. 7A Samaritan woman came to
the well to get some water. Jesus said to her,
"Please give me a drink." 8(This happened
while Jesus' followers were in town buying
some food.)

9The woman said, "I am surprised that
you ask me for a drink. You are a Jew and I
am a Samaritan." (Jews are not friends with
Samaritans.)

10Jesus said, "You don't know what God
gives. And you don't know who asked you
for a drink. If you knew, you would have
asked me, and I would have given you living water."

11The woman said, "Sir, where will you
get that living water? The well is very deep,
and you have nothing to get water with.
12Are you greater than Jacob, our father?
Jacob is the one who gave us this well. He
drank from it himself. Also, his sons and
flocks drank from this well."

13Jesus answered, "Every person who
drinks this water will be thirsty again.
14But whoever drinks the water I give will
never be thirsty again. The water I give will
become a spring of water flowing inside
him. It will give him eternal life."

LET'S PRAY!

Thank you for my friend next door,
And my friend across the street,
And please help me to be a friend
To everyone I meet.

—Unknown

SPECIAL WORDS: Living water *refers to the Holy Spirit.*

Did You Know?
Jacob's well is one of the few places from the life of Jesus that can still be identified today. It is one hundred feet deep and nine feet across.[32]

Going Deeper

Read It! Jesus told his disciples that when he left them he would send the Holy Spirit to help them. Read this promise in John 14:16.

Do It! The Samaritans believed they were worshiping the same God as the Jews even though some of their beliefs were very different. Notice that Jesus did not scold the woman at the well for her beliefs; he simply told her what she needed. What can we learn from this about how to share Jesus with others?

Jesus Teaches His Disciples to Pray

Matthew 6:5–18

Do you talk to God in prayer before you go to bed at night, or when you wake up each morning, or before meals? Some people just rattle through their prayers quickly, without really thinking about what they are saying or to whom they are speaking.

Imagine driving to your grandma's house, running inside to her favorite chair, shouting, "Hi, Grandma! How are you? I'm fine. Bye!" and then running back to your car again. She would wonder what was wrong!

You show your love for your grandmother by taking time to speak to her from the heart and then listening for her answer. In the same way, you show God that you love him by thinking carefully about what you say to him and then sitting quietly in his presence, listening for what he has to say to your heart. Whether the words are your own or you pray with these words of Jesus, the most important thing is to think about the one who hears them.

"When you pray, don't be like the hypocrites.
They love to stand in the synagogues and on
the street corners and pray loudly. They want
people to see them pray. I tell you the truth.
They already have their full reward. [6]When
you pray, you should go into your room and
close the door. Then pray to your Father who
cannot be seen. Your Father can see what is
done in secret, and he will reward you.

[7]"And when you pray, don't be like those
people who don't know God. They continue
saying things that mean nothing. They
think that God will hear them because of
the many things they say. [8]Don't be like
them. Your Father knows the things you
need before you ask him. [9]So when you
pray, you should pray like this:

'Our Father in heaven,
we pray that your name will always be
kept holy.
[10]We pray that your kingdom will come.
We pray that what you want will be done,
here on earth as it is in heaven.
[11]Give us the food we need for each day.
[12]Forgive the sins we have done,
just as we have forgiven those who did
wrong to us.
[13]Do not cause us to be tested;
but save us from the Evil One.'

[14]Yes, if you forgive others for the things
they do wrong, then your Father in heaven
will also forgive you for the things you do
wrong. [15]But if you don't forgive the wrongs
of others, then your Father in heaven will
not forgive the wrong things you do.

[16]"When you give up eating, don't put on
a sad face like the hypocrites. They make
their faces look strange to show people
that they are giving up eating. I tell you the
truth, those hypocrites already have their
full reward. [17]So when you give up eating,
comb your hair and wash your face. [18]Then
people will not know that you are giving up
eating. But your Father, whom you cannot
see, will see you. Your Father sees what is
done in secret, and he will reward you."

Quote of the Day:
Prayer is simply a two-way conversation between you and God.
—Billy Graham

Let's Pray!

Father, thank you for teaching me to pray, and thank you for hearing my prayers. Help me want to pray to you each and every day. In Jesus' name, amen.

Going Deeper

Read It! Many of the psalms are prayers to God. One of the most beautiful is Psalm 139. Read it today!

Do It! Write your own prayer, and turn it into a card. Send it to someone you love.

Don't Worry!

Matthew 6:24–34

Do you ever worry—about tests at school or how you'll do at the ball game? Have you ever been so afraid you wouldn't do well that you couldn't think of anything else? If you let worry and fear take over your life, you'll miss out on all the happiness God wants you to have. But if you do your part—like studying for the test or practicing for the game—you can leave the outcome in God's hands. When you choose to trust God, nothing can take away your joy!

"No one can be a slave to two masters. He will hate one master and love the other. Or he will follow one master and refuse to follow the other. So you cannot serve God and money at the same time.

25"So I tell you, don't worry about the food you need to live. And don't worry about the clothes you need for your body. Life is more important than food. And the body is more important than clothes. 26Look at the birds in the air. They don't plant or harvest or store food in barns. But your heavenly Father feeds the birds. And you know that you are worth much more than the birds. 27You cannot add any time to your life by worrying about it.

28"And why do you worry about clothes? Look at the flowers in the field. See how they grow. They don't work or make clothes for themselves. 29But I tell you that even Solomon with his riches was not dressed as beautifully as one of these flowers. 30God clothes the grass in the field like that. The grass is living today, but tomorrow it is thrown into the fire to be burned. So you can be even more sure that God will clothe you. Don't have so little faith! 31Don't worry and say, 'What will we eat?' or 'What will we drink?' or 'What will we wear?' 32All the people who don't know God keep trying to get these things. And your Father in heaven knows that you need them. 33The thing you should want most is God's kingdom and doing what God wants. Then all these other things you need will be given to you. 34So don't worry about tomorrow. Each day has enough trouble of its own. Tomorrow will have its own worries."

Let's Pray!

Thank you, Father, for taking care of my every need. When I start to worry, help me remember your faithfulness. In Jesus' name, amen.

Quote of the Day:
"I leave you peace. My peace I give you. I do not give it to you as the world does. So don't let your hearts be troubled. Don't be afraid."
—Jesus, in John 14:27

Going Deeper

Read It! God sometimes provides for his people in amazing ways. The Israelites wandered in the desert for forty years. Read about how God took care of their clothes and shoes in Deuteronomy 8:4.

Do It! Sometimes we get into the habit of worrying because we forget to ask God to help us, or we don't think about all the times he has helped us before. Make a prayer journal to help you remember. Use a small, blank book to write down your prayers, and give your worries to God. Don't forget to leave space to write down how God answered your prayers!

Jesus Heals the Official's Son

John 4:46–54

Think of a time when you were sick. What did your parents do to help you feel better? Did they take you to the doctor and get you medicine, or did they bring you chicken soup or Popsicles? Parents love their children, and they do everything they can to keep them healthy. In today's story, a rich man had a son who was very sick. Then the man heard about Jesus. Would Jesus be able to heal his son? The man just had to find out!

Jesus went to visit Cana in Galilee again.
This is where Jesus had changed the water
into wine. One of the king's important
officers lived in the city of Capernaum.
This man's son was sick. 47The man heard
that Jesus had come from Judea and was
now in Galilee. He went to Jesus and
begged him to come to Capernaum and
heal his son. His son was almost dead.
48Jesus said to him, "You people must see
signs and miracles before you will believe
in me."
49The officer said, "Sir, come before my
child dies."
50Jesus answered, "Go. Your son will live."
The man believed what Jesus told him
and went home. 51On the way the man's
servants came and met him. They told him,
"Your son is well."
52The man asked, "What time did my son
begin to get well?"
They answered, "It was about one o'clock
yesterday when the fever left him."
53The father knew that one o'clock was
the exact time that Jesus had said, "Your
son will live." So the man and all the people
of his house believed in Jesus.
54That was the second miracle that Jesus
did after coming from Judea to Galilee.

Let's Pray!

He heals the brokenhearted.
He bandages their wounds.

—Psalm 147:3

Dear Lord, please be with all those who are hurting and sick. Hold them close to your heart. Heal and comfort them. In Jesus' name, amen.

Going Deeper

READ IT! Jesus could heal with just a word or a touch. But in the Old Testament, God told Naaman to do something unusual to be healed. Find out what it was in 2 Kings 5:1–14.

DO IT! Have a canned food drive or bake sale to raise money for St. Jude Children's Hospital or your local children's hospital.

Quote of the Day:
A happy heart is
like good medicine.
But a broken spirit
drains your strength.
—Proverbs 17:22

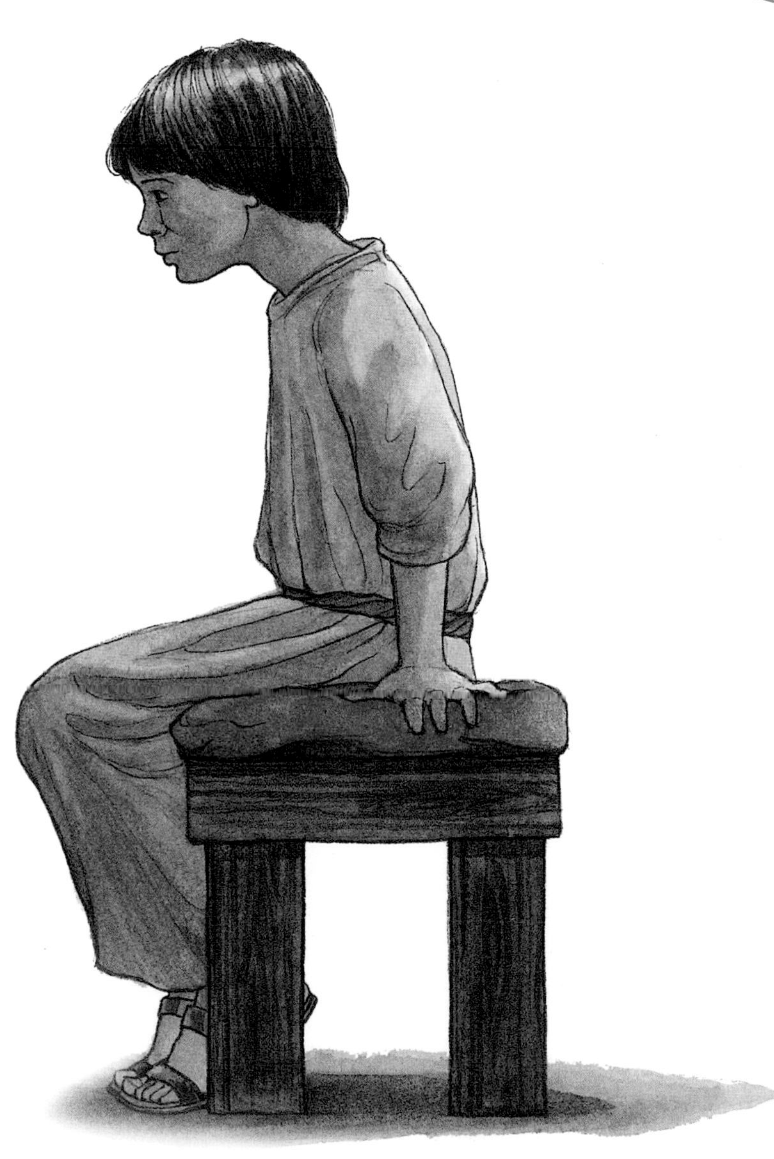

Jesus Heals the Sick

Mark 1:21–34

When Adam and Eve gave in to the devil's temptation, sin and sickness and death came into the world. But God sent his Son, Jesus, to save the world. Jesus had the power to forgive sin, to heal the sick, and even to raise the dead. During his time on earth, Jesus often used his healing powers to help people see that he was truly the Son of God.

Jesus and his followers went to Capernaum. On the Sabbath day Jesus went to the synagogue and began to teach. 22The people there were amazed at his teaching. He did not teach like their teachers of the law. He taught like a person who had authority. 23While he was in the synagogue, a man was there who had an evil spirit in him. The man shouted, 24"Jesus of Nazareth! What do you want with us? Did you come to destroy us? I know who you are—God's Holy One!"

25Jesus said strongly, "Be quiet! Come out of the man!" 26The evil spirit made the man shake violently. Then the spirit gave a loud cry and came out of him.

27The people were amazed. They asked each other, "What is happening here? This man is teaching something new. And he teaches with authority. He even gives commands to evil spirits, and they obey him." 28And the news about Jesus spread quickly everywhere in the area of Galilee.

29Jesus and his followers left the synagogue. They all went at once with James and John to the home of Simon and Andrew. 30Simon's mother-in-law was sick in bed with a fever. The people there told Jesus about her. 31So Jesus went to her bed, took her hand, and helped her up. Immediately the fever left her, and she was healed. Then she began serving them.

32That night, after the sun went down, the people brought to Jesus all who were sick. They also brought those who had demons in them. 33The whole town gathered at the door of the house. 34Jesus healed many who had different kinds of sicknesses. He also forced many demons to leave people. But he would not allow the demons to speak, because they knew who he was.

LET'S PRAY!

Lord, my God, I
prayed to you.
And you healed me. . . .
You changed my sorrow
into dancing.

—Psalm 30:2, 11

Special Words:
Evil spirit *in verse 23 refers to a demon or fallen angel.*

Going Deeper

Read It! Jesus hurt for those who were sick. Read other healing stories in Matthew 8:16–17 and Luke 4:40–41.

Do It! What are some ways you can help people with special needs? Consider volunteering with the Special Olympics or another local center that helps the developmentally disabled.

Jesus Feeds 5,000

Mark 6:30–44

Have you ever shared your lunch at school with someone who had forgotten his? In today's story, more than five thousand men (plus women and children) seemed to have forgotten their lunches! How would Jesus be able to feed all those people?

The apostles that Jesus had sent out to
preach returned. They gathered around
him and told him about all the things they
had done and taught. [31]Crowds of people
were coming and going. Jesus and his followers did not even have time to eat. He
said to them, "Come with me. We will go to
a quiet place to be alone. There we will get
some rest."

[32]So they went in a boat alone to a place
where there were no people. [33]But many
people saw them leave and recognized
them. So people from all the towns ran
to the place where Jesus was going. They
got there before Jesus arrived. [34]When he
landed, he saw a great crowd waiting. Jesus
felt sorry for them, because they were like
sheep without a shepherd. So he taught
them many things.

[35]It was now late in the day. Jesus' followers came to him and said, "No one lives in
this place. And it is already very late. [36]Send
the people away. They need to go to the
farms and towns around here to buy some
food to eat."

[37]But Jesus answered, "You give them
food to eat."

They said to him, "We can't buy enough
bread to feed all these people! We would
all have to work a month to earn enough
money to buy that much bread!"

[38]Jesus asked them, "How many loaves of
bread do you have now? Go and see."

When they found out, they came to him
and said, "We have five loaves and two fish."

[39]Then Jesus said to the followers, "Tell
all the people to sit in groups on the green
grass." [40]So all the people sat in groups.
They sat in groups of 50 or groups of 100.
[41]Jesus took the five loaves and two fish. He
looked up to heaven and thanked God for
the bread. He divided the bread and gave it
to his followers for them to give to the people. Then he divided the two fish among
them all. [42]All the people ate and were satisfied. [43]The followers filled 12 baskets with
the pieces of bread and fish that were not
eaten. [44]There were about 5,000 men there
who ate.

Let's Pray!

The Lord is good to me,
  and so I thank the Lord
For giving me the things I need:
  the sun, the rain, and the apple tree!
The Lord is good to me.

—Traditional

GOING DEEPER

READ IT! Read John 6:8–9 to find out where the disciples got the five loaves and two fish!

DO IT! Have fish sandwiches for dinner tonight and talk about which of Jesus' miracles is your favorite.

DID YOU KNOW?

Verse 44 tells us that more than 5,000 men ate the bread and fishes. But that number doesn't include the women and children. Jesus may have fed many thousands more!

Jesus Teaches About the Family

Mark 10:2–9, 13–16

God loves families! He created men and women to get married and to love each other for their whole lives. God hates divorce because he knows how much it hurts families. God created children to love, learn from, honor, and respect their parents always. When we follow God's order for the family, we help each other grow in God's family. And that is a good thing!

Some Pharisees came to Jesus and tried to
trick him. They asked, "Is it right for a man
to divorce his wife?"
3 Jesus answered, "What did Moses command you to do?"
4 They said, "Moses allowed a man to write
out divorce papers and send her away."
5 Jesus said, "Moses wrote that command
for you because you refused to accept God's
teaching. 6 But when God made the world,
'he made them male and female.' 7 'So a
man will leave his father and mother and
be united with his wife. 8 And the two people
will become one body.' So the people are
not two, but one. 9 God has joined the two
people together. So no one should separate
them." . . .
13 Some people brought their small children to Jesus so he could touch them. But
his followers told the people to stop bringing their children to him. 14 When Jesus saw
this, he was displeased. He said to them,
"Let the little children come to me. Don't
stop them. The kingdom of God belongs to
people who are like these little children.
15 I tell you the truth. You must accept the
kingdom of God as a little child accepts
things, or you will never enter it." 16 Then
Jesus took the children in his arms. He put
his hands on them and blessed them.

Let's Pray!

Bless, O Lord Jesus, my parents,
And all who love me and take care of me.
Make me loving to them.
Polite and obedient, helpful and kind.
Amen.

—Unknown

Going Deeper

Read It! God had a plan for the family from the very beginning. Find out what it was in Genesis 2:18–24.

Do It! Movie night! Watch a good family movie, such as *Life with Father.*

Quote of the Day:
Bless all parents in their children, and all children in their parents.
—Christina Rossetti

Jesus Walks on Water

Matthew 14:22–36

Do you ever get scared in your bedroom at night? Do shadows and noises make you wish for a brighter night-light? Everyone gets scared sometimes—even Jesus' disciples! Those brave fishermen had been out on the sea hundreds of times and had been through lots of storms. But this storm scared even them! What would they do?

Then Jesus made his followers get into the
boat. He told them to go ahead of him to the
other side of the lake. Jesus stayed there to
tell the people they could go home. 23After
he said good-bye to them, he went alone up
into the hills to pray. It was late, and Jesus
was there alone. 24By this time, the boat was
already far away on the lake. The boat was
having trouble because of the waves, and
the wind was blowing against it.
25Between three and six o'clock in the
morning, Jesus' followers were still in the
boat. Jesus came to them. He was walking
on the water. 26When the followers saw him
walking on the water, they were afraid. They
said, "It's a ghost!" and cried out in fear.
27But Jesus quickly spoke to them. He said,
"Have courage! It is I! Don't be afraid."
28Peter said, "Lord, if that is really you,
then tell me to come to you on the water."
29Jesus said, "Come."
And Peter left the boat and walked on
the water to Jesus. 30But when Peter saw the
wind and the waves, he became afraid and
began to sink. He shouted, "Lord, save me!"
31Then Jesus reached out his hand and
caught Peter. Jesus said, "Your faith is
small. Why did you doubt?"
32After Peter and Jesus were in the boat,
the wind became calm. 33Then those who
were in the boat worshiped Jesus and said,
"Truly you are the Son of God!"
34After they crossed the lake, they came to
the shore at Gennesaret. 35The people there
saw Jesus and knew who he was. So they
told people all around there that Jesus had
come. They brought all their sick to him.
36They begged Jesus to let them just touch
the edge of his coat to be healed. And all the
sick people who touched it were healed.

Let's Pray!

I will listen to God the Lord.
He has ordered peace for his people who
worship him.

—Psalm 85:8

Lord, when my heart is troubled, help me to see you and to remember that you are more powerful than any storm. In Jesus' name, amen.

Going Deeper

Read It! God controls the wind and the waves because he made them. Read about another time God controlled the seas in Exodus 14.

Do It! Find the Sea of Galilee on a map. Then find Gennesaret. Did you know this body of water was also called by other names? Find out what they are.

Special Words:
The town of Gennesaret was on the northwest shore of the Sea of Galilee, which was also called the Sea of Gennesaret.[33]

Simon Becomes Peter

Matthew 16:13–24

Do you have a nickname? A name that tells something about you? Jesus gave one of his disciples—Simon—a new name, a name that would tell something about him. Jesus named him Cephas (in Aramaic), which is Petros *in Greek. But you probably know him better as Peter. In today's story, Jesus asked Peter whom he believes Jesus really is.*

Jesus went to the area of Caesarea Philippi. He said to his followers, "I am the Son of Man. Who do the people say I am?"

[14]They answered, "Some people say you are John the Baptist. Others say you are Elijah. And others say that you are Jeremiah or one of the prophets."

[15]Then Jesus asked them, "And who do you say I am?"

[16]Simon Peter answered, "You are the Christ, the Son of the living God."

[17]Jesus answered, "You are blessed, Simon son of Jonah. No person taught you that. My Father in heaven showed you who
I am. [18]So I tell you, you are Peter. And I will build my church on this rock. The power of death will not be able to defeat my church.
[19]I will give you the keys of the kingdom of heaven. The things you don't allow on earth will be the things that God does not allow. The things you allow on earth will be
the things that God allows." [20]Then Jesus warned his followers not to tell anyone that he was the Christ.

[21]From that time on Jesus began telling his followers that he must go to Jerusalem. He explained that the Jewish elders, the leading priests, and the teachers of the law would make him suffer many things. And he told them that he must be killed. Then, on the third day, he would be raised from death.

[22]Peter took Jesus aside and began to criticize him. Peter said, "God save you from those things, Lord! Those things will never happen to you!"

[23]Then Jesus said to Peter, "Go away from me, Satan! You are not helping me! You don't care about the things of God. You care only about things that men think are important."

[24]Then Jesus said to his followers, "If anyone wants to follow me, he must say 'no' to the things he wants. He must be willing even to die on a cross, and he must follow me."

Let's Pray!

Jesus said, "If anyone wants to follow me, he must say 'no' to the things he wants. Every day he must be willing even to die on a cross, and he must follow me" (Luke 9:23).

Lord, I don't like to think about suffering for my faith. But I know that if I must, then you will give me the strength to get through it. Thank you for your faithfulness to me! In Jesus' name, amen.

GOING DEEPER

READ IT! Read about how Jesus first called his disciples in Matthew 4:17–22; Mark 1:14–20; Luke 5:4–11; and John 1:35–51.

DO IT! Who is your favorite disciple? Is it Peter or one of the others? Get out some crayons and paper, and draw a picture of your favorite disciple spending time with Jesus.

QUOTE OF THE DAY:
Until you have given up your self to Him you will not have a real self.
—C. S. Lewis

Jairus's Daughter

Mark 5:21–43

In today's story, there is a miracle within a miracle! Both a grown woman and a young girl needed Jesus' healing touch. Doctors could no longer help them. But as Jesus stopped to heal one, the other died. And that's when the people saw Jesus' true power!

Jesus went in the boat back to the other side of the lake. . . . 22A ruler from the synagogue, named Jairus . . . saw Jesus and bowed before him. 23The ruler begged Jesus again and again. He said, "My little daughter is dying. Please come and put your hands on her. Then she will be healed and will live." 24So Jesus went with the ruler, and many people followed Jesus. They were pushing very close around him.

25A woman was there who had been bleeding for the past 12 years. 26She had suffered very much. Many doctors had tried to help her. She had spent all the money she had, but she was not improving. She was getting worse. 27When the woman heard about Jesus, she followed him with the people and touched his coat. 28The woman thought, "If I can even touch his coat, that will be enough to heal me." 29When she touched his coat, her bleeding stopped. She could feel in her body that she was healed.

30At once Jesus felt power go out from him. So he stopped and turned around. Then he asked, "Who touched my clothes?"

31The followers said, "There are so many people pushing against you! And you ask, 'Who touched me?'"

32But Jesus continued looking around to see who had touched him. 33The woman knew that she was healed. So she came and bowed at Jesus' feet. Shaking with fear, she told him the whole story. 34Jesus said to the woman, "Dear woman, you are made well because you believed. Go in peace. You will have no more suffering."

35Jesus was still speaking to her when some men came from the house of Jairus, the synagogue ruler. The men said, "Your daughter is dead. There is now no need to bother the teacher."

36But Jesus paid no attention to what the men said. He said to the synagogue ruler, "Don't be afraid; only believe."

37Jesus let only Peter, James, and John the brother of James go with him to Jairus's house. 38They came to the house of the synagogue ruler. . . . 39Jesus entered the house and said to the people, "Why are you crying and making so much noise? This child is not dead. She is only asleep." 40But they only laughed at Jesus. He told all the people to leave. Then he went into the room where the child was. He took the child's father and mother and his three followers into the room with him. 41Then he took hold of the girl's hand and said to her, "Talitha, koum!" (This means, "Little girl, I tell you to stand up!") 42The girl stood right up and began walking. (She was 12 years old.) The father and mother and the followers were amazed. 43Jesus gave the father and mother strict orders not to tell people about this. Then he told them to give the girl some food.

Quote of the Day:
Little deeds of kindness,
little words of love,
help to make our pleasant
earth below,
like the heaven above.
—Julia Carney

Let's Pray!

Father in heaven,
Reach down from above.
Touch my heart and heal it,
And seal it with your love.
Amen.

Going Deeper

Read It! Jesus raised people from the dead at least two other times that are recorded in the New Testament. Find out who in Luke 7:11–17 and John 11:1–44.

Do It! As a family, pray for the sick and hurting in your church.

The Centurion's Servant

Luke 7:1–10

Have you ever prayed for something and been surprised when God answered that prayer with a big yes? In today's story, a powerful man sent friends to ask Jesus to heal his servant. He knew that Jesus was a busy man and that many people wanted his time and attention. Would Jesus have time to help him?

When Jesus finished saying all these things to the people, he went to Capernaum. [2]In Capernaum there was an army officer. He had a servant who was so sick he was nearly dead. The officer loved the servant very much. [3]When the officer heard about Jesus, he sent some Jewish elders to him. The officer wanted the leaders to ask Jesus to come and heal his servant. [4]The men went to Jesus and begged him saying, "This officer is worthy of your help. [5]He loves our people, and he built us a synagogue."

[6]So Jesus went with the men. He was getting near the officer's house when the officer sent friends to say, "Lord, you don't need to come into my house. I am not good enough for you to be under my roof. [7]That is why I did not come to you myself. You only need to say the word, and my servant will be healed. [8]I, too, am a man under the authority of other men. And I have soldiers under my command. I tell one soldier, 'Go,' and he goes. And I tell another soldier, 'Come,' and he comes. And I say to my servant, 'Do this,' and my servant obeys me."

[9]When Jesus heard this, he was amazed. He turned to the crowd following him and said, "I tell you, this is the greatest faith I have seen anywhere, even in Israel."

[10]The men who had been sent to Jesus went back to the house. There they found that the servant was healed.

Let's Pray!

Lord, thank you for the gift of my brothers and sisters who pray for me. I lift them up to you. Bless and protect them, O Lord. In Jesus' name, amen.

Special Words:
A centurion was a Roman officer who led a unit of one hundred soldiers.[34]

Did You Know?
The homes of Gentiles (or non-Jewish people) were considered unclean by the Jews. So when the centurion urged Jesus not to come to his house, he was showing his respect for Jewish law.

Going Deeper

Read It! One of the greatest friendships in the Bible is that of David and Jonathan. Read about it in 1 Samuel 18:1–4 and 1 Samuel 20.

Do It! Be a friend to a soldier. Send a care package or a card of encouragement to a soldier from your hometown.

THE LORD'S PRAYER

Our Father in heaven,

we pray that your name will always be
kept holy.

We pray that your kingdom will come.

We pray that what you want will be done,
here on earth as it is in heaven.

Give us the food we need for each day.
Forgive the sins we have done,
just as we have forgiven those who did
wrong to us.
Do not cause us to be tested;
but save us from the Evil One.

—Matthew 6:9–13

Forgiven

Luke 7:36–50

One of the most wonderful things about Jesus was how he made friends with all kinds of people—rich and poor, men and women, grown-ups and children. Jesus was especially kind to those who had no other friends. When we show kindness to others, including those who are not very popular, we are being like Jesus! In today's story, a woman repaid Jesus' kindness to her in an amazing and unexpected way. She also taught some important men about the true meaning of forgiveness. Let's find out how she did it.

One of the Pharisees asked Jesus to eat with him. Jesus went into the Pharisee's house and sat at the table. 37A sinful woman in the town learned that Jesus was eating at the Pharisee's house. So she brought an alabaster jar of perfume. 38She stood at Jesus' feet, crying, and began to wash his feet with her tears. She dried his feet with her hair, kissed them many times and rubbed them with the perfume. 39The Pharisee who asked Jesus to come to his house saw this. He thought to himself, "If Jesus were a prophet, he would know that the woman who is touching him is a sinner!"

40Jesus said to the Pharisee, "Simon, I have something to say to you."

Simon said, "Teacher, tell me."

41Jesus said, "There were two men. Both men owed money to the same banker. One man owed the banker 500 silver coins. The other man owed the banker 50 silver coins. 42The men had no money; so they could not pay what they owed. But the banker told the men that they did not have to pay him. Which one of the two men will love the banker more?"

43Simon, the Pharisee, answered, "I think it would be the one who owed him the most money."

Jesus said to Simon, "You are right." 44Then Jesus turned toward the woman and said to Simon, "Do you see this woman? When I came into your house, you gave me no water for my feet. But she washed my feet with her tears and dried my feet with her hair. 45You did not kiss me, but she has been kissing my feet since I came in! 46You did not rub my head with oil, but she rubbed my feet with perfume. 47I tell you that her many sins are forgiven. This is clear because she showed great love. But the person who has only a little to be forgiven will feel only a little love."

48Then Jesus said to her, "Your sins are forgiven."

49The people sitting at the table began to think to themselves, "Who is this man? How can he forgive sins?"

50Jesus said to the woman, "Because you believed, you are saved from your sins. Go in peace."

Let's Pray!

"Those people who know they have great spiritual needs are happy. The kingdom of heaven belongs to them."

—Matthew 5:3

Lord, I know that I have many things—a home, family, friends, and food. But sometimes I forget about my spiritual needs. Help me to always love and worship you. And help me to reach out to those around me who are in need. In Jesus' name, amen.

QUOTE OF THE DAY:
The greatest thing a man can do for his heavenly Father is to be kind to some of His other children.
—Henry Drummond

GOING DEEPER

READ IT! God wants us to help those who are poor. See what he said about it in Proverbs 14:31.

DO IT! What can you do to show kindness to the poor this week? Consider donating some clothes and toys to a local shelter.

The Man Born Blind

John 9:1–3, 6–7, 13–22, 24–25

Whose fault is it?" When bad things happen, do you look around for someone to blame, or do you look for a way to fix the problem? In today's story, some people wanted to know whose fault it was that a man was blind. But Jesus just wanted to show him—and the others—the love and power of God.

As Jesus was walking along, he saw a man
who had been born blind. 2His followers
asked him, "Teacher, whose sin caused this
man to be born blind—his own sin or his
parents' sin?"

3Jesus answered, "It is not this man's sin
or his parents' sin that made him blind.
This man was born blind so that God's
power could be shown in him." . . .

6After Jesus said this, he spit on the
ground and made some mud with it. He
put the mud on the man's eyes. 7Then he
told the man, "Go and wash in the Pool
of Siloam." (Siloam means Sent.) So the
man went to the pool. He washed and came
back. And he was able to see. . . .

13Then the people took to the Pharisees
the man who had been blind. 14The day Jesus
had made mud and healed his eyes was a
Sabbath day. 15So now the Pharisees asked
the man, "How did you get your sight?"

He answered, "He put mud on my eyes. I
washed, and now I can see."

16Some of the Pharisees were saying,
"This man does not keep the Sabbath day.
He is not from God!"

Others said, "But a man who is a sinner
can't do miracles like these." So they could
not agree with each other.

17They asked the man again, "What do you
say about him? It was your eyes he opened."

The man answered, "He is a prophet."

18The Jews did not believe that he had
been blind and could now see again. So
they sent for the man's parents 19and asked
them, "Is this your son? You say that he was
born blind. Then how does he see now?"

His parents answered, "We know that
this is our son, and we know that he was
born blind. 21But we don't know how he can
see now. We don't know who opened his
eyes. Ask him. He is old enough to answer
for himself." 22His parents said this because they were afraid of the Jews. . . .

24So for the second time, they called the
man who had been blind. They said, "You
should give God the glory by telling the
truth. We know that this man is a sinner."

25He answered, "I don't know if he is
a sinner. But one thing I do know. I was
blind, and now I can see."

Let's Pray!

Lord, help me see your gifts all around me each and every day. Don't let me be blind to your many blessings! In Jesus' name, amen.

Did You Know?
Part of the Pool of Siloam still exists in the southern tip of the Old City of Jerusalem.[35]

Going Deeper

READ IT! Too often, the Pharisees looked at only the outside of a person, but God doesn't just look at the outside. To find out what God thinks is important, read 1 Samuel 16:7.

DO IT! Imagine how wonderful it must have been for the blind man to be able to see! Close your eyes for a moment; then open them. Count how many blessings you can see right in front of you!

Lazarus

John 11:23, 25–29, 32–44

Lazarus was a dear friend of Jesus. He and his sisters—Mary and Martha—often invited Jesus and his disciples into their home at Bethany. So when Lazarus became sick, Mary and Martha sent for Jesus. They thought Jesus would come quickly and heal their brother. But Jesus didn't come quickly, and Lazarus died. It was all "for the glory of God," Jesus said (John 11:4). But how? Let's find out!

Jesus said, "Your brother will rise and live again."...

25Jesus said to her, "I am the resurrection and the life. He who believes in me will have life even if he dies. 26And he who lives and believes in me will never die. Martha, do you believe this?"

27Martha answered, "Yes, Lord. I believe that you are the Christ, the Son of God. You are the One who was coming to the world."

28After Martha said this, she went back to her sister Mary. She talked to Mary alone. Martha said, "The Teacher is here and he is asking for you." 29When Mary heard this, she got up quickly and went to Jesus. . . . 32When she saw him, she fell at his feet and said, "Lord, if you had been here, my brother would not have died."

33Jesus saw that Mary was crying and that the Jews who came with her were crying, too. Jesus felt very sad in his heart and was deeply troubled. 34He asked, "Where did you bury him?"

"Come and see, Lord," they said.

35Jesus cried.

36So the Jews said, "See how much he loved him."

37But some of them said, "If Jesus healed the eyes of the blind man, why didn't he keep Lazarus from dying?"

38Again Jesus felt very sad in his heart. He came to the tomb. The tomb was a cave with a large stone covering the entrance. 39Jesus said, "Move the stone away."

Martha said, "But, Lord, it has been four days since he died. There will be a bad smell." Martha was the sister of the dead man.

40Then Jesus said to her, "Didn't I tell you that if you believed, you would see the glory of God?"

41So they moved the stone away from the entrance. Then Jesus looked up and said, "Father, I thank you that you heard me. 42I know that you always hear me. But I said these things because of the people here around me. I want them to believe that you sent me." 43After Jesus said this, he cried out in a loud voice, "Lazarus, come out!" 44The dead man came out. His hands and feet were wrapped with pieces of cloth, and he had a cloth around his face.

Jesus said to them, "Take the cloth off of him and let him go."

Let's Pray!

Thank you for being the kind of God who is sad when your children are sad. Please comfort all those who are sad today just as you did Martha and Mary. In Jesus' name, amen.

GOING DEEPER

READ IT! Elijah—through God's power—also raised someone from the dead. Find out who in 1 Kings 17:17–24.

DO IT! Get out your craft supplies, and make "Jesus gives me new life!" Bible bookmarks for you and your family.

Faith of a Child

Mark 10:13–16

Jesus loves all people—rich and poor, young and old. But he has a special place in his heart for children—and they have a special place in his kingdom.

Some people brought their small children to Jesus so he could touch them. But his followers told the people to stop bringing their children to him. [14]When Jesus saw this, he was displeased. He said to them, "Let the little children come to me. Don't stop them. The kingdom of God belongs to people who are like these little children. [15]I tell you the truth. You must accept the kingdom of God as a little child accepts things, or you will never enter it." [16]Then Jesus took the children in his arms. He put his hands on them and blessed them.

GOING DEEPER

READ IT! Jesus warned about causing young believers to stumble in their faith. Read what he said in Mark 9:42.

DO IT! Even though you are young, you can tell other children about Jesus. Offer to tell a Bible story or teach a song to your church's toddler class.

LET'S PRAY!

God who made the earth,
The air, the sky, the sea,
Who gave the light its birth,
Careth for me.

God who made the grass,
The flower, the fruit, the tree,
The day and night to pass,
Careth for me.

God who made the sun,
The moon, the stars, is He
Who, when life's clouds come on,
Careth for me.

God who made all things
On earth, in air, in sea,
Who changing seasons brings,
Careth for me.

—Sarah Betts Rhodes

Thank you, God, for caring for me. In Jesus' name, amen.

Quote of the Day:
"Be careful. Don't think these little children are worth nothing. I tell you that they have angels in heaven who are always with my Father in heaven."
—Jesus, in Matthew 18:10

Two Parables of Jesus

Luke 15:1–10

Have you ever lost a mitten, a shoe, or even a favorite toy? Have you ever searched your room from top to bottom to find what was lost? Remember how happy you were when you finally found what you were looking for? In today's reading, Jesus told two parables, little stories that teach a lesson. These parables remind us of how much God tries to help those who wander away from his love—and how happy he is when they are found!

Many tax collectors and "sinners" came
to listen to Jesus. 2The Pharisees and the
teachers of the law began to complain:
"Look! This man welcomes sinners and
even eats with them!"

3Then Jesus told them this story:
4"Suppose one of you has 100 sheep, but he
loses 1 of them. Then he will leave the other
99 sheep alone and go out and look for the
lost sheep. The man will keep on search-
ing for the lost sheep until he finds it. 5And
when he finds it, the man is very happy. He
puts it on his shoulders 6and goes home. He
calls to his friends and neighbors and says,
'Be happy with me because I found my lost
sheep!' 7In the same way, I tell you there is
much joy in heaven when 1 sinner changes
his heart. There is more joy for that 1 sinner than there is for 99 good people who
don't need to change.

8"Suppose a woman has ten silver coins,
but she loses one of them. She will light
a lamp and clean the house. She will look
carefully for the coin until she finds it. 9And
when she finds it, she will call her friends
and neighbors and say, 'Be happy with me
because I have found the coin that I lost!' 10In
the same way, there is joy before the angels
of God when 1 sinner changes his heart."

Let's Pray!

Amazing grace, how sweet the sound,
That saved a wretch like me.
I once was lost but now am found,
Was blind, but now, I see.

—John Newton

I praise you, Lord, for you always search for those who are lost. Help me never to wander from you. In Jesus' name, amen.

Did You Know?
"Silver coins" were drachmas, Greek coins much like a Roman denarius. One denarius would have been a day's pay for a soldier.[36]

Did You Know?
When a lamb wandered away and hurt itself, the shepherd would often place the lamb around his neck and carry it until it was healed. This extra love and care bonded the lamb to the shepherd, so it would not run away again!

Going Deeper

Read It! Sometimes we may wander away from God, but God is always waiting to be found by us. Read his promise to us in Jeremiah 29:11–13.

Do It! Do you need to clean out your closet? Give it a careful cleaning today—and see how many "lost" things you can find!

The Good Samaritan

Luke 10:25–37

Who is my neighbor?" the teacher of the law asked. He wanted to trick Jesus into giving a wrong answer. But instead Jesus told a story about a most unlikely hero, a Samaritan man whose name is never given, but whose example has lasted for thousands of years. The story of the good Samaritan is one of the best known of all Jesus' parables. In telling this story, Jesus reminded that we are to care for all people—not just the ones we love and who are like us.

Then a teacher of the law stood up. He was
trying to test Jesus. He said, "Teacher, what
must I do to get life forever?"
26 Jesus said to him, "What is written in
the law? What do you read there?"
27 The man answered, "Love the Lord your
God. Love him with all your heart, all your
soul, all your strength, and all your mind."
Also, "You must love your neighbor as you
love yourself."
28 Jesus said to him, "Your answer is right.
Do this and you will have life forever."
29 But the man wanted to show that the
way he was living was right. So he said to
Jesus, "And who is my neighbor?"
30 To answer this question, Jesus said,
"A man was going down the road from
Jerusalem to Jericho. Some robbers
attacked him. They tore off his clothes and
beat him. Then they left him lying there,
almost dead. 31 It happened that a Jewish
priest was going down that road. When the
priest saw the man, he walked by on the
other side of the road. 32 Next, a Levite came
there. He went over and looked at the man.
Then he walked by on the other side of the
road. 33 Then a Samaritan traveling down the
road came to where the hurt man was lying.
He saw the man and felt very sorry for him.
34 The Samaritan went to him and poured
olive oil and wine on his wounds and ban-
daged them. He put the hurt man on his
own donkey and took him to an inn. At the
inn, the Samaritan took care of him. 35 The
next day, the Samaritan brought out two silver coins and gave them to the innkeeper.
The Samaritan said, 'Take care of this man.
If you spend more money on him, I will pay
it back to you when I come again.'"
36 Then Jesus said, "Which one of these
three men do you think was a neighbor to
the man who was attacked by the robbers?"
37 The teacher of the law answered, "The
one who helped him."

Jesus said to him, "Then go and do the same thing he did!"

Let's Pray!

Lord, you give me so many blessings! Help me see the needs of those around me, and give me a heart that wants to help them. In Jesus' name, amen.

Did You Know?
The Samaritans were considered enemies of the Jewish people even though they were both neighbors and distant relatives. By showing that the Samaritan man was the hero of the story, Jesus was gently scolding the lawyer who was trying to trick him.

Going Deeper

Read It! How can you be a good neighbor? Jesus tells us in Matthew 5:43–48.

Do It! Think of something you can do to help a "neighbor" in need. Collect cans of food for the hungry or shampoo and soap for the homeless shelter.

The Rich Fool

Luke 12:13–21

That's mine!" "No, it's mine!" How often do you fuss over your toys instead of sharing them with others? In today's story, Jesus warned against the dangers of selfishness and of keeping things for ourselves when we could use them to bless others. Sometimes those are physical things—such as money or food. Other times the gifts God gives us are ones that we can't see and hold, but they are still very important to share—such as the gifts of our time and friendship. What happens if we won't share our gifts? Let's find out what happened to one rich, but selfish man!

One of the men in the crowd said to Jesus,
"Teacher, tell my brother to divide with me
the property our father left us."
14But Jesus said to him, "Who said that
I should be your judge or decide how to
divide the property between you two?"
15Then Jesus said to them, "Be careful and
guard against all kinds of greed. A man's
life is not measured by the many things he
owns."
16Then Jesus used this story: "There was
a rich man who had some land, which grew
a good crop of food. 17The rich man thought
to himself, 'What will I do? I have no place
to keep all my crops.' 18Then he said, 'I
know what I will do. I will tear down my
barns and build bigger ones! I will put all
my grain and other goods together in my
new barns. 19Then I can say to myself, I have
enough good things stored to last for many
years. Rest, eat, drink, and enjoy life!'
20"But God said to that man, 'Foolish
man! Tonight you will die. So who will
get those things you have prepared for
yourself?'
21"This is how it will be for anyone who
stores things up only for himself and is not
rich toward God."

Let's Pray!

Lord, I want to have a giving heart. Please show me when I am being selfish and help me choose to share instead. In Jesus' name, amen.

Going Deeper

READ IT! You can't out-give God. When you bless others, he blesses you even more. Read his promise in Malachi 3:10.

DO IT! What can you share with others today—your money, time, or friendship?

Quote of the Day:
You can give without loving, but you cannot love without giving.
—Amy Carmichael

The Widow and the Judge

Luke 18:1–8

Sometimes God answers our prayers right away. But other times he does not. Sometimes he says yes, sometimes no, and sometimes "Wait." But no matter what God's answer is, the important thing to remember is that God knows what is best for us. Trust him to give you the perfect answer at the perfect time. In today's reading, Jesus used the story of a widow to teach us to keep praying until God answers.

Then Jesus used this story to teach his followers that they should always pray and
never lose hope. 2"Once there was a judge
in a town. He did not care about God. He
also did not care what people thought about
him. 3In that same town there was a widow
who kept coming to this judge. She said,
'There is a man who is not being fair to me.
Give me my rights!' 4But the judge did not
want to help the widow. After a long time,
he thought to himself, 'I don't care about
God. And I don't care about what people
think. 5But this widow is bothering me. I
will see that she gets her rights, or she will
bother me until I am worn out!'"

6The Lord said, "Listen to what the bad
judge said. 7God's people cry to him night
and day. God will always give them what
is right, and he will not be slow to answer
them. 8I tell you, God will help his people
quickly! But when the Son of Man comes
again, will he find those on earth who believe in him?"

LET'S PRAY!

I look up to the hills.
  But where does my help come from?
My help comes from the Lord.
  He made heaven and earth.
He will not let you be defeated.
  He who guards you never sleeps.

—Psalm 121:1–3

Lord, I look to you for all the answers in my life, for I know that you only want what is best for me. In Jesus' name, amen.

Quote of the Day:
Faith sees the invisible,
believes the unbelievable, and
receives the impossible.
—Corrie ten Boom

Going Deeper

Read It! God always hears you when you pray to him. Read his promise in Psalm 18:6.

Do It! What does your family need right now? Gather together and pray every day to ask God for those things.

Zacchaeus

Luke 19:1–10

Every class seems to have one or two kids who are much smaller—or much bigger!—than everyone else. Sometimes those kids use humor or other special talents to help them fit in, but other times they can end up feeling left out. In today's story, a rich man who was very short wanted to see Jesus. But first he had to find a way to see over the crowds!

Jesus was going through the city of Jericho. 2In Jericho there was a man named Zacchaeus. He was a wealthy, very important tax collector. 3He wanted to see who Jesus was, but he was too short to see above the crowd. 4He ran ahead to a place where he knew Jesus would come. He climbed a sycamore tree so he could see Jesus. 5When Jesus came to that place, he looked up and saw Zacchaeus in the tree. He said to him, "Zacchaeus, hurry and come down! I must stay at your house today."

6Zacchaeus came down quickly. He was pleased to have Jesus in his house. 7All the people saw this and began to complain, "Look at the kind of man Jesus stays with. Zacchaeus is a sinner!"

8But Zacchaeus said to the Lord, "I will give half of my money to the poor. If I have cheated anyone, I will pay that person back four times more!"

9Jesus said, "Salvation has come to this house today. This man truly belongs to the family of Abraham. 10The Son of Man came to find lost people and save them."

Let's Pray!

Today, God, I pray for our leaders—those who make the laws, those who enforce them, and those who represent us around the world. Give each of them your wisdom. Guide them to do your will. Help them to serve you first, the people second, and themselves last. In Jesus' name, amen.

Special Words:
Restitution *is the giving back of something you stole, either the thing itself or the money to replace it. When Zacchaeus wanted to pay back those he had cheated out of their money, he gave them back four times what he had taken.*

Did You Know?
At that time, tax collectors were hated because the people's tax money went to the Roman government. Tax collectors were also hated because they often took more money than what the people really owed in taxes. And yet, here in Jericho, Jesus chose to stay with one of the most hated men in town! Jesus' love and mercy are for all people.

Going Deeper

READ IT! One of Jesus' twelve apostles was a tax collector. Find out who in Matthew 9:9.

DO IT! It takes a big person to admit doing something wrong! Can you think of a time when you cheated—when you didn't point out a mistake you'd made on your test or when a cashier gave you back too much change and you kept it? What should you have done, and how can you make it right?

The Lost Son

Luke 15:11–32

Today's story is the third parable in the "lost" chapter—the stories of the lost sheep, the lost coins, and the lost son. God created families to love and care for one another all the way to heaven. But in today's story, one son wanted to leave his family—and he did! When he finally decided to return, would his father welcome him back or turn him away?

Then Jesus said, "A man had two sons. [12]The younger son said to his father, 'Give me my share of the property.' So the father divided the property between his two sons. [13]Then the younger son gathered up all that was his and left. He traveled far away to another country. There he wasted his money in foolish living. [14]He spent everything that he had. Soon after that, the land became very dry, and there was no rain. There was not enough food to eat anywhere in the country. The son was hungry and needed money. [15]So he got a job with one of the citizens there. The man sent the son into the fields to feed pigs. [16]The son was so hungry that he was willing to eat the food the pigs were eating. But no one gave him anything. [17]The son realized that he had been very foolish. He thought, 'All of my father's servants have plenty of food. But I am here, almost dying with hunger. [18]I will leave and return to my father. I'll say to him: Father, I have sinned against God and against you. [19]I am not good enough to be called your son. But let me be like one of your servants.' [20]So the son left and went to his father.

"While the son was still a long way off, his father saw him coming. He felt sorry for his son. So the father ran to him, and hugged and kissed him. [21]The son said, 'Father, I have sinned against God and have done wrong to you. I am not good enough to be called your son.' [22]But the father said to his servants, 'Hurry! Bring the best clothes and put them on him. Also, put a ring on his finger and sandals on his feet. [23]And get our fat calf and kill it. Then we can have a feast and celebrate! [24]My son was dead, but now he is alive again! He was lost, but now he is found!' So they began to celebrate.

[25]"The older son was in the field. As he came closer to the house, he heard the sound of music and dancing. [26]So he called to one of the servants and asked, 'What does all this mean?' [27]The servant said, 'Your brother has come back. Your father killed the fat calf to eat because your brother came home safely!' [28]The older son was angry and would not go in to the feast. So his father went out and begged him to come in. [29]The son said to his father, 'I have served you like a slave for many years! I have always obeyed your commands. But you never even killed a young goat for me to have a feast with my friends. [30]But your other son . . . comes home, and you kill the fat calf for him!' [31]The father said to him, 'Son, you are always with me. All that I have is yours. [32]We had to celebrate and be happy because your brother was dead, but now he is alive. He was lost, but now he is found.'"

Let's Pray!

Lord, tell me your ways.
Show me how to live.
Guide me in your truth.
Teach me, my God, my Savior.
I trust you all day long.
Lord, remember your mercy and love.
You have shown them since long ago.
Do not remember the sins
and wrong things I did when I was
young.
But remember to love me always
because you are good, Lord.

—Psalm 25:4–7

Going Deeper

READ IT! How does God want you to live your life and treat others? Read his answer in Matthew 5:43–48.

DO IT! Is there someone in your life who is hard to love or to forgive—maybe someone right in your own family? Take a step toward making things better. Think of something special and kind you can do just for that person.

Sheep and Goats

Matthew 25:31–46

No one knows when Jesus will come back to take his people home to heaven. And until he does come back, Jesus has work for us to do here on earth. In Matthew 28:19–20, Jesus told us to go throughout the whole world, telling people about him and about how to get to heaven. And in today's reading Jesus told us how we should treat others. Because when Jesus does return, all people will be separated into one of two groups—sheep or goats. Let's find out which ones Jesus said we should be!

"The Son of Man will come again in his great glory. . . . He will be King and sit on his great throne. 32All the people of the world will be gathered before him. Then he will separate them into two groups as a shepherd separates the sheep from the goats. 33The Son of Man will put the sheep, the good people, on his right and the goats, the bad people, on his left.

34"Then the King will say to the good people on his right, 'Come. My Father has given you his blessing. . . . 35I was hungry, and you gave me food. I was thirsty, and you gave me something to drink. I was alone and away from home, and you invited me into your house. 36I was without clothes, and you gave me something to wear. I was sick, and you cared for me. I was in prison, and you visited me.'

37"Then the good people will answer, 'Lord, when did we see you hungry and give you food? When did we see you thirsty and give you something to drink? 38When did we see you alone and away from home and invite you into our house? When did we see you without clothes and give you something to wear? 39When did we see you sick or in prison and care for you?'

40"Then the King will answer, 'I tell you the truth. Anything you did for any of my people here, you also did for me.'

41"Then the King will say to those on his left, 'Go away from me. God has said that you will be punished. Go into the fire that burns forever. That fire was prepared for the devil and his helpers. 42I was hungry, and you gave me nothing to eat. I was thirsty, and you gave me nothing to drink. 43I was alone and away from home, and you did not invite me into your house. I was without clothes, and you gave me nothing to wear. I was sick and in prison, and you did not care for me.'

44"Then those people will answer, 'Lord, when did we see you hungry or thirsty? When did we see you alone and away from home? Or when did we see you without clothes or sick or in prison? When did we see these things and not help you?'

45"Then the King will answer, 'I tell you the truth. Anything you refused to do for any of my people here, you refused to do for me.'

46"These people will go off to be punished forever. But the good people will go to live forever."

Quote of the Day:
The true calling of a Christian is not to do extraordinary things, but to do ordinary things in an extraordinary way.
—A. P. Stanley

LET'S PRAY!

Dear God, there is nothing more important in this life than knowing you and serving you. Help me to do your will so you will count me as one of your sheep when Jesus comes back again. In Jesus' name, amen.

GOING DEEPER

READ IT! The Bible often describes God as our Shepherd. Read how the Shepherd cares for his sheep in Ezekiel 34:11–16.

DO IT! The greatest thing you can do for someone is to tell him or her about Jesus. Who can you tell about Jesus today?

The Good Shepherd

John 10:7–18

In the Gospels, Jesus often compared himself to people and things to show something true about himself as well as something true about us: "I am the Bread of Life." "I am the Vine." "I am the Great Physician." In today's story, Jesus revealed another way he shows his love and care for us: as our Good Shepherd, who gives his life for his sheep.

So Jesus said again, "I tell you the truth. I am the door for the sheep. [8]All the people who came before me were thieves and robbers. The sheep did not listen to them. [9]I am the door. The person who enters through me will be saved. He will be able to come in and go out and find pasture. [10]A thief comes to steal and kill and destroy. But I came to give life—life in all its fullness.

[11]"I am the good shepherd. The good shepherd gives his life for the sheep. [12]The worker who is paid to keep the sheep is different from the shepherd who owns them. So when the worker sees a wolf coming, he runs away and leaves the sheep alone. Then the wolf attacks the sheep and scatters them. [13]The man runs away because he is only a paid worker. He does not really care for the sheep.

[14]"I am the good shepherd. I know my sheep, as the Father knows me. And my sheep know me, as I know the Father. [16]I have other sheep that are not in this flock here. I must bring them also. They will listen to my voice, and there will be one flock and one shepherd. [17]The Father loves me because I give my life. I give my life so that I can take it back again. [18]No one takes it away from me. I give my own life freely. I have the right to give my life, and I have the right to take it back. This is what my Father commanded me to do."

LET'S PRAY!

The Lord is my shepherd.
I have everything I need.
He gives me rest in green pastures.
  He leads me to calm water.
He gives me new strength.
For the good of his name,
  he leads me on paths that are right.
Even if I walk
  through a very dark valley,
I will not be afraid
  because you are with me.
Your rod and your walking stick
    comfort me.
You prepare a meal for me
  in front of my enemies.
You pour oil on my head.
  You give me more than I can hold.
Surely your goodness and love will be with
    me
  all my life.
And I will live in the house of the Lord
    forever.

—Psalm 23

Did You Know?
The "other sheep" (verse 16) means the Gentiles. Jesus came to first give his message to the Jews, God's chosen people. But Jesus' mercy was for the Gentiles (non-Jews) too. All people who believe in Jesus and obey his word are joined together in his church.

Going Deeper

READ IT! One day God will lead his sheep to the promised land of heaven. But long ago God first led his people from the slavery of Egypt to the promised land of Canaan. Read about it in Psalm 78:52–55.

DO IT! Is there a sheep farm or petting zoo in your area? Try to visit one soon.

The Transfiguration

Matthew 17:1–13

Some people believed that Jesus was Elijah or one of the prophets (Matthew 16:14). But in today's story—called "The Transfiguration"—Jesus showed his disciples who he truly is.

Six days later, Jesus took Peter, James, and John the brother of James up on a high mountain. They were all alone there. 2While they watched, Jesus was changed. His face became bright like the sun. And his clothes became white as light. 3Then two men were there, talking with him. The men were Moses and Elijah.

4Peter said to Jesus, "Lord, it is good that we are here. If you want, I will put three tents here—one for you, one for Moses, and one for Elijah."

5While Peter was talking, a bright cloud covered them. A voice came from the cloud. The voice said, "This is my Son and I love him. I am very pleased with him. Obey him!"

6The followers with Jesus heard the voice. They were so frightened that they fell to the ground. 7But Jesus went to them and touched them. He said, "Stand up. Don't be afraid." 8When the followers looked up, they saw Jesus was now alone.

9When Jesus and the followers were coming down the mountain, Jesus commanded them, "Don't tell anyone about the things you saw on the mountain. Wait until the Son of Man has been raised from death. Then you may tell."

10The followers asked Jesus, "Why do the teachers of the law say that Elijah must come first, before the Christ comes?"

11Jesus answered, "They are right to say that Elijah is coming. And it is true that Elijah will make everything the way it should be. 12But I tell you, Elijah has already come. People did not know who he was. They did to him everything they wanted to do. It will be the same with the Son of Man. Those same people will make the Son of Man suffer." 13Then the followers understood that Jesus was talking about John the Baptist.

Let's Pray!

Everything on earth, shout with joy to God!
Sing about his glory!
  Make his praise glorious!
Say to God, "Your works are amazing!
  Your power is great."

—Psalm 66:1–3

Going Deeper

Read It! Moses' face also shone after he spoke with God. Read about it in Exodus 34:29–35.

Do It! Make signs for your home or garden to remind you of God's love and care. Get some scrap wood (Mom or Dad may want to sand the edges for little ones) or wooden paint sticks. Cover them with craft paint. Write sayings or verses on them, and put them where everyone will be sure to see them!

Jesus, tender Shepherd, hear me;
Bless Thy little lamb tonight;
Through the darkness be Thou near me;
Watch my sleep till morning light.

All this day Thy hand has led me,
And I thank Thee for Thy care;
Thou hast clothed me, warmed and fed me,
Listen to my evening prayer.

Let my sins be all forgiven;
Bless the friends I love so well;
Take me, when I die, to Heaven,
Happy there with Thee to dwell.

—Mary L. Duncan

Who Is the Greatest?

Matthew 18:1–6

Think for a moment about all the people you are important to. Your parents and grandparents, teachers and coaches, friends, and all the other people who work together for your good. In today's story, we discover an important truth: you are important to God too! In fact, Jesus said that the kingdom of God belongs to those who become just like you!

At that time the followers came to Jesus and
asked, "Who is greatest in the kingdom of
heaven?"
2Jesus called a little child to him. He
stood the child before the followers. 3Then
he said, "I tell you the truth. You must
change and become like little children. If
you don't do this, you will never enter the
kingdom of heaven. 4The greatest person
in the kingdom of heaven is the one who
makes himself humble like this child.
5"Whoever accepts a little child in my
name accepts me. 6If one of these little
children believes in me, and someone
causes that child to sin, then it will be very
bad for that person. It would be better for
him to have a large stone tied around his
neck and be drowned in the sea."

LET'S PRAY!

Thank you, God, for all the people in my life who help me grow as a Christian. Thank you for my family and friends, teachers and preachers. And thank you for loving me right now, just as I am at this moment. Even if I were the only one in the world, you would have died for me! Help me live in a way that pleases you always. In Jesus' name, amen.

GOING DEEPER

READ IT! Jesus loves little children. Read about it in Matthew 19:13–14.

DO IT! Did you know there are thousands of children in the United States in need of new homes and families? Please pray for their "forever families" to find them soon!

QUOTE OF THE DAY:
You may speak but a word to a child, and in that child there may be slumbering a noble heart which shall stir the Christian Church in years to come.
—Charles H. Spurgeon

Jesus Rides into Jerusalem

Matthew 21:1–14

As Jesus and his disciples neared Jerusalem for Passover, Jesus told his disciples to go into the village, get a donkey, and bring it him. Long ago the prophet Zechariah had promised that the Messiah would into the city on a donkey (Zechariah 9:9). King Solomon had ridden to his coronation on the colt that had belonged to his father, David (1 Kings 1:33–44), so Jesus entered the City of David, ready to do the will of his Father.

Jesus and his followers were coming closer
to Jerusalem. But first they stopped at
Bethphage at the hill called the Mount of
Olives. From there Jesus sent two of his followers into the town. 2He said to them, "Go to
the town you can see there. When you enter it,
you will find a donkey tied there with its colt.
Untie them and bring them to me. 3If anyone
asks you why you are taking the donkeys, tell
him, 'The Master needs them. He will send
them back soon.'" 4This was to make clear the
full meaning of what the prophet said:

5"Tell the people of Jerusalem,
'Your king is coming to you.
He is gentle and riding on a donkey.
He is on the colt of a donkey.'"
Isaiah 62:11; Zechariah 9:9

6The followers went and did what Jesus
told them to do. 7They brought the donkey
and the colt to Jesus. They laid their coats
on the donkeys, and Jesus sat on them.
8Many people spread their coats on the road
before Jesus. Others cut branches from the
trees and spread them on the road. 9Some
of the people were walking ahead of Jesus.
Others were walking behind him. All the
people were shouting,

"Praise to the Son of David!
God bless the One who comes in the
name of the Lord! *Psalm 118:26*
Praise to God in heaven!"

10Then Jesus went into Jerusalem. The
city was filled with excitement. The people
asked, "Who is this man?"

11The crowd answered, "This man is
Jesus. He is the prophet from the town of
Nazareth in Galilee."

12Jesus went into the Temple. He threw
out all the people who were buying and
selling there. He turned over the tables that
belonged to the men who were exchanging
different kinds of money. And he upset the
benches of those who were selling doves.
13Jesus said to all the people there, "It is
written in the Scriptures, 'My Temple will
be a house where people will pray.' But you
are changing God's house into a 'hideout
for robbers.'"

14The blind and crippled people came
to Jesus in the Temple, and Jesus healed
them.

SPECIAL WORDS: The Hebrew word for praise *in verse 9 is* Hosanna, *which means "Save us now!"*[37]

Let's Pray!

You are my God, and I will thank you.
You are my God, and I will praise your greatness.
—Psalm 118:28

Did You Know?

This event is often called the "Triumphal Entry." It happened on the Sunday before Jesus was crucified. This day is also known as Palm Sunday, because the people spread palm branches on the road before Jesus.

Going Deeper

Read It! There are many prophecies about Jesus in the Old Testament. Jeremiah 23:5–6 prophesied that the Christ would be a descendant of David—just as the people say in verse 9.

Do It! Act out this story with your family or friends. Lay out your coats (or pieces of cloth or towels) for the person pretending to be Jesus to walk on. Shout "Hosanna" as he passes by.

Jesus Washes the Disciples' Feet

John 13:1–17

In Bible times, people usually wore some type of sandal on their feet. Because the roads were made of dirt, their feet became very dirty. It was a servant's job to wash the people's feet before a feast. It was a dirty job, and it was usually given to the lowliest of servants. So what was Jesus doing washing the disciples' feet?

It was almost time for the Jewish Passover Feast. Jesus knew that it was time for him to leave this world and go back to the Father. He had always loved those who were his own in the world, and he loved them all the way to the end.

[2]Jesus and his followers were at the evening meal. The devil had already persuaded Judas Iscariot to turn against Jesus. (Judas was the son of Simon.) [3]Jesus knew that the Father had given him power over everything. He also knew that he had come from God and was going back to God. [4]So during the meal Jesus stood up and took off his outer clothing. Taking a towel, he wrapped it around his waist. [5]Then he poured water into a bowl and began to wash the followers' feet. He dried them with the towel that was wrapped around him.

[6]Jesus came to Simon Peter. But Peter said to Jesus, "Lord, are you going to wash my feet?"

[7]Jesus answered, "You don't understand what I am doing now. But you will understand later."

[8]Peter said, "No! You will never wash my feet."

Jesus answered, "If I don't wash your feet, then you are not one of my people."

[9]Simon Peter answered, "Lord, after you wash my feet, wash my hands and my head, too!"

[10]Jesus said, "After a person has had a bath, his whole body is clean. He needs only to wash his feet. And you men are clean, but not all of you." [11]Jesus knew who would turn against him. That is why Jesus said, "Not all of you are clean."

[12]When he had finished washing their feet, he put on his clothes and sat down again. Jesus asked, "Do you understand what I have just done for you? [13]You call me 'Teacher' and 'Lord.' And this is right, because that is what I am. [14]I, your Lord and Teacher, have washed your feet. So you also should wash each other's feet. [15]I did this as an example for you. So you should do as I have done for you. [16]I tell you the truth. A servant is not greater than his master. A messenger is not greater than the one who sent him. [17]If you know these things, you will be happy if you do them."

Let's Pray!

Take my life and let it be
  Consecrated, Lord, to Thee.
Take my hands and let them move
  At the impulse of Thy love.
Take my feet and let them be
  Swift and beautiful for Thee!
Take my voice and let me sing
  Always, only, for my King.

—Frances Havergal

Quote of the Day:
Jesus said, "I am the living bread that came down from heaven. If anyone eats this bread, he will live forever. This bread is my flesh. I will give my flesh so that the people in the world may have life."
—John 6:51

Going Deeper

Read It! The first Passover feast was prepared in Egypt as the Israelites waited for God's final plague to "pass over" them. Read about it in Exodus 12:1–14.

Do It! What is the worst chore in your house, the one everyone hates to do? It may be something different for each person. This week, be like Jesus and do that chore out of love for someone in your family.

The Lord's Supper

Mark 14:17–26

As Jesus and his disciples gathered together for the Passover meal, Jesus knew that his time on earth was almost over. For three years, he had taught the twelve disciples. Now it was almost time for them to take his message to the whole world. But this last night he had many more things to tell them, and he gave them—and us—a very special way to remember him.

In the evening, Jesus went to that house
with the 12. 18While they were all eating,
Jesus said, "I tell you the truth. One of you will give me to my enemies—one of you eating with me now."

19The followers were very sad to hear this. Each one said to Jesus, "I am not the one, am I?"

20Jesus answered, "The man who is against me is 1 of the 12. He is the 1 who dips
his bread into the bowl with me. 21The Son
of Man must go and die. The Scriptures say this will happen. But how terrible it will be for the person who gives the Son of Man to be killed. It would be better for that person if he had never been born."

22While they were eating, Jesus took some bread. He thanked God for it and broke it. Then he gave it to his followers and said, "Take it. This bread is my body."

23Then Jesus took a cup. He thanked God for it and gave it to the followers. All the followers drank from the cup.

24Then Jesus said, "This is my blood which begins the new agreement that God makes with his people. This blood is
poured out for many. 25I tell you the truth. I
will not drink of this fruit of the vine again until that day when I drink it new in the kingdom of God."

26They sang a hymn and went out to the Mount of Olives.

Let's Pray!

Savior, teach me, day by day,
Love's sweet lesson, to obey;
Sweeter lesson cannot be,
Loving Him who first loved me.

—Jane Elizabeth Leeson

Going Deeper

Read It! The early Christians broke bread together to remember Jesus. Read about it in Acts 2:46 and 1 Corinthians 11:23–26.

Do It! The seder meal marks the beginning of the Jewish Passover celebration. Celebrate a seder meal with your family. Check online for directions.

Did You Know?
The bread that Jesus and his disciples ate was unleavened bread. That means it was made without any yeast. This was done to remember the Exodus, when the Israelites fled Egypt and did not have time to let the yeast in the bread rise.

Jesus Prays

John 17:1, 6–8, 11–16, 20–23

After the Passover meal, Jesus and his disciples made their way to Gethsemane to pray. Along the way, Jesus spoke to them about what was ahead and what they must do: keep the commandments, love one another, and wait for the Holy Spirit to come. Although Jesus dreaded the pain and suffering of the cross, he was also concerned about his disciples. So in the final hours before the cross, Jesus prayed for them.

Jesus prayed, "Father, the time has come.
Give glory to your Son so that the Son can
give glory to you. . . .
6"You gave me some men from the world.
I have shown them what you are like. Those
men belonged to you, and you gave them
to me. They have obeyed your teaching.
7Now they know that everything you gave
me comes from you. 8I gave these men
the teachings that you gave me. They accepted those teachings. They know that I
truly came from you. . . . 11Now I am coming to you. I will not stay in the world now.
But these men are still in the world. Holy
Father, keep them safe. Keep them safe
by the power of your name (the name you
gave me), so that they will be one, the same
as you and I are one. 12While I was with
them, I kept them safe. I kept them safe
by the power of your name—the name you
gave me. I protected them. And only one
of them, the one who is going to hell, was
lost. He was lost so that what was said in the
Scripture would happen.
13"I am coming to you now. But I pray
these things while I am still in the world.
I say these things so that these men can
have my joy. I want them to have all of my
joy. 14I have given them your teaching. And
the world has hated them. The world hated
these men, because they don't belong to
the world, the same as I don't belong to the
world. 15I am not asking you to take them
out of the world. But I am asking that you
keep them safe from the Evil One. 16They
don't belong to the world, the same as I
don't belong to the world. . . .
20"I pray for these men. But I am also
praying for all people who will believe in
me because of the teaching of these men.
21Father, I pray that all people who believe
in me can be one. You are in me and I am
in you. I pray that these people can also be
one in us, so that the world will believe that
you sent me. 22I have given these people
the glory that you gave me. I gave them this
glory so that they can be one, the same as
you and I are one. 23I will be in them and
you will be in me. So they will be completely one. Then the world will know that
you sent me. And the world will know that
you loved these people the same as you
loved me."

Did You Know?
In his prayer, Jesus prayed both for the original apostles (17:6–19) and for future ones—like you (17:20–21)!

LET'S PRAY!

All through the day,
I humbly pray,
Be Thou my Guard and Guide;
My sins forgive
And let me live,
Blest Jesus, near Thy side. Amen.
—Anonymous

SPECIAL WORDS:
Gethsemane *means "olive press." The Garden of Gethsemane was filled with olive trees.*[38]

GOING DEEPER

READ IT! Jesus often prayed alone (Luke 5:16). Read about how Jesus wants you to pray in Matthew 6:5–6.

DO IT! Find a quiet place of your own to pray. Perhaps it is in your room, in your closet, or even outside under a tree. Try to pray there every day.

Judas Betrays Christ

Luke 22:39–53

Have you ever heard of a "fair-weather friend"? Some people like to have fun with you and play with you until you need help or are in trouble—and then they are nowhere to be found! Sadly, one of the twelve disciples was such a "friend." Judas Iscariot was happy to be with Jesus when times were good, but when the people turned against Jesus, Judas did too!

Jesus left the city and went to the Mount of Olives. His followers went with him. (Jesus went there often.) He said to his followers, "Pray for strength against temptation."

41Then Jesus went about a stone's throw away from them. He kneeled down and prayed, 42"Father, if it is what you want, then let me not have this cup of suffering. But do what you want, not what I want."
43Then an angel from heaven appeared to him to help him. 44Jesus was full of pain; he prayed even more. Sweat dripped from his face as if he were bleeding. 45When he finished praying, he went to his followers. They were asleep. (Their sadness had made them very tired.) 46Jesus said to them, "Why are you sleeping? Get up and pray for strength against temptation."

47While Jesus was speaking, a crowd came up. One of the 12 apostles was leading them. He was Judas. He came close to Jesus so that he could kiss him.

48But Jesus said to him, "Judas, are you using the kiss to give the Son of Man to his enemies?"

49The followers of Jesus were standing there too. They saw what was happening. They said to Jesus, "Lord, should we use our swords?" 50And one of them did use his sword. He cut off the right ear of the servant of the high priest.

51Jesus said, "Stop!" Then he touched the servant's ear and healed him.

52Those who came to arrest Jesus were the leading priests, the soldiers who guarded the Temple, and the older Jewish leaders. Jesus said to them, "Why did you come out here with swords and sticks? Do you think I am a criminal? 53I was with you every day in the Temple. Why didn't you try to arrest me there? But this is your time—the time when darkness rules."

Let's Pray!

A friend loves you all the time.

—Proverbs 17:17

Thank you, Lord, for my friends. I pray that you would help me be a true friend, especially when people I love are in trouble. In Jesus' name, amen.

Going Deeper

Read It! Even before the creation of the world, God had a plan to save his people. Read his promise in Ephesians 1:4–5.

Do It! Do you have a friend who could use a little cheering up today? Call, set up a time to play, or just offer a listening ear.

Peter's Mistake

Matthew 26:57–59, 69–75

When the soldiers arrested Jesus, the frightened and confused disciples ran away. But Peter quickly came to his senses and began to follow the soldiers from a safe distance. At the Last Supper, Jesus had predicted that Peter would deny being one of his followers, not just once, but three times (Mark 14:30)! Peter could not imagine such a thing! Was Jesus right? Let's find out.

Those men who arrested Jesus led him to
the house of Caiaphas, the high priest. The
teachers of the law and the Jewish leaders
were gathered there. 58Peter followed Jesus
but did not go near him. He followed Jesus
to the courtyard of the high priest's house.
He sat down with the guards to see what
would happen to Jesus.

59The leading priests and the Jewish
council tried to find something false against
Jesus so that they could kill him. . . .

69At that time, Peter was sitting in the
courtyard. A servant girl came to him and
said, "You were with Jesus, that man from
Galilee."

70But Peter said that he was never with
Jesus. He said this to all the people there.
Peter said, "I don't know what you are talk-
ing about."

71Then he left the courtyard. At the gate,
another girl saw him. She said to the people there, "This man was with Jesus of
Nazareth."

72Again, Peter said that he was never with
Jesus. Peter said, "I swear that I don't know
this man Jesus!"

73A short time later, some people standing there went to Peter. They said, "We
know you are one of those men who followed Jesus. We know this because of the
way you talk."

74Then Peter began to curse. He said,
"May a curse fall on me if I'm not telling
the truth. I don't know the man." After
Peter said this, a rooster crowed. 75Then
he remembered what Jesus had told him:
"Before the rooster crows, you will say
three times that you don't know me." Then
Peter went outside and cried painfully.

Let's Pray!

Father, thank you for loving me and always being faithful to me, even when I am not faithful to you. Please forgive me and help me to do better. I love you, Lord! In Jesus' name, amen.

Quote of the Day:
God send me a friend that will tell me of my faults.
—Thomas Fuller

Did You Know?
John's gospel says that "another one of Jesus' followers" (most likely John himself) was also present and was able to get the two of them into the courtyard of the high priest, Caiaphas (John 18:15).

Going Deeper

Read It! The story of Peter's denials is found in all four gospels (Matthew 26:69–75; Mark 14:66–72; Luke 22:54–62; and John 18:15–18, 25–27). One of the Old Testament prophecies about Jesus tells that his followers will desert him. Check it out in Zechariah 13:7.

Do It! Romans 8:28 says, "We know that in everything God works for the good of those who love him." What good do you think came out of Peter's mistake?

Jesus Goes Before Pilate

Matthew 27:15–26

Have you ever waited to be chosen to be on a team? Standing there, hoping your name will be called, as first one team captain and then the other chooses one kid, then the next, and the next. It feels great if your name is called right away, but not so good if you have to wait. In today's story, there was a much more important choice to be made. Jesus went before Pilate, who was going to release one prisoner. Pilate asked the people to choose between Jesus and another prisoner, named Barabbas. Which one would be punished, and which one would be released?

Every year at the time of Passover the governor would free one person from prison.
This was always a person the people wanted
to be set free. 16At that time there was a man
in prison who was known to be very bad. His
name was Barabbas. 17All the people gathered at Pilate's house. Pilate said, "Which
man do you want me to free: Barabbas, or
Jesus who is called the Christ?" 18Pilate
knew that they gave Jesus to him because
they were jealous.
19Pilate said these things while he was sitting on the judge's seat. While he was sitting
there, his wife sent a message to him. The
message said, "Don't do anything to that
man. He is not guilty. Today I had a dream
about him, and it troubled me very much."
20But the leading priests and elders told
the crowd to ask for Barabbas to be freed
and for Jesus to be killed.
21Pilate said, "I have Barabbas and Jesus.
Which do you want me to set free for you?"
The people answered, "Barabbas!"
22Pilate asked, "What should I do with
Jesus, the one called the Christ?"
They all answered, "Kill him on a cross!"
23Pilate asked, "Why do you want me to
kill him? What wrong has he done?"
But they shouted louder, "Kill him on a
cross!"
24Pilate saw that he could do nothing
about this, and a riot was starting. So he
took some water and washed his hands in
front of the crowd. Then he said, "I am not
guilty of this man's death. You are the ones
who are causing it!"
25All the people answered, "We will be
responsible. We accept for ourselves and for
our children any punishment for his death."
26Then Pilate freed Barabbas. Pilate told
some of the soldiers to beat Jesus with
whips. Then he gave Jesus to the soldiers to
be killed on a cross.

Let's Pray!

The Lord is king. He is clothed with
majesty.
The Lord is clothed in majesty
and armed with strength.
The world is set,
and it cannot be moved.
Lord, your kingdom was set up long ago.
You are everlasting.

—Psalm 93:1–2

Dear God, you sent your only Son to die so I could live with you in heaven forever. I can never thank you enough for that—but help me to live my life trying. In Jesus' name, amen.

Did You Know?
Because the Jews were under Roman law, they could not execute anyone themselves. That is why they brought Jesus to Pilate. Pilate did not want to kill Jesus, but the Jewish leaders threatened to tell the Roman emperor that Jesus was a king. This could start a riot, so Pilate gave in and ordered that Jesus be crucified.

Going Deeper

READ IT! Read the other gospel accounts of Jesus going before Pilate in Mark 15:1–15 and Luke 23:1–25.

DO IT! Movie Night! Watch *The Story of Jesus for Children* film together as a family.

Jesus Carries His Cross

Mark 15:16–27

Jesus, the Son of God, suffered through all the pain and the shame of the cross so we could be saved from our sins and one day live with him in heaven. After he had been beaten and mocked by the Roman soldiers, Jesus was forced to carry his own cross to the place where he would be crucified. But Jesus was so weak from the beatings that he stumbled under the weight of the cross. Who would carry it for him?

Pilate's soldiers took Jesus into the governor's palace (called the Praetorium). They
called all the other soldiers together. [17]They
put a purple robe on Jesus. Then they used
thorny branches to make a crown. They put
it on his head. [18]Then they called out to him,
"Hail, King of the Jews!" [19]The soldiers beat
Jesus on the head many times with a stick.
They also spit on him. Then they made fun
of him by bowing on their knees and worshiping him. [20]After they finished making
fun of him, the soldiers took off the purple
robe and put his own clothes on him again.
Then they led Jesus out of the palace to be
killed on a cross.

[21]There was a man from Cyrene coming
from the fields to the city. The man was
Simon, the father of Alexander and Rufus.
The soldiers forced Simon to carry the
cross for Jesus. [22]They led Jesus to the place
called Golgotha. (Golgotha means the
Place of the Skull.) [23]At Golgotha the soldiers tried to give Jesus wine to drink. This
wine was mixed with myrrh. But he refused
to drink it. [24]The soldiers nailed Jesus to a
cross. Then they divided his clothes among
themselves. They threw lots to decide
which clothes each soldier would get.

[25]It was nine o'clock in the morning when
they nailed Jesus to the cross. [26]There was a
sign with the charge against Jesus written
on it. The sign read: "THE KING OF THE JEWS."
[27]They also put two robbers on crosses beside Jesus, one on the right, and the other
on the left.

LET'S PRAY!

Lord, help me to remember today and every day the sacrifice you made for me.

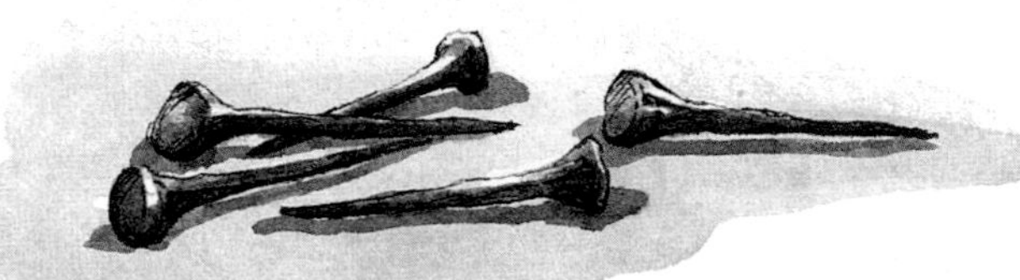

Quote of the Day:
There is a green
hill far away
Outside a city wall
Where the dear
Lord was crucified
Who died to save us all.
—Mrs. Cecil F. Alexander

Did You Know?
Simon was probably a Jew who had come to Jerusalem to celebrate the Passover. At that time, Cyrene was an important city in North Africa.[39]

GOING DEEPER

READ IT! The Old Testament prophets told how Jesus would die. Isaiah said he would die with criminals (Isaiah 53:12), and Zechariah said his hands and feet would be pierced (Zechariah 12:10).

DO IT! This week think about all that Jesus suffered to save you. Do something extra nice for someone as a way of saying thank you to Jesus.

Jesus Is Crucified

John 19:16–24

Crucifixion was so cruel and so terrible that the Romans only crucified slaves and criminals. The person's hands and feet were nailed to the cross. Not only was it very painful, but it was also very shameful. Jesus suffered all of that for us. He took the punishment for all our sins, so we would not have to be punished.

So Pilate gave Jesus to them to be killed on
a cross.
The soldiers took charge of Jesus.
17Carrying his own cross, Jesus went out
to a place called The Place of the Skull.
(In the Jewish language this place is called
Golgotha.) 18There they nailed Jesus to
the cross. They also put two other men on
crosses, one on each side of Jesus with Jesus
in the middle. 19Pilate wrote a sign and put
it on the cross. It read: "JESUS OF NAZARETH,
THE KING OF THE JEWS." 20The sign was written in the Jewish language, in Latin, and in
Greek. Many of the Jews read the sign, because this place where Jesus was killed was
near the city. 21The leading Jewish priests
said to Pilate, "Don't write, 'The King of the
Jews.' But write, 'This man said, I am the
King of the Jews.'"
22Pilate answered, "What I have written, I
have written!"
23After the soldiers nailed Jesus to the
cross, they took his clothes. They divided
them into four parts. Each soldier got one
part. They also took his long shirt. It was all
one piece of cloth, woven from top to bottom. 24So the soldiers said to each other,
"We should not tear this into parts. We
should throw lots to see who will get it."
This happened to give full meaning to the
Scripture:

"They divided my clothes among them.
And they threw lots for my clothing."
Psalm 22:18

So the soldiers did this.

Let's Pray!
"The Tax Collector's Prayer"
God, have mercy on me. I am a sinner!
—Luke 18:13

Going Deeper

Read It! Isaiah 53:1–12 is an Old Testament prophecy of what Jesus would suffer on the cross—and why he did it. Read it for yourself.

Do It! Write a prayer or poem to Jesus, telling him how you feel when you think of all he did to save you.

Quote of the Day:
At the heart of the story stands the cross of Christ where evil did its worst and met its match.
—John W. Wenham

Jesus of Nazareth
King of the Jews

"Here Is Your Mother"

John 19:25–30

For six long hours Jesus hung on the cross, suspended between heaven and earth. During that time, his mother, Mary, and a small group of his followers stood nearby. They would not leave him, no matter how much it hurt to stay. But even on the cross, Jesus thought of others. Read of how Jesus took care of his mother.

Jesus' mother stood near his cross. His
mother's sister was also standing there,
with Mary the wife of Clopas, and Mary
Magdalene. 26Jesus saw his mother. He also
saw the follower he loved standing there.
He said to his mother, "Dear woman, here
is your son." 27Then he said to the follower,
"Here is your mother." From that time on,
this follower took her to live in his home.

28After this, Jesus knew that everything
had been done. To make the Scripture
come true, he said, "I am thirsty." 29There
was a jar full of vinegar there, so the soldiers
soaked a sponge in it. Then they put
the sponge on a branch of a hyssop plant
and lifted it to Jesus' mouth. 30Jesus tasted
the vinegar. Then he said, "It is finished."
He bowed his head and died.

Let's Pray!

As I think about the cross, God, I understand how much you must have loved each of us. Help me to love and serve others as you have loved and served me. In Jesus' name, amen.

Did You Know?
Historians believe that Mary was a widow by the time Jesus went to the cross. She would have had very little or no money of her own. Since Jesus was her oldest son, it was his responsibility to take care of his mother. Jesus trusted John, one of his closest friends and disciples, to take care of her.

Going Deeper

READ IT! By making sure that Mary was taken care of, Jesus was fulfilling the fifth commandment. What was it? Read Exodus 20:12 to find out.

DO IT! Mothers are such a special blessing from God. Give your mom a great big hug, and thank God for hcr!

Jesus Is Buried

John 19:38–42

Have you ever lost a pet or a family member you loved very much? It's one of the hardest things in the world. Death leaves a big hole in your heart. For a long time you may think that pain will never go away. That's how it felt when Jesus died too. His friends and family didn't understand why he had died—or that, three days later, they would be happy again when he rose from the grave. At that moment, all they could do was bury Jesus with great love and great sadness.

Later, a man named Joseph from Arimathea asked Pilate if he could take the body of Jesus. (Joseph was a secret follower of Jesus, because he was afraid of the Jews.) Pilate gave his permission. So Joseph came and took Jesus' body away. [39]Nicodemus went with Joseph. Nicodemus was the man who earlier had come to Jesus at night. He brought about 75 pounds of spices. This was a mixture of myrrh and aloes. [40]These two men took Jesus' body and wrapped it with the spices in pieces of linen cloth. (This is how the Jews bury people.) [41]In the place where Jesus was killed, there was a garden. In the garden was a new tomb where no one had ever been buried. [42]The men laid Jesus in that tomb because it was near, and the Jews were preparing to start their Sabbath day.

Let's Pray!

Savior, teach me, day by day,
Love's sweet lesson to obey;
Sweeter lesson cannot be,
Loving Him who first loved me.

—Jane Elizabeth Leeson

Did You Know?

Jesus' tomb was sealed with a great stone, and soldiers stood guard over it. Why? Because the Jewish leaders were afraid that the disciples would steal Jesus' body and pretend he had risen from the grave (Matthew 27:62–66). But Jesus is more powerful than any stone or any guard!

Did You Know?
Joseph of Arimathea was a member of the Jewish Sanhedrin. Nicodemus was the same man who went to Jesus in the night to ask him questions. Both men had secretly followed Jesus because they were afraid of the Jewish leaders.

Going Deeper

Read It! When a person is baptized, he is acting out Jesus' death and burial. When the person comes up out of the water, that is like the resurrection—the beginning of a new life in Jesus. Read about it in Romans 6:4.

Do It! Tonight, when you say your prayers, thank God for his love for you—a love so great that he sent his Son to die for you.

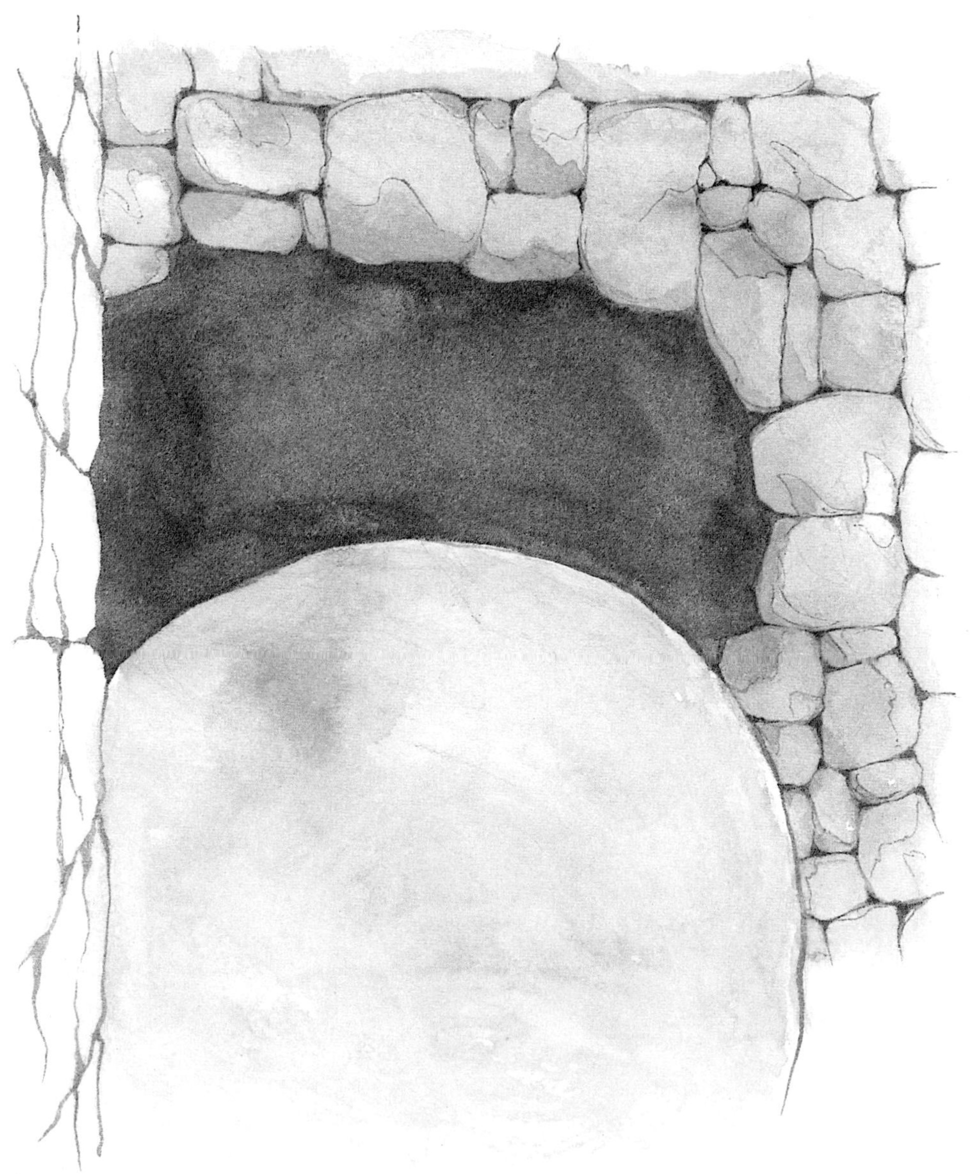

I cry out to God Most High,
to the God who does everything for me.
He sends help from heaven and saves me.

—Psalm 57:2–3

My God, in whom arc all the springs
Of boundless love, and grace unknown,
Hide me beneath Thy spreading wings,
Till the dark cloud is overblown.

Up to the heavens I send my cry,
The Lord will my desires perform;
He sends His angel from the sky,
And saves me from the threatening storm.

Be Thou exalted, O my God,
Above the heavens, where angels dwell;
Thy power on earth be known abroad,
And land to land Thy wonders tell.

—Isaac Watts

Jesus' Last Week on Earth

(Matthew 21–28; Mark 11–16; Luke 19–24; John 13–20)

Sunday	Jesus rides into Jerusalem on a donkey's colt.
Monday	Jesus drives the money changers out of the temple.
Tuesday	Jesus teaches in the temple.
Wednesday	Judas agrees to betray Jesus.
Thursday	Jesus and his disciples share the Passover meal.
Thursday night	Jesus prays in the Garden of Gethsemane.
Friday before dawn	Jesus is arrested and tried.
Friday morning	Pilate gives the order for Jesus to be killed.
Friday	Jesus is crucified on the cross.
Friday to Sunday	Jesus is buried in the grave.
Sunday	Jesus' tomb is found empty.
Sunday	Mary sees Jesus.
Sunday	Jesus is seen on the road to Emmaus by two believers.
Sunday	Jesus appears before his disciples.

The Empty Tomb

Matthew 28:1–4; John 20:1–10

Imagine that you were a Roman soldier, put in charge of guarding the tomb of Jesus the Nazarene. In the marketplace and on the street, everyone was talking about the trial and crucifixion of this man, who had been so loved by some and so hated by others. He had said that he would rise from the dead after three days, and your job was to make sure he didn't. Then suddenly, in a flash of blinding light, the tomb was empty! What now?

The day after the Sabbath day was the first
day of the week. . . . 2At that time there was
a strong earthquake. An angel of the Lord
came down from heaven. The angel went
to the tomb and rolled the stone away from
the entrance. Then he sat on the stone.
3He was shining as bright as lightning. His
clothes were white as snow. 4The soldiers
guarding the tomb were very frightened of
the angel. They shook with fear and then
became like dead men.

John 20:1Early on the first day of the week,
Mary Magdalene went to the tomb. It was
still dark. Mary saw that the large stone had
been moved away from the tomb. 2So Mary
ran to Simon Peter and the other follower
(the one Jesus loved). Mary said, "They
have taken the Lord out of the tomb. We
don't know where they have put him."

3So Peter and the other follower started for
the tomb. 4They were both running, but the
other follower ran faster than Peter. So the
other follower reached the tomb first. 5He
bent down and looked in. He saw the strips
of linen cloth lying there, but he did not go
in. 6Then following him came Simon Peter.
He went into the tomb and saw the strips of
linen lying there. 7He also saw the cloth that
had been around Jesus' head. The cloth was
folded up and laid in a different place from
the strips of linen. 8Then the other follower,
who had reached the tomb first, also went
in. He saw and believed. 9(These followers
did not yet understand from the Scriptures
that Jesus must rise from death.)

10Then the followers went back home.

LET'S PRAY!

Dear Lord, how amazed the disciples must have been when they found the tomb empty! Each day, help me to remember the empty tomb and to be as amazed as the disciples were. In Jesus' name, amen.

Did You Know?

Although John only mentions Mary Magdalene at the tomb, the use of "we" (verse 2) suggests she was not alone. Matthew 28:1 says she went with "another woman named Mary," who was probably the mother of the disciple James. And Mark 16:1 says that "Mary Magdalene, Mary the mother of James, and Salome "bought some sweet-smelling spices to put on Jesus' body."

Going Deeper

Read It! The Old Testament has many prophecies about Jesus—even about his resurrection. Find one of them in Psalm 16:10.

Do It! Using the letters of the word *resurrection*, make an acrostic that tells what Jesus' resurrection means to you. For example, *R* might be for "rejoicing," *E* for "excited," and *S* for "Savior."

Mary Sees Jesus

John 20:11–18

Several women were among the followers of Jesus. They helped support Jesus and his disciples during his ministry (Luke 8:1–3). One was Mary Magdalene, from whom Jesus had driven away seven evil spirits (Luke 8:2). How she loved Jesus for freeing her from those evil spirits! When Jesus was arrested and crucified, Mary stayed nearby. Then, early Sunday morning, she and some other women went to Jesus' tomb to prepare his body. When she discovered that the stone had been rolled away and the tomb was empty, she ran to get Peter and the others. They came and found the empty tomb. Still they did not understand what had happened, so the disciples returned home. But all Mary could do was stand by the tomb and weep. What have they done with Jesus? she wondered.

But Mary stood outside the tomb, crying.
While she was still crying, she bent down
and looked inside the tomb. 12She saw two
angels dressed in white. They were sitting
where Jesus' body had been, one at the
head and one at the feet.
13They asked her, "Woman, why are you
crying?"
She answered, "They have taken away
my Lord. I don't know where they have put
him." 14When Mary said this, she turned
around and saw Jesus standing there. But
she did not know that it was Jesus.
15Jesus asked her, "Woman, why are you
crying? Whom are you looking for?"
Mary thought he was the gardener. So
she said to him, "Did you take him away,
sir? Tell me where you put him, and I will
get him."
16Jesus said to her, "Mary."
Mary turned toward Jesus and said in the
Jewish language, "Rabboni." (This means
Teacher.)
17Jesus said to her, "Don't hold me. I have
not yet gone up to the Father. But go to my
brothers and tell them this: 'I am going
back to my Father and your Father. I am
going back to my God and your God.'"
18Mary Magdalene went and said to the
followers, "I saw the Lord!" And she told
them what Jesus had said to her.

Let's Pray!

You can look for the Lord your God. And you will find him if you look. But you must look for him with your whole being.

—Deuteronomy 4:29

Dear Lord, all over the world, people are sad and feeling far away from you. Help them reach out to you, because I know you will receive them. In Jesus' name, amen.

Going Deeper

Read It! The Jewish leaders did not want the people to know that Jesus had risen from the grave. Read in Matthew 28:11–15 about what they did to hide the truth.

Do It! A giant stone covered the entrance to Jesus' tomb. It was rolled away when he rose from the grave. Find a large stone and paint a cross on it to remind you that Jesus is alive!

Doubting Thomas

John 20:19–29

"Prove it!" That's what you might say if someone tells you that something amazing has just happened—something you find hard to believe. In today's story, Thomas—or "doubting Thomas," as he is sometimes called—has a hard time believing the news that Jesus is alive and that the disciples had seen him (verse 25). Thomas said he would not believe it unless he saw see Jesus too. So what do you think happened?

It was the first day of the week. That evening [Jesus'] followers were together. The doors were locked, because they were afraid of the Jews. Then Jesus came and stood among them. He said, "Peace be with you!" [20]After he said this, he showed them his hands and his side. His followers were very happy when they saw the Lord.

[21]Then Jesus said again, "Peace be with you! As the Father sent me, I now send you." [22]After he said this, he breathed on them and said, "Receive the Holy Spirit. [23]If you forgive anyone his sins, they are forgiven. If you don't forgive them, they are not forgiven."

[24]Thomas (called Didymus) was not with the followers when Jesus came. Thomas was 1 of the 12. [25]The other followers told Thomas, "We saw the Lord."

But Thomas said, "I will not believe it until I see the nail marks in his hands. And I will not believe until I put my finger where the nails were and put my hand into his side."

[26]A week later the followers were in the house again. Thomas was with them. The doors were locked, but Jesus came in and stood among them. He said, "Peace be with you!" [27]Then he said to Thomas, "Put your finger here. Look at my hands. Put your hand here in my side. Stop doubting and believe."

[28]Thomas said to him, "My Lord and my God!"

[29]Then Jesus told him, "You believe because you see me. Those who believe without seeing me will be truly happy."

Let's Pray!

Lord, fill me with your Spirit so that even though I have never seen Jesus face-to-face my faith in him will never weaken. Then, one day, I really will see him face-to-face. In Jesus' name, amen.

Quote of the Day:
Our old history ends with the cross; our new history begins with the resurrection.
—Watchman Nee

Going Deeper

Read It! Thomas wasn't the only one in the Bible to doubt. In the middle of all his troubles, Job doubted God and questioned him. Read God's answer to him in Job 38. We only have to remember the power of God to trust him.

Do It! Do you ever doubt God's love for you? When you do, read John 3:16–17. That's how much God loves you!

Jesus Forgives Peter

John 21:2–19

"Tonight you will say you don't know me. You will say this three times before the rooster crows," Jesus had warned Peter at the Last Supper. Peter had declared that he would never deny Jesus (Mark 14:30–31). But on the night Jesus was arrested, Peter did deny Jesus. Three times Peter said he did not know his dear Friend. When Peter heard the rooster crow, he realized what he had done, and he ran away and wept bitterly. Now that Jesus had risen from the grave, Peter wondered if Jesus could ever forgive him. What would happen when they met again?

Some of the followers were together.
They were Simon Peter, Thomas (called
Didymus), Nathanael from Cana in Galilee,
the two sons of Zebedee, and two other followers. 3Simon Peter said, "I am going out
to fish."

The other followers said, "We will go with
you." . . . They fished that night but caught
nothing.

4Early the next morning Jesus stood on
the shore. But the followers did not know
that it was Jesus. 5Then he said to them,
"Friends, have you caught any fish?"

They answered, "No."

6He said, "Throw your net into the water
on the right side of the boat, and you will
find some." So they did this. They caught so
many fish that they could not pull the net
back into the boat.

7The follower whom Jesus loved said to
Peter, "It is the Lord!" When Peter heard
him say this, he wrapped his coat around
himself. (Peter had taken his clothes off.)
Then he jumped into the water. 8The other
followers went to shore in the boat, drag-
ging the net full of fish. They were not
very far from shore, only about 100 yards.
9When the followers stepped out of the boat
and onto the shore, they saw a fire of hot
coals. There were fish on the fire, and there
was bread.

10Then Jesus said, "Bring some of the fish
that you caught."

11Simon Peter went into the boat and
pulled the net to the shore. It was full of
big fish. There were 153. Even though there
were so many, the net did not tear. 12Jesus
said to them, "Come and eat." None of the
followers dared ask him, "Who are you?"
They knew it was the Lord. 13Jesus came and
took the bread and gave it to them. He also
gave them the fish.

14This was now the third time Jesus
showed himself to his followers after he
was raised from death.

15When they finished eating, Jesus said
to Simon Peter, "Simon son of John do you
love me more than these?"

He answered, "Yes, Lord, you know that
I love you."

Jesus said, "Take care of my lambs."

16Again Jesus said, "Simon son of John do
you love me?"

He answered, "Yes, Lord, you know that
I love you."

Jesus said, "Take care of my sheep."

17A third time he said, "Simon son of
John do you love me?"

Peter was hurt because Jesus asked him the third time, "Do you love me?" Peter said, "Lord, you know everything. You know that I love you!"

He said to him, "Take care of my sheep.
18 I tell you the truth. When you were younger, you tied your own belt and went where you wanted. But when you are old, you will put out your hands and someone else will tie them. They will take you where you don't want to go."
19 (Jesus said this to show how Peter would die to give glory to God.) Then Jesus said to Peter, "Follow me!"

Quote of the Day:
Courage is fear that has said its prayers.
—Unknown

Let's Pray!

Father, thank you for forgiving my sins. Help me be strong in my faith in you, and help me not be afraid to tell everyone that you are the one true God. In Jesus' name, amen.

Going Deeper

Read It! You can be strong and courageous for God. Read Joshua 1:9 to find out how!

Do It! Have you ever been embarrassed to talk about Jesus? Ask your parents what you can do to not be afraid to talk about Jesus. Then pray for another chance to tell someone about him.

Travelers to Emmaus

Luke 24:13–20, 25–31

The same day the disciples discovered the empty tomb, believers several miles away also saw the risen Jesus. Just like Mary Magdalene, they did not know who he was at first. Let's read about their miraculous visit with Jesus.

That same day two of Jesus' followers
were going to a town named Emmaus.
It is about seven miles from Jerusalem.
14They were talking about everything that
had happened. 15While they were discuss-
ing these things, Jesus himself came near
and began walking with them. 16(They were
not allowed to recognize Jesus.) 17Then he
said, "What are these things you are talking
about while you walk?"

The two followers stopped. Their faces
were very sad. 18The one named Cleopas
answered, "You must be the only one in
Jerusalem who does not know what just
happened there."

19Jesus said to them, "What are you talking about?"

The followers said, "It is about Jesus of
Nazareth. He was a prophet from God to all
the people. He said and did many powerful things. 20Our leaders and the leading
priests gave him up to be judged and killed.
They nailed him to a cross. . . .

25Then Jesus said to them, "You are foolish and slow to realize what is true. You
should believe everything the prophets
said. 26They said that the Christ must suffer these things before he enters his glory."
27Then Jesus began to explain everything
that had been written about himself in the
Scriptures. He started with Moses, and
then he talked about what all the prophets
had said about him.

28They came near the town of Emmaus,
and Jesus acted as if he did not plan to stop
there. 29But they begged him, "Stay with us.
It is late; it is almost night." So he went in
to stay with them.

30Jesus sat down with them and took
some bread. He gave thanks for the food
and divided it. Then he gave it to them.
31And then, they were allowed to recognize
Jesus. But when they saw who he was, he
disappeared.

Let's Pray!

O help me, Lord, this day to be
Thy own dear child and follow Thee;
And lead me, Savior, by Thy hand
Until I reach the heavenly land. Amen.

—Anonymous

Going Deeper

READ IT! In verse 27, Jesus used the Old Testament to explain to the disciples who he really was. Read one of the Old Testament verses about Jesus in Genesis 22:18.

DO IT! Take time today to pray for the leaders and teachers of your church.

The Ascension

Luke 24:36–51

After the disciples at Emmaus realized who Jesus was, they got up right away and hurried back to Jerusalem. They wanted to tell Peter and the others what had happened: they had seen Jesus! But then something even more amazing happened.

While the two followers were telling this, Jesus himself stood among those gathered. He said to them, "Peace be with you."

37 They were fearful and terrified. They thought they were seeing a ghost. 38 But Jesus said, "Why are you troubled? Why do you doubt what you see? 39 Look at my hands and my feet. It is I myself! Touch me. You can see that I have a living body; a ghost does not have a body like this."

40 After Jesus said this, he showed them his hands and feet. 41 The followers were amazed and very happy. They still could not believe it. Jesus said to them, "Do you have any food here?" 42 They gave him a piece of cooked fish. 43 While the followers watched, Jesus took the fish and ate it.

44 He said to them, "Remember when I was with you before? I said that everything written about me must happen—everything in the law of Moses, the books of the prophets, and the Psalms."

45 Then Jesus opened their minds so they could understand the Scriptures. 46 He said to them, "It is written that the Christ would be killed and rise from death on the third day. 47–48 You saw these things happen—you are witnesses. You must tell people to change their hearts and lives. If they do this, their sins will be forgiven. You must start at Jerusalem and preach these things in my name to all nations. 49 Listen! My Father has promised you something; I will send it to you. But you must stay in Jerusalem until you have received that power from heaven."

50 Jesus led his followers out of Jerusalem almost to Bethany. He raised his hands and blessed them. 51 While he was blessing them, he was separated from them and carried into heaven.

Let's Pray!

Let us pray, for God loves us;
Let us pray, for God hears us;
Let us pray, for God is our God,
And we are all His children.
—Unknown

Going Deeper

Read It! Did you know that Jesus defends you to God? Read about it in Romans 8:34.

Do It! Learn "Jesus Loves Me" in sign language. Check online for instructions.

Did You Know?
Jesus stayed on earth for forty days after he rose from the grave (Acts 1:3). He was seen by hundreds of people, including Mary Magdalene, the disciples, and hundreds of people in Galilee (1 Corinthians 15:6).

Other Apostles

Acts 1:12–17, 21–26

When Judas died (Matthew 27:5), the apostles gathered to name someone to take his place. Very little is known about Matthias, the man who took Judas's place. These men—who had met Jesus himself—had special authority to teach and to defend the teachings of the Lord. Soon the church began to grow all over the world!

Then they went back to Jerusalem from the Mount of Olives. (This mountain is about half a mile from Jerusalem.) [13]When they entered the city, they went to the upstairs room where they were staying. Peter, John, James, Andrew, Philip, Thomas, Bartholomew, Matthew, James son of Alphaeus, Simon (known as the Zealot), and Judas son of James were there. [14]They all continued praying together. Some women, including Mary the mother of Jesus, and Jesus' brothers were also there with the apostles.

[15]During this time there was a meeting of the believers. (There were about 120 of them.) Peter stood up and said, [16–17]"Brothers, in the Scriptures the Holy Spirit said through David that something must happen. The Spirit was talking about Judas, one of our own group, who served together with us. The Spirit said that Judas would lead men to arrest Jesus. . . .

[21–22]"So now a man must join us and become a witness of Jesus' being raised from death. He must be one of the men who were part of our group during all the time the Lord Jesus was with us. He must have been with us from the time John began to baptize people until the day when Jesus was taken up from us to heaven."

[23]They put the names of two men before the group. One was Joseph Barsabbas, who was also called Justus. The other was Matthias. [24–25]The apostles prayed, "Lord, you know the minds of everyone. Show us which one of these two you have chosen to do this work. Judas turned away from it and went where he belongs. Lord, show us which one should take his place as an apostle!" [26]Then they used lots to choose between them, and the lots showed that Matthias was the one. So he became an apostle with the other 11.

Let's Pray!

God be in my head
And in my understanding;
God be in my eyes
And in my looking;
God be in my mouth
And in my speaking;
God be in my heart
And in my thinking.

—from the Sarum Primer

Did You Know?
Among the seventy closest followers of Jesus, Matthias was with Jesus from his baptism to his ascension (Acts 1:21–22).

GOING DEEPER

READ IT! Before Jesus rose up into heaven, he gave his disciples a job to do. It is called the "Great Commission." Read about it in Mark 16:15–16.

DO IT! The Great Commission wasn't just for Jesus' first followers. It's for you too! What will you do to share Jesus with someone today?

Pentecost

Acts 2:1–11

Fifty days after Jesus' resurrection, and just ten days after Jesus ascended into heaven, the Holy Spirit came upon the apostles. And then amazing things began to happen!

When the day of Pentecost came, they were all together in one place. 2Suddenly a noise came from heaven. It sounded like a strong wind blowing. This noise filled the whole house where they were sitting. 3They saw something that looked like flames of fire. The flames were separated and stood over each person there. 4They were all filled with the Holy Spirit, and they began to speak different languages. The Holy Spirit was giving them the power to speak these languages.

5There were some religious Jews staying in Jerusalem who were from every country in the world. 6When they heard this noise, a crowd came together. They were all surprised, because each one heard them speaking in his own language. 7They were completely amazed at this. They said, "Look! Aren't all these men that we hear speaking from Galilee? 8But each of us hears them in his own language. How is this possible? We are from different places: 9Parthia, Media, Elam, Mesopotamia, Judea, Cappadocia, Pontus, Asia, 10Phrygia, Pamphylia, Egypt, the areas of Libya near Cyrene, Rome 11(both Jews and those who had become Jews), Crete and Arabia. But we hear these men telling in our own languages about the great things God has done!"

Let's Pray!

Lord, thank you for sending your Holy Spirit to be with me at all times. Help me to be guided by your Spirit in all I do and say. And please use me to spread your Word everywhere I go. In Jesus' name, amen.

Going Deeper

READ IT! How should you tell others about God? With joy and singing! Read about it in Psalm 98.

DO IT! Missionaries take God's Word to people all over the world. Make and send a card to encourage a missionary from your church.

Did You Know?

Pentecost was also called the "Feast of Firstfruits" and the "Feast of Harvest."

Peter Heals the Lame Man

Acts 3:1–10

The Beautiful Gate was a favorite entrance to the temple. Since many people passed by it every day, it was a good place for a beggar to sit and ask for money. But when one beggar asked Peter and John for money, he got much more!

One day Peter and John went to the Temple.
It was three o'clock in the afternoon. This
was the time for the daily prayer service.
2There, at the Temple gate called Beautiful
Gate, was a man who had been crippled all
his life. Every day he was carried to this
gate to beg. He would ask for money from
the people going into the Temple. 3The man
saw Peter and John going into the Temple
and asked them for money. 4Peter and John
looked straight at him and said, "Look at
us!" 5The man looked at them; he thought
they were going to give him some money.
6But Peter said, "I don't have any silver or
gold, but I do have something else I can
give you: By the power of Jesus Christ from
Nazareth—stand up and walk!" 7Then Peter
took the man's right hand and lifted him
up. Immediately the man's feet and ankles
became strong. 8He jumped up, stood on
his feet, and began to walk. He went into the
Temple with them, walking and jumping,
and praising God. 9–10All the people recognized him. They knew he was the crippled
man who always sat by the Beautiful Gate
begging for money. Now they saw this same
man walking and praising God. The people
were amazed. They could not understand
how this could happen.

LET'S PRAY!

Keep my little tongue today,
Keep it gentle while I play;
Keep my hands from doing wrong.
Keep my feet the whole day long;
Keep me all, O Jesus mild,
Keep me ever Thy dear child. Amen.

—Anonymous

Special Words:
The "Beautiful Gate" (or "Golden Gate") is on the east side of the temple. Some think it was in the temple court between the court of Gentiles and the court of women.

GOING DEEPER

READ IT! Jesus gave the power to heal to the first apostle. Read about it in Matthew 10:1.

DO IT! Thank God for your legs today! As a family, go outside and play a game of tag, kickball, baseball, or another active game.

Peter and John Arrested

Acts 4:1–5, 7–13, 21–22

As the early church quickly grew from just a handful of believers to more than 5,000, the Jewish religious leaders became very nervous about the power that the apostles had. Early Christians were Jews who continued to observe the Jewish Sabbath. They were watched with suspicion because of their gatherings on Sunday (the day of resurrection) to "break bread." This was a special worry for the Sadducees, a Jewish group who did not believe in the resurrection. The Jewish leaders decided they needed to stop those who believed in God—but God had other plans!

While Peter and John were speaking to the
people, a group of men came up to them.
There were Jewish priests, the captain of
the soldiers that guarded the Temple, and
some Sadducees. 2They were upset because
the two apostles were teaching the people.
Peter and John were preaching that people
will rise from death through the power of
Jesus. 3The Jewish leaders grabbed Peter
and John and put them in jail. It was already night, so they kept them in jail until
the next day. 4But many of those who heard
Peter and John preach believed the things
they said. There were now about 5,000
men in the group of believers.

5The next day the Jewish rulers, the older
Jewish leaders, and the teachers of the law
met in Jerusalem. . . . 7They made Peter and
John stand before them. The Jewish leaders asked them: "By what power or authority did you do this?"

8Then Peter was filled with the Holy Spirit.
He said to them, "Rulers of the people and
you elders, 9are you questioning us about a
good thing that was done to a crippled man?
Are you asking us who made him well? 10We
want all of you and all the Jewish people to
know that this man was made well by the
power of Jesus Christ from Nazareth! You
nailed him to a cross, but God raised him
from death. This man was crippled, but he
is now well and able to stand here before
you because of the power of Jesus! 11Jesus is

'the stone that you builders did not want.
It has become the cornerstone.'

Psalm 118:22

12Jesus is the only One who can save
people. . . .

13The Jewish leaders saw that Peter and
John were not afraid to speak. They understood that these men had no special train-
ing or education. So they were amazed.
Then they realized that Peter and John had
been with Jesus. . . .

21–22The Jewish leaders could not find a
way to punish them because all the people
were praising God for what had been done.
(This miracle was a proof from God. The
man who was healed was more than 40
years old!) So the Jewish leaders warned
the apostles again and let them go free.

Let's Pray!

I will rejoice in God my Savior.
The Lord God gives me my strength.
He makes me like a deer, which does not stumble.
He leads me safely on the steep mountains.

—Habakkuk 3:18–19

Quote of the Day:
Prayer in private results in boldness in public.
—Edwin Louis Cole

Going Deeper

Read It! Peter and John had such good news to share that they just couldn't keep quiet about it. When you declare to others that you believe in Jesus, Jesus promises you something very special. Find out what it is in Matthew 10:32.

Do It! Take a walk together as a family, and pray for your neighbors.

Ananias and Sapphira

Acts 4:32–35; 5:1–11

In the early Christian church, believers often put their money and supplies together, so those with greater wealth could help those who had less. This was especially important because some new believers lost everything—including family ties—when they chose to worship Jesus and be followers of "the Way." No one was forced to give up their wealth, but those who chose to make this sacrifice were greatly admired by the church. But one couple was more interested in being admired than in truly helping others. Their selfishness led them to make a very bad choice!

The group of believers were joined in their hearts, and they had the same spirit. No person in the group said that the things he had were his own. Instead, they shared everything. [33]With great power the apostles were telling people that the Lord Jesus was truly raised from death. And God blessed all the believers very much. [34]They all received the things they needed. Everyone that owned fields or houses sold them. They brought the money [35]and gave it to the apostles. Then each person was given the things he needed. . . .

[5:1]A man named Ananias and his wife Sapphira sold some land. [2]But he gave only part of the money to the apostles. He secretly kept some of it for himself. His wife knew about this, and she agreed to it. [3]Peter said, "Ananias, why did you let Satan rule your heart? You lied to the Holy Spirit. Why did you keep part of the money you received for the land for yourself? [4]Before you sold the land, it belonged to you. And even after you sold it, you could have used the money any way you wanted. Why did you think of doing this? You lied to God, not to men!" [5–6]When Ananias heard this, he fell down and died. Some young men came in, wrapped up his body, carried it out, and buried it. And everyone who heard about this was filled with fear.

[7]About three hours later his wife came in. She did not know what had happened. [8]Peter said to her, "Tell me how much money you got for your field. Was it this much?"

Sapphira answered, "Yes, that was the price."

[9]Peter said to her, "Why did you and your husband agree to test the Spirit of the Lord? Look! The men who buried your husband are at the door! They will carry you out." [10]At that moment Sapphira fell down by his feet and died. The young men came in and saw that she was dead. They carried her out and buried her beside her husband. [11]The whole church and all the others who heard about these things were filled with fear.

Let's Pray!

Lord, I thank you and I praise you for your many gifts to me. Help me see the needs of others and how I can help them. I want to do good with all that you have given me. In Jesus' name, amen.

Going Deeper

Read It! Check out Matthew 6:2–4 to see how God wants you to give to others.

Do It! It's important to give to others for the right reasons—to give honor to God and not to yourself. Make sure you're giving for the right reasons by giving in secret. Who can you secretly bless today?

Quote of the Day:
"Give, and you will receive. You will be given much. It will be poured into your hands—more than you can hold. You will be given so much that it will spill into your lap. The way you give to others is the way God will give to you."
—Jesus, in Luke 6:38

A LITTLE CHILD MAY KNOW

A little child may know
Our Father's name of love;
'Tis written o'er the earth below
And on the sky above.

Around me when I look,
His handiwork I see;
This world is like a picture book
To teach His love to me.

The birds that sweetly sing,
The moon that shines by night,
With every tiny living thing
Rejoicing in the light;

And every star above,
Set in the deep blue sky,
Assure me that our God is love
And tell me He is nigh.

—Jane Elizabeth Leeson

The Great Escape

Acts 5:12–26

As the apostles faced greater and greater trouble from the Jewish leaders, and more and more praise from the people, they had to make a choice. If they kept preaching and teaching as Jesus had told them to do, their lives might be in danger. Should they be quiet, or should they keep preaching the gospel no matter what happened? The apostles decided to obey God—and he took care of them in a miraculous way!

The apostles did many signs and miracles
among the people. And they would all meet
together on Solomon's Porch. [13]None of
the others dared to stand with them. All
the people were saying good things about
them. [14]More and more men and women
believed in the Lord and were added to the
group of believers. [15]As Peter was passing
by, the people brought their sick into the
streets. They put their sick on beds and
mats so at least Peter's shadow might fall
on them. [16]Crowds came from all the towns
around Jerusalem. They brought their sick
and those who were bothered by evil spirits. All of them were healed.

[17]The high priest and all his friends (a
group called the Sadducees) became very
jealous. [18]They took the apostles and put
them in jail. [19]But during the night, an angel
of the Lord opened the doors of the jail. He
led the apostles outside and said, [20]"Go
and stand in the Temple. Tell the people
everything about this new life." [21]When the
apostles heard this, they obeyed and went
into the Temple. It was early in the morning, and they began to teach.

The high priest and his friends arrived.
They called a meeting of the Jewish leaders
and all the important older men of the Jews.
They sent some men to the jail to bring the
apostles to them. [22]When the men went to
the jail, they could not find the apostles. So
they went back and told the Jewish leaders
about this. [23]They said, "The jail was closed
and locked. The guards were standing at
the doors. But when we opened the doors,
the jail was empty!" [24]Hearing this, the
captain of the Temple guards and the leading priests were confused. They wondered,
"What will happen because of this?"

[25]Then someone came and told them,
"Listen! The men you put in jail are standing in the Temple. They are teaching the
people!" [26]Then the captain and his men
went out and brought the apostles back. But
the soldiers did not use force, because they
were afraid that the people would kill them
with stones.

Let's Pray!

Lord, give me the courage to share your Word, just as Peter and the other apostles did. I will trust you to take care of me, just as you took care of them! In Jesus' name, amen.

Special Words:
The Sadducees were very powerful. They came from the leading Jewish families. The high priests and the most powerful members of the priesthood were Sadducees. Because the Sadducees did not believe in the resurrection, they wanted to stop Jesus' disciples.[40]

Going Deeper

Read It! This isn't the first time an angel of the Lord rescued prisoners. Read about Shadrach, Meshach, and Abednego in Daniel 3.

Do It! In many parts of the world, Christians are still put into prison, hurt, or even killed for their faith! Take time today to pray for those believers who are suffering for Jesus.

Wise Gamaliel

Acts 5:27–42

In today's story, a wise Jewish rabbi who may have been a secret follower of Christ helps the apostles.

The soldiers brought the apostles to the meeting and made them stand before the Jewish leaders. The high priest questioned them. 28He said, "We gave you strict orders not to go on teaching in that name. But . . . you have filled Jerusalem with your teaching. You are trying to make us responsible for this man's death."

29Peter and the other apostles answered, "We must obey God, not men! 30You killed Jesus. You hung him on a cross. But God, the same God our ancestors had, raised Jesus up from death! 31Jesus is the One whom God raised to be on his right side. God made Jesus our Leader and Savior. God did this so that all Jews could change their hearts and lives and have their sins forgiven. 32We saw all these things happen. The Holy Spirit also proves that these things are true. God has given the Spirit to all who obey him."

33When the Jewish leaders heard this, they became very angry and wanted to kill them. 34A Pharisee named Gamaliel stood up in the meeting. He was a teacher of the law, and all the people respected him. He ordered the apostles to leave the meeting for a little while. 35Then he said to them, "Men of Israel, be careful of what you are planning to do to these men! 36Remember when Theudas appeared? He said that he was a great man, and about 400 men joined him. But he was killed. And all his followers were scattered. They were able to do nothing. 37Later, a man named Judas came from Galilee at the time of the registration. He led a group of followers, too. He was also killed, and all his followers were scattered. 38And so now I tell you: Stay away from these men. Leave them alone. If their plan comes from men, it will fail. 39But if it is from God, you will not be able to stop them. You might even be fighting against God himself!"

The Jewish leaders agreed with what Gamaliel said. 40They called the apostles in again. They beat the apostles and told them not to speak in the name of Jesus again. Then they let them go free. 41The apostles left the meeting full of joy because they were given the honor of suffering disgrace for Jesus. 42The apostles did not stop teaching people. Every day in the Temple and in people's homes they continued to tell the Good News—that Jesus is the Christ.

Let's Pray!

O Lord our God, grant us grace to desire you with our whole heart. that so desiring we may seek and find you; and so finding you, may love you; and loving you, may hate those sins from which you have redeemed us.

—Anselm

Did You Know?
Rabbi Gamaliel was one of the most honored Jewish teachers of all time. He taught Saul of Tarsus (Acts 22:3). According to the historian Photius, Gamaliel was baptized by Peter and John and was a secret follower of Christ.

Going Deeper

Read It! Jesus made a promise to those who obey God's laws and teach them to others. He also warned about what will happen to those who do not. Find out what that promise—and that warning—is in Matthew 5:19.

Do It! Even in our own country, laws that dishonor God are sometimes made. When you hear of such a law, ask your parents to help you write a letter to your government leaders.

The First Deacons

Acts 6:1–7

Have you ever thought about how busy the apostles must have been? They were teaching and preaching, as well as trying to take care of all the others needs of the church and its members. It was just too much for them to do—they needed help!

More and more people were becoming followers of Jesus. But during this same time, the Greek-speaking followers had an argument with the other Jewish followers. The Greek-speaking Jews said that their widows were not getting their share of the food that was given out every day. [2]The 12 apostles called the whole group of followers together. They said, "It is not right for us to stop our work of teaching God's word in order to serve tables. [3]So, brothers, choose seven of your own men. They must be men who are good. They must be full of wisdom and full of the Spirit. We will put them in charge of this work. [4]Then we can use all our time to pray and to teach the word of God."

[5]The whole group liked the idea. So they chose these seven men: Stephen (a man with great faith and full of the Holy Spirit), Philip, Procorus, Nicanor, Timon, Parmenas, and Nicolas (a man from Antioch who had become a Jew). [6]Then they put these men before the apostles. The apostles prayed and laid their hands on the men.

[7]The word of God was reaching more and more people. The group of followers in Jerusalem became larger and larger. A great number of the Jewish priests believed and obeyed.

Let's Pray!

Lord, make me an instrument of your
peace.
Where there is hatred, let me sow love.
Where there is injury, pardon.
Where there is doubt, faith.
Where there is despair, hope.
Where there is darkness, light.
Where there is sadness, joy.

—St. Francis

God, help me to be an instrument of your peace and love. Give to me the gift of your grace, so I may bring others to you. In Jesus' name, amen.

Special Words:
The word deacon *means "service" or "ministry." Deacons are leaders who serve other people in Jesus' church.*[4']

Did You Know?
Moses also needed help taking care of all the people. In Exodus 18:13–23, his father-in-law, Jethro, advised Moses to choose men to help him.

Going Deeper

Read It! Deacons are still used in the church today. Read 1 Timothy 3:8–13 to see what kind of people deacons must be.

Do It! Send a thank-you note to the deacons in your church for all the good work they do.

The First Martyr

Acts 6:8–15; 7:54–8:1

Stephen was one of the first deacons chosen by the apostles. His faith was very great. It was so great that he preached about Jesus even when he faced death!

Stephen was richly blessed by God. God
gave him the power to do great miracles
and signs among the people. 9But some
Jews were against him. They belonged to
a synagogue of Free Men (as it was called).
(This synagogue was also for Jews from
Cyrene and from Alexandria.) Jews from
Cilicia and Asia were also with them. They
all came and argued with Stephen.

10But the Spirit was helping him to speak
with wisdom. His words were so strong that
they could not argue with him. 11So they
paid some men to say, "We heard him say
things against Moses and against God!"

12This upset the people, the older Jewish
leaders, and the teachers of the law. They
came to Stephen, grabbed him and brought
him to a meeting of the Jewish leaders.
13They brought in some men to tell lies
about Stephen. They said, "This man is
always saying things against this holy place
and the law of Moses. 14We heard him say
that Jesus from Nazareth will destroy this
place. He also said that Jesus will
change the things that Moses told
us to do." 15All the people in the
meeting were watching Stephen
closely. His face looked like the
face of an angel. . . .

7:54When the leaders heard
Stephen saying all these
things, they became
very angry. They were so mad that they
were grinding their teeth at Stephen. 55But
Stephen was full of the Holy Spirit. He
looked up to heaven and saw the glory of
God. He saw Jesus standing at God's right
side. 56He said, "Look! I see heaven open.
And I see the Son of Man standing at God's
right side!"

57Then they all shouted loudly. They covered their ears with their hands and all ran
at Stephen. 58They took him out of the city
and threw stones at him until he was dead.
The men who told lies against Stephen
left their coats with a young man named
Saul. 59While they were throwing stones,
Stephen prayed, "Lord Jesus, receive my
spirit!" 60He fell on his knees and cried
in a loud voice, "Lord, do not hold this sin
against them!" After Stephen said this, he
died.

8:1Saul agreed that the killing of Stephen
was a good thing.

LET'S PRAY!

Lord, you taught that "those who are treated badly for doing good are happy" and that "the kingdom of heaven belongs to them" (Matthew 5:10). Send your special blessings to all those who are suffering because they believe in you. In Jesus' name, amen.

Did You Know?
Saul in chapter 8, verse 1 is the same man who later became known as Paul, one of the greatest all-time preachers of Jesus.

Going Deeper

Read It! A *martyr* is someone who dies because of what he or she believes. Read John 15:13. How does this verse apply to martyrs?

Do It! Hold a bake sale, wash cars, or do extra chores. Give the money you earn to an organization that buys Bibles for people in other countries.

The Church Spreads

Acts 8:2–8

The Jewish leaders believed that the followers of Jesus were wrong. They did everything they could to stop them—even arresting and killing believers! This is called persecution, and it was a terrible time for God's people. Yet God was able to use even this persecution for good (Romans 8:28). Thanks to Saul and the others who were persecuting the church, the apostles and other believers fled from Jerusalem. They scattered all over the known world—and so began the first missionary journeys of the apostles!

Some religious men buried Stephen. They
cried very loudly for him. On that day
people began trying to hurt the church in
Jerusalem and make it suffer. Saul was also
trying to destroy the church. He went from
house to house. He dragged out men and
women and put them in jail. All the believers, except the apostles, went to different
places in Judea and Samaria. 4And everywhere they were scattered, they told people
the Good News.

5Philip went to the city of Samaria and
preached about the Christ. 6The people
there heard Philip and saw the miracles he
was doing. They all listened carefully to the
things he said. 7Many of these people had
evil spirits in them. But Philip made the
evil spirits leave them. The spirits made a
loud noise when they came out. There were
also many weak and crippled people there.
Philip healed them, too. 8So the people in
that city were very happy.

LET'S PRAY!

Lord God, those who loved you best often suffered because of their love for you. Yet you used their suffering to spread your message. When I am suffering, help me see it as a chance to trust you more. In Jesus' name, amen!

Quote of the Day:
We are the Bibles the world is reading.
—Billy Graham

Going Deeper

Read It! Jesus wants you to be the light of the world. Read his words to you in Matthew 5:14–16.

Do It! The actions of the Jewish leaders spread darkness and fear, but God used those same actions to spread his light and his Word. Ask God to use you to spread his light to someone today.

Simon the Magician

Acts 8:9–24

Today's magicians use their tricks to make us laugh and to entertain us. Their tricks are just that—tricks. But in Bible times, magicians and sorcerers wanted to be powerful, like God. They used their tricks to draw people away from God. Today's story is about a magician who met the apostles Peter and John. What would happen when a man of wickedness met the men of God? Let's read and find out!

But there was a man named Simon in that city. Before Philip came there, Simon had practiced magic. He amazed all the people of Samaria with his magic. He bragged and called himself a great man. [10]All the people—the least important and the most important—paid attention to what Simon said. They said, "This man has the power of God, called 'the Great Power'!" [11]Simon had amazed them with his magic tricks so long that the people became his followers. [12]But Philip told them the Good News about the kingdom of God and the power of Jesus Christ. Men and women believed Philip and were baptized. [13]Simon himself believed and was baptized. He stayed very close to Philip. When he saw the miracles and the very powerful things that Philip did, Simon was amazed.

[14]The apostles were still in Jerusalem. They heard that the people of Samaria had accepted the word of God. So they sent Peter and John to them. [15]When Peter and John arrived, they prayed that the Samaritan believers might receive the Holy Spirit. [16]These people had been baptized in the name of the Lord Jesus. But the Holy Spirit had not yet entered any of them. [17]Then, when the two apostles began laying their hands on the people, they received the Holy Spirit.

[18]Simon saw that the Spirit was given to people when the apostles laid their hands on them. So he offered the apostles money. [19]He said, "Give me also this power so that when I lay my hands on a person, he will receive the Holy Spirit."

[20]Peter said to him, "You and your money should both be destroyed! You thought you could buy God's gift with money. [21]You cannot share with us in this work. Your heart is not right before God. [22]Change your heart! Turn away from this evil thing you have done. Pray to the Lord. Maybe he will forgive you for thinking this. [23]I see that you are full of bitter jealousy and ruled by sin."

[24]Simon answered, "Both of you pray for me to the Lord. Pray that the things you have said will not happen to me!"

Let's Pray!

Lord, teach me all that I should know;
In grace and wisdom I may grow;
The more I learn to do Thy will,
The better may I love Thee still.

—Isaac Watts

Quote of the Day:
God, examine me and know my heart. Test me and know my thoughts. See if there is any bad thing in me. Lead me in the way you set long ago.
—Psalm 139:23–24

Going Deeper

Read It! Read what God thinks of magic and witchcraft in Deuteronomy 18:9–13.

Do It! Do you have any supernatural games like tarot cards or Ouija boards? Time to do a little housecleaning! These things are not for Christians!

Philip and the Ethiopian

Acts 8:26–39

Philip traveled and preached among the Samaritan people of Judea, baptizing them in the name of the Lord. Then, one day, an angel of the Lord appeared to Philip with a message. God had a special job for Philip to do. Let's read about what happened!

An angel of the Lord spoke to Philip. The
angel said, "Get ready and go south. Go
to the road that leads down to Gaza from
Jerusalem—the desert road." 27So Philip got
ready and went. On the road he saw a man
from Ethiopia, a eunuch. . . . He had gone to
Jerusalem to worship, and 28now he was on
his way home. He was sitting in his chariot
and reading from the book of Isaiah, the
prophet. 29The Spirit said to Philip, "Go to
that chariot and stay near it."

30So Philip ran toward the chariot. He
heard the man reading from Isaiah, the
prophet. Philip asked, "Do you understand
what you are reading?"

31He answered, "How can I understand? I
need someone to explain it to me!" Then he
invited Philip to climb in and sit with him.
32The verse of Scripture that he was reading
was this:

"He was like a sheep being led to be
killed.
He was quiet, as a sheep is quiet while
its wool is being cut.
He said nothing.
33He was shamed and was treated
unfairly.
He died without children to continue his
family.
His life on earth has ended."

Isaiah 53:7–8

34The officer said to Philip, "Please tell
me, who is the prophet talking about? Is
he talking about himself or about someone
else?" 35Philip began to speak. He started
with this same Scripture and told the man
the Good News about Jesus.

36While they were traveling down the
road, they came to some water. The officer
said, "Look! Here is water! What is stop-
ping me from being baptized?" 37[Philip
answered, "If you believe with all your
heart, you can." The officer said, "I believe
that Jesus Christ is the Son of God."] 38Then
the officer commanded the chariot to stop.
Both Philip and the officer went down into
the water, and Philip baptized him. 39When
they came up out of the water, the Spirit of
the Lord took Philip away; the officer never
saw him again. The officer continued on
his way home, full of joy.

Let's Pray!

All of you who fear God, come and listen.
I will tell you what he has done for me.
I cried out to him with my mouth.
I praised him with my tongue.
If I had known of any sin in my heart,
the Lord would not have listened to me.
But God has listened.
He has heard my prayer.
Praise God.
He did not ignore my prayer.
He did not hold back his love from me.

—Psalm 66:16–20

Lord, let me never be too afraid to go where you send me. In Jesus' name, amen.

QUOTE OF THE DAY:
"You will call my name. You will come to me and pray to me. And I will listen to you. You will search for me. And when you search for me with all your heart, you will find me!"
—Jeremiah 29:12–13

GOING DEEPER

READ IT! Romans 10:15 tells us how God sees those who share his good news. Check it out!

DO IT! The Bible is God's living Word. That means that each time you read it, you learn something new. Is God showing you something from the Bible today that you didn't know before? What is it?

Damascus Road

Acts 9:1–9

Saul of Tarsus was a man with a bright future ahead of him. He was born to the tribe of Benjamin and raised a Roman citizen in one of the ancient world's three most important centers of learning. As a Pharisee, he knew both Greek and Roman culture, and he followed the law of Moses very carefully. Sadly, though, Saul was involved in the first great persecution of the church. He did his best to stamp out all traces of Christianity in Jerusalem and the country around it! Yes, Saul was a brilliant man, but when it came to Jesus, it took a real miracle for him to see the light of truth!

In Jerusalem Saul was still trying to frighten the followers of the Lord by saying he would kill them. So he went to the high priest [2]and asked him to write letters to the synagogues in the city of Damascus. Saul wanted the high priest to give him the authority to find people in Damascus who were followers of Christ's Way. If he found any there, men or women, he would arrest them and bring them back to Jerusalem.

[3]So Saul went to Damascus. As he came near the city, a bright light from heaven suddenly flashed around him. [4]Saul fell to the ground. He heard a voice saying to him, "Saul, Saul! Why are you doing things against me?"

[5]Saul said, "Who are you, Lord?"

The voice answered, "I am Jesus. I am the One you are trying to hurt. [6]Get up now and go into the city. Someone there will tell you what you must do."

[7]The men traveling with Saul stood there, but they said nothing. They heard the voice, but they saw no one. [8]Saul got up from the ground. He opened his eyes, but he could not see. So the men with Saul took his hand and led him into Damascus. [9]For three days Saul could not see, and he did not eat or drink.

Let's Pray!

Open my eyes, Lord. I want to see Jesus! And open my ears, Lord. I want to hear your Word. In Jesus' name, amen.

Going Deeper

Read It! Saul—who became known as Paul—even went on to preach about Jesus' resurrection. Read what he said in 1 Corinthians 15:3–8.

Do It! Saul's blindness made him become "like a little child." To see what this was like, gather some family and friends and go into the backyard. Divide into teams, blindfold the grown-ups, and see how long it takes the children to lead the grown-ups from one end of the yard to the other.

Did You Know?

Like Abraham and Simon Peter, Saul's name was changed. His name was changed to show that his heart had changed. But, he was still called "Saul" during his first missionary journey.

Ananias Faces Saul

Acts 9:10–22

Imagine that someone at school or in your neighborhood was a bully, saying mean things to you or to one of your brothers or sisters. How easy would it be for you to show love to that person, to offer to help if he or she were in trouble? In today's story, that is exactly the situation the Christians at Damascus found themselves in. God asked one of the Christians there, Ananias, to do something incredible—to help the man who had done so much to hurt other Christians! Would Ananias have the courage to do as God asked?

There was a follower of Jesus in Damascus named Ananias. The Lord spoke to Ananias in a vision, "Ananias!"

Ananias answered, "Here I am, Lord."

11The Lord said to him, "Get up and go to the street called Straight Street. Find the house of Judas. Ask for a man named Saul from the city of Tarsus. He is there now,
praying. 12Saul has seen a vision. In it a man named Ananias comes to him and lays his hands on him. Then he sees again."

13But Ananias answered, "Lord, many people have told me about this man and the terrible things he did to your people
in Jerusalem. 14Now he has come here to Damascus. The leading priests have given him the power to arrest everyone who worships you."

15But the Lord said to Ananias, "Go! I have chosen Saul for an important work. He must tell about me to non-Jews, to kings, and to
the people of Israel. 16I will show him how much he must suffer for my name."

17So Ananias went to the house of Judas. He laid his hands on Saul and said, "Brother Saul, the Lord Jesus sent me. He is the one you saw on the road on your way here. He sent me so that you can see again and be
filled with the Holy Spirit." 18Immediately, something that looked like fish scales fell from Saul's eyes. He was able to see again!
Then Saul got up and was baptized. 19After eating some food, his strength returned.

Saul stayed with the followers of Jesus in
Damascus for a few days. 20Soon he began to preach about Jesus in the synagogues, saying, "Jesus is the Son of God!"

21All the people who heard him were amazed. They said, "This is the man who was in Jerusalem. He was trying to destroy those who trust in this name! He came here to do the same thing. He came here to arrest the followers of Jesus and take them back to the leading priests."

22But Saul became more and more powerful. His proofs that Jesus is the Christ were so strong that the Jews in Damascus could not argue with him.

Let's Pray!

At the close of every day,
Lord, to Thee I kneel and pray.
Look upon Thy little child,
Look in love and mercy mild.
O forgive and wash away
All my naughtiness this day,
And both when I sleep and wake
Bless me for my Savior's sake. Amen.

—Anonymous

Did You Know?
The first followers of Christ to be called "Christians" were from the church at Antioch (Acts 11:26).

GOING DEEPER

READ IT! God tells us that it is important to forgive others. Find out why in Matthew 6:14–15.

DO IT! Matthew 6:12 says, "Forgive the sins we have done, just as we have forgiven those who did wrong to us." When you say these words, who comes to mind? Is it someone you need to forgive? Ask God to help you forgive.

Saul Escapes Damascus

Acts 9:23–31

Saul had not been preaching in Damascus long before the Jews decided to kill him. He sneaked out of the city and went to Arabia, where he spent three years (Galatians 1:18). He then returned to Jerusalem, where he spent two weeks before the Jews again tried to kill this newest apostle. How would he escape this time? And would he dare to keep preaching about Jesus?

After many days, the Jews made plans to
kill Saul. [24]They were watching the city
gates day and night. They wanted to kill
him, but Saul learned about their plan.
[25]One night some followers of Saul helped
him leave the city. They lowered him in a
basket through an opening in the city wall.
[26]Then Saul went to Jerusalem. He tried to
join the group of followers, but they were all
afraid of him. They did not believe that he was
really a follower. [27]But Barnabas accepted Saul
and took him to the apostles. Barnabas told
them that Saul had seen the Lord on the road.
He explained how the Lord had spoken to
Saul. Then he told them how boldly Saul had
preached in the name of Jesus in Damascus.
[28]And so Saul stayed with the followers. He
went everywhere in Jerusalem, preaching
boldly in the name of Jesus. [29]He would often
talk and argue with the Jews who spoke Greek.
But they were trying to kill him. [30]When the
brothers learned about this, they took Saul to
Caesarea. From there they sent him to Tarsus.
[31]The church everywhere in Judea, Galilee,
and Samaria had a time of peace. With the
help of the Holy Spirit, the group became
stronger. The believers showed that they
respected the Lord by the way they lived.
Because of this, the group of believers grew
larger and larger.

Let's Pray!

Lord, there is no one like you.
You are great.
Your name is great and powerful.
Everyone should respect you, King of all nations.
You deserve their respect.
There are many wise men among the nations.
And there are wise men in all the kingdoms.
But none of them are as wise as you. . . .
But the Lord is the only true God.
He is the only living God, King forever.

—Jeremiah 10:6–7, 10

Going Deeper

Read It! David wrote many songs to God. Psalm 18 was written to praise God for helping him escape from his enemies. Read verses 1–3, and remember that God will be your fortress too.

Do It! Write your own song of praise for God and all that he means to you. Share it with your family and friends.

Did You Know?
At first, the believers at Damascus did not believe that Saul had truly changed and was a follower of Jesus. At the same time, the Jews hated him for leaving their side! It must have been a lonely time for Paul, a time when he had to depend on God alone.

God bless the field and bless the furrow,
Stream and branch and rabbit burrow,
Bless the sun and bless the sleet,
Bless the land and bless the street,
Bless the minnow, bless the whale,
Bless the rainbow and the hail,
Bless the nest and bless the leaf,
Bless the righteous and the thief,
Bless the wing and bless the fin,
Bless the air I travel in,
Bless the mill and bless the mouse,
Bless the miller's bricken house,
Bless the earth and bless the sea,
God bless you and God bless me!

—Old English Rhyme

Tabitha

Acts 9:32–43

In the early church, those who had money often helped meet the needs of those who had less. These people were loved by all for their kindness and giving. Today's story is about one such woman named Tabitha. In the Greek language, she was called Dorcas. Let's find out what happened to her.

As Peter was traveling through all the area, he visited God's people who lived in Lydda. 33There he met a paralyzed man named Aeneas. Aeneas had not been able to leave his bed for the past eight years. 34Peter said to him, "Aeneas, Jesus Christ heals you. Stand up and make your bed!" Aeneas stood up immediately. 35All the people living in Lydda and on the Plain of Sharon saw him. These people turned to the Lord.

36In the city of Joppa there was a follower named Tabitha. (Her Greek name, Dorcas, means "a deer.") She was always doing good and helping the poor. 37While Peter was in Lydda, Tabitha became sick and died. Her body was washed and put in a room upstairs. 38The followers in Joppa heard that Peter was in Lydda. (Lydda is near Joppa.) So they sent two men to Peter. They begged him, "Hurry, please come to us!" 39Peter got ready and went with them. When he arrived, they took him to the upstairs room. All the widows stood around Peter, crying. They showed him the shirts and coats that Tabitha had made when she was still alive. 40Peter sent everyone out of the room. He kneeled and prayed. Then he turned to the body and said, "Tabitha, stand up!" She opened her eyes, and when she saw Peter, she sat up. 41He gave her his hand and helped her up. Then he called the saints and the widows into the room. He showed them Tabitha; she was alive! 42People everywhere in Joppa learned about this, and many believed in the Lord. 43Peter stayed in Joppa for many days with a man named Simon who was a leatherworker.

Let's Pray!

Whoever is cruel to the poor insults their
 Maker.
But anyone who is kind to the needy
 honors God.

—Proverbs 14:31

Lord, open my eyes to the needs of those around me, and show me how I can best help them. In Jesus' name, amen.

Quote of the Day:
Never be afraid of giving up your best, and God will give you His better.
—James Hinton

Going Deeper

READ IT! The apostles were able to heal people and to raise people from the dead. But their power didn't come from themselves. Read about how they were able to do these things in Matthew 10:1.

DO IT! James 1:27 says, "Caring for orphans or widows who need help. . . . This is the kind of religion that God accepts as pure and good." As a family, plan something to help the widows or orphans in your hometown.

Angels to the Rescue

Acts 12:1–11

Angels are the messengers of God. Sometimes, though, they did more than just deliver a message. In today's story, an angel of the Lord came to Peter's rescue—and just in the nick of time! Let's find out more.

During that same time King Herod began to
do terrible things to some who belonged to
the church. 2He ordered James, the brother
of John, to be killed by the sword. 3Herod
saw that the Jews liked this, so he decided
to arrest Peter, too. (This happened during
the time of the Feast of Unleavened Bread.)
4After Herod arrested Peter, he put him
in jail and handed him over to be guarded
by 16 soldiers. Herod planned to bring
Peter before the people for trial after the
Passover Feast. 5So Peter was kept in jail.
But the church kept on praying to God for
him.
6The night before Herod was to bring
him to trial, Peter was sleeping. He was between two soldiers, bound with two chains.
Other soldiers were guarding the door of
the jail. 7Suddenly, an angel of the Lord
stood there. A light shined in the room.
The angel touched Peter on the side and
woke him up. The angel said, "Hurry! Get
up!" And the chains fell off Peter's hands.
8The angel said to him, "Get dressed and
put on your sandals." And so Peter did this.
Then the angel said, "Put on your coat and
follow me." 9So the angel went out, and
Peter followed him. Peter did not know
if what the angel was doing was real. He
thought he might be seeing a vision. 10They
went past the first and the second guard.
They came to the iron gate that separated
them from the city. The gate opened itself
for them. They went through the gate and
walked down a street. And the angel suddenly left him.
11Then Peter realized what had happened.
He thought, "Now I know that the Lord
really sent his angel to me. He rescued me
from Herod and from all the things the
Jewish people thought would happen."

LET'S PRAY!

He has put his angels in charge of you.
They will watch over you wherever you go.
—Psalm 91:11

Thank you, God, for angels—your messengers of light and truth! In Jesus' name, amen.

Quote of the Day:
If instead of a gem, or even a flower, we should cast the gift of a loving thought into the heart of a friend, that would be giving as the angels give.
—George MacDonald

Going Deeper

READ IT! The Bible tells us to be kind to everyone. Find out why in Hebrews 13:1–2.

DO IT! Get out an angel from your Christmas decorations. Set it in your room to remind you of God's angels watching over you.

"It's Peter!"

Acts 12:12–19

The believers knew that James had been killed. Now Peter was in prison, waiting to be killed as well. So they did the only thing they knew to do—they gathered to pray. But what did they do when Peter turned up on their doorstep? Let's read and find out!

When [Peter] realized [that an angel had helped him escape from prison], he went to the home of Mary. She was the mother of John. (John was also called Mark.) Many people were gathered there, praying. 13Peter knocked on the outside door. A servant girl named Rhoda came to answer it. 14She recognized Peter's voice, and she was very happy. She even forgot to open the door. She ran inside and told the group, "Peter is at the door!"

15They said to her, "You are crazy!" But she kept on saying that it was true. So they said, "It must be Peter's angel."

16Peter continued to knock. When they opened the door, they saw him and were amazed. 17Peter made a sign with his hand to tell them to be quiet. He explained how the Lord led him out of the jail. And he said, "Tell James and the other believers what happened." Then he left to go to another place.

18The next day the soldiers were very upset. They wondered what had happened to Peter. 19Herod looked everywhere for Peter but could not find him. So he questioned the guards and ordered that they be killed.

Let's Pray!

Please give me what I ask, dear Lord,
If You'd be glad about it.
But if You think it's not for me,
Please help me do without it.

—Traditional

Quote of the Day:
To be a Christian without prayer is no more possible than to be alive without breathing.
—Martin Luther

Going Deeper

Read It! With God, nothing is impossible! To whom did the angel say this in Luke 1:37?

Do It! First Thessalonians 5:17 says, "Never stop praying." That means we don't ever want to go a day without praying to God. Many people pray first thing in the morning, at mealtimes, and at bedtime. But try other times too. For example, when you get in the car, pray for safe travels. When you wash your hands or take a bath, pray for God to cleanse your heart. And when you see a fire truck, pray for all those who protect us.

Paul and Barnabas Preach

Acts 13:42–49

Paul became a leader in the church at Antioch. It was one of leading churches among the Gentiles, and it was also Paul's home church. He often began his missionary journeys from there. After one such journey, Paul and Barnabas returned to Antioch. On the Sabbath day, they went into the synagogue. There they began to preach about Jesus, and many Jews and Gentiles became believers. But those who did not believe began to cause trouble!

While Paul and Barnabas were leaving the synagogue, the people asked them to tell them more about these things on the next Sabbath.
43After the meeting, many Jews followed Paul and Barnabas from that place. With the Jews there were many who had changed to the Jewish religion and worshiped God. Paul and Barnabas were persuading them to continue trusting in God's kindness.

44On the next Sabbath day, almost all the people in the city came to hear the word of the Lord.
45Seeing the crowd, the Jews became very jealous. They said insulting things and argued against what Paul said.
46But Paul and Barnabas spoke very boldly. They said, "We must speak the message of God to you first. But you refuse to listen. You are judging yourselves not worthy of having eternal life! So we will now go to the people of other nations!
47This is what the Lord told us to do. The Lord said:

'I have made you a light for the non-Jewish nations.
You will show people all over the world the way to be saved.'" *Isaiah 49:6*

48When the non-Jewish people heard Paul say this, they were happy. They gave honor to the message of the Lord. And many of the people believed the message. They were the ones chosen to have life forever.

49And so the message of the Lord was spreading through the whole country.

LET'S PRAY!

Dear Lord, thank you for all those who boldly share your message. Help me do the same. In Jesus' name, amen.

GOING DEEPER

READ IT! In the Garden of Gethsemane, Jesus prayed that his believers would all be one in faith. Read his prayer in John 17:20–23.

DO IT! Pretend two friends are fighting. What should you do—take sides or make peace?

SPECIAL WORDS:

Barnabas *means "son of encouragement." He helped Paul start in ministry. Together they traveled and shared the good news of Jesus. But then they argued over his cousin, John Mark (Acts 15:37–40). They later made up, and John Mark wrote the gospel of Mark.*

The Stoning of Paul

Acts 14:8–21

To show the Gentiles the truth of his message, Paul healed a lame man—a miracle much like the one Peter did in Acts 3:2–10. But instead of believing in Jesus, this time the people said Paul and Barnabas were gods! What would they do now?

In Lystra there sat a man who had been
born crippled; he had never walked. 9This
man was listening to Paul speak. Paul
looked straight at him and saw that the
man believed God could heal him. 10So he
cried out, "Stand up on your feet!" The
man jumped up and began walking around.
11When the crowds saw what Paul did, they
shouted in their own Lycaonian language.
They said, "The gods have become like
men! They have come down to us!" 12And
the people began to call Barnabas "Zeus."
They called Paul "Hermes," because he
was the main speaker. 13The temple of Zeus
was near the city. The priest of this temple
brought some bulls and flowers to the city
gates. The priest and the people wanted
to offer a sacrifice to Paul and Barnabas.
14But when the apostles, Barnabas and
Paul, understood what they were about to
do, they tore their clothes in anger. Then
they ran in among the people and shouted,
15"Men, why are you doing these things? We
are only men, human beings like you! We
are bringing you the Good News. We are
telling you to turn away from these worthless things and turn to the true living God.
He is the One who made the sky, the earth,
the sea, and everything that is in them. 16In
the past, God let all the nations do what
they wanted. 17Yet he did things to prove
he is real: He shows kindness to you. He
gives you rain from heaven and crops at the
right times. He gives you food and fills your
hearts with joy." 18Even with these words,
they were barely able to keep the crowd
from offering sacrifices to them.

19Then some Jews came from Antioch
and Iconium. They persuaded the people to
turn against Paul. And so they threw stones
at Paul and dragged him out of town. They
thought that they had killed him. 20But the
followers gathered around him, and he got
up and went back into the town. The next
day, he and Barnabas left and went to the
city of Derbe.

21Paul and Barnabas told the Good News
in Derbe and many became followers. Paul
and Barnabas returned to Lystra, Iconium,
and Antioch.

Let's Pray!

Dear God, soften the hearts of those who do not believe in you. Open their eyes to see your Presence in the world around them. Open their ears to hear the truth in your Word. And open their hearts to feel your love for them. In Jesus' name, amen.

Did You Know?
To tear one's clothes was a sign of great sadness or anger or other extreme emotion.

Going Deeper

Read It! It isn't good to take credit for what God has done. Find out what happened to Herod in Acts 12:21–23!

Do It! Many people have heard God's Word, but they refuse to believe. Maybe you know someone like that. Pray that God will bring people and events into their lives that will help them see that he truly is Lord of all!

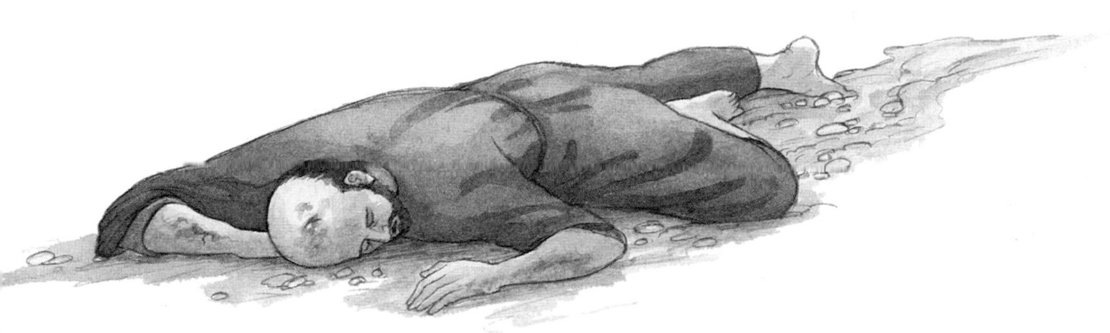

Peter Speaks

Acts 15:1–12

The Jewish people had many rules and traditions. Some of the Jews who became Christians tried to bring those same rules and traditions into the Christian church. They began to tell the Gentile believers that they had to follow the law of Moses in order to be saved. But this was not what Jesus had taught. How would the apostles sort this out?

Then some men came to Antioch from
Judea. They began teaching the non-Jewish brothers: "You cannot be saved if you
are not circumcised. Moses taught us to
do this." 2Paul and Barnabas were against
this teaching and argued with the men
about it. So the group decided to send
Paul, Barnabas, and some other men to
Jerusalem. There they could talk more
about this with the apostles and elders.

3The church helped the men leave on
the trip. They went through the countries
of Phoenicia and Samaria, telling all about
how the non-Jewish people had turned to
God. This made all the believers very happy.
4When they arrived in Jerusalem, the apostles, the elders, and the church welcomed
them. Paul, Barnabas, and the others told
about all the things that God had done with
them. 5But some of the believers who had
belonged to the Pharisee group came forward. They said, "The non-Jewish believers must be circumcised. We must tell them
to obey the law of Moses!"

6The apostles and the elders gathered
to study this problem. 7There was a long
debate. Then Peter stood up and said to
them, "Brothers, you know what happened
in the early days. God chose me from
among you to preach the Good News to
the non-Jewish people. They heard the
Good News from me, and they believed.
8God, who knows the thoughts of all men,
accepted them. He showed this to us by giving them the Holy Spirit, just as he did to
us. 9To God, those people are not different
from us. When they believed, he made their
hearts pure. 10So now why are you testing
God? You are putting a heavy load around
the necks of the non-Jewish brothers. It is
a load that neither we nor our fathers were
able to carry. 11But we believe that we and
they too will be saved by the grace of the
Lord Jesus!"

12Then the whole group became quiet.
They listened to Paul and Barnabas speak.
Paul and Barnabas told about all the miracles and signs that God did through them
among the non-Jewish people.

LET'S PRAY!

Lord, I know there is nothing I can do to get myself to heaven. Only your mercy and grace will save me. Help me trust and obey you in all things. In Jesus' name, amen.

Special Words:
Grace is when God gives us what we do not deserve—forgiveness and heaven. Mercy is when he does not give us what we do deserve—punishment for our sins.

Going Deeper

Read It! No one is better than anyone else. We are all equal in Jesus. Read that promise in Galatians 3:28.

Do It! Church leaders have a difficult job. Write a thank-you note to one of your church's leaders today.

Paul and Timothy

Acts 16:1–10

After Paul and Barnabas went their separate ways, Paul set out on another missionary journey. This time he traveled with Silas. But before many miles passed, Paul met another young man—Timothy—who became like a son to him.

Paul came to Derbe and Lystra. A follower
named Timothy was there. Timothy's
mother was Jewish and a believer. His
father was a Greek.
2The brothers in Lystra and Iconium
respected Timothy and said good things
about him. 3Paul wanted Timothy to travel
with him. But all the Jews living in that area
knew that Timothy's father was Greek. So
Paul circumcised Timothy to please the
Jews. 4Paul and the men with him traveled
from town to town. They gave the decisions made by the apostles and elders in
Jerusalem for the people to obey. 5So the
churches became stronger in the faith and
grew larger every day.
6Paul and the men with him went through
the areas of Phrygia and Galatia. The Holy
Spirit did not let them preach the Good
News in Asia. 7When they came near the
country of Mysia, they tried to go into
Bithynia. But the Spirit of Jesus did not let
them. 8So they passed by Mysia and went
to Troas. 9That night Paul had a vision. In
the vision, a man from Macedonia came
to him. The man stood there and begged,
"Come over to Macedonia. Help us!"
10After Paul had seen the vision, we immediately prepared to leave for Macedonia.
We understood that God had called us to
tell the Good News to those people.

Let's Pray!

How beautiful is the person who comes to bring good news!

—Romans 10:15

Lord, you tell us that true beauty comes from what we do and what is in our hearts. Please help me to be truly beautiful in all I do and say. In Jesus' name, amen.

Quote of the Day:
When I want to speak let me think first: Is it true? Is it kind? Is it necessary? If not, let it be left unsaid.
—Maltbie Davenport Babcock

Going Deeper

Read It! Even young people can lead others to Jesus. Read what Paul had to say about it in 1 Timothy 4:12.

Do It! On a map, find the cities from this story, and track Paul and Silas's journey.

Lydia

Acts 16:11–15

In Philippi, Paul met a wealthy woman from the seaside town of Thyatira. Her name was Lydia. In today's reading, we find out what happened when she heard the good news of Jesus!

We left Troas in a ship, and we sailed
straight to the island of Samothrace. The
next day we sailed to Neapolis. 12Then we
went by land to Philippi, the leading city in
that part of Macedonia. It is also a Roman
colony. We stayed there for several days.
13On the Sabbath day we went outside the
city gate to the river. There we thought we
would find a special place for prayer. Some
women had gathered there, so we sat down
and talked with them. 14There was a woman
named Lydia from the city of Thyatira. Her
job was selling purple cloth. She worshiped
the true God. The Lord opened her mind to
pay attention to what Paul was saying. 15She
and all the people in her house were baptized. Then Lydia invited us to her home.
She said, "If you think I am truly a believer
in the Lord, then come stay in my house."
And she persuaded us to stay with her.

LET'S PRAY!

Lord, help me open my heart and my home to those around me. In Jesus' name, amen.

Did You Know?
The dye used for purple cloth was probably Tyrian dye. This dye was highly prized because it was so expensive to make. Each drop had to be painstakingly collected from a certain kind of sea snail. Because each snail produced only a tiny drop of dye, it could take thousands of them to dye a single garment![42]

Going Deeper

Read It! Many people think giving is only about money, but it's also about giving your time and attention. In 2 Corinthians 9:7, find out what kind of giver God likes.

Do It! First Peter 4:9 says, "Open your homes to one another, without complaining." Lydia opened her home to Paul and those traveling with him. Open your home to someone. Have a friend over to play, or invite your Sunday school teacher over for cookies and tea.

Paul's Good News

Acts 16:22–34

Paul and Silas never missed a chance to preach the gospel. Even when they ended up in prison, they trusted God to bring some good out of it. But what would it be this time?

The crowd joined the attack against them. The Roman officers tore the clothes of Paul and Silas and had them beaten with rods again and again. 23Then Paul and Silas were thrown into jail. The jailer was ordered to guard them carefully. 24When he heard this order, he put them far inside the jail. He pinned down their feet between large blocks of wood.

25About midnight Paul and Silas were praying and singing songs to God. The other prisoners were listening to them. 26Suddenly, there was a big earthquake. It was so strong that it shook the foundation of the jail. Then all the doors of the jail broke open. All the prisoners were freed from their chains. 27The jailer woke up and saw that the jail doors were open. He thought that the prisoners had already escaped. So he got his sword and was about to kill himself. 28But Paul shouted, "Don't hurt yourself! We are all here!"

29The jailer told someone to bring a light. Then he ran inside. Shaking with fear, he fell down before Paul and Silas. 30Then he brought them outside and said, "Men, what must I do to be saved?"

31They said to him, "Believe in the Lord Jesus and you will be saved—you and all the people in your house." 32So Paul and Silas told the message of the Lord to the jailer and all the people in his house. 33At that hour of the night the jailer took Paul and Silas and washed their wounds. Then he and all his people were baptized immediately. 34After this the jailer took Paul and Silas home and gave them food. He and his family were very happy because they now believed in God.

Let's Pray!

Lord, even when my life doesn't go the way I plan, I know that nothing takes you by surprise. Help me use each moment as a chance to praise you and to share your goodness with the world. In Jesus' name, amen.

Going Deeper

READ IT! God made great things happen for another prisoner. Read the story of Joseph in Genesis 39–41.

DO IT! Collect small bottles of shampoo and other toiletries for the local prison.

Quote of the Day:

"I was hungry, and you gave me food. I was thirsty, and you gave me something to drink. I was alone and away from home, and you invited me into your house. I was without clothes, and you gave me something to wear. I was sick, and you cared for me. I was in prison, and you visited me."
—Jesus, in Matthew 25:35–36

Paul Speaks in Athens

Acts 17:16–25, 34

Inside every heart is a longing for God. It is a longing that God put there, so we would search for him. Only God can fill that longing. But some people try to fill that longing with false gods—sometimes many false gods! In today's story, Paul took the good news to some Greeks who worshiped many different gods—even one whose name they didn't know!

Paul was waiting for Silas and Timothy in Athens. He was troubled because he saw that the city was full of idols. 17In the synagogue, he talked with the Jews and the Greeks who worshiped the true God. He also talked every day with people in the marketplace.

18Some of the Epicurean and Stoic philosophers argued with him. Some of them said, "This man doesn't know what he is talking about. What is he trying to say?" Paul was telling them the Good News of Jesus' rising from death. They said, "He seems to be telling us about some other gods." 19They got Paul and took him to a meeting of the Areopagus. They said, "Please explain to us this new idea that you have been teaching. 20The things you are saying are new to us. We want to know what this teaching means." 21(All the people of Athens and those from other countries always used their time talking about all the newest ideas.)

22Then Paul stood before the meeting of the Areopagus. He said, "Men of Athens, I can see that you are very religious in all things. 23I was going through your city, and I saw the things you worship. I found an altar that had these words written on it: 'TO A GOD WHO IS NOT KNOWN.' You worship a god that you don't know. This is the God I am telling you about! 24He is the God who made the whole world and everything in it. He is the Lord of the land and the sky. He does not live in temples that men build! 25This God is the One who gives life, breath, and everything else to people. He does not need any help from them. He has everything he needs." . . .

34But some of the people believed Paul and joined him.

Let's Pray!

Jesus, help my eyes to see
All the good Thou sendest me.
Jesus, help my ears to hear
Calls for help from far and near.
Jesus, help my feet to go
In the way that Thou wilt show.
Jesus, help my hands to do
All things loving, kind, and true.
Jesus, may I helpful be,
Growing every day like Thee. Amen.

—Anonymous

Going Deeper

Read It! All creation declares God's existence, but especially "this" in Psalm 19:1–4.

Do It! What parts of nature help you to best see God's handiwork? Is it the animals or trees? The sunrise or the seas? Thank God for all those things today!

Special Words:
The Areopagus was a court for criminal and civil trials. It was also known as Ares Hill after the Greek god Ares, who was supposed to have been tried here for murdering Poseidon's son. To the Romans, Ares was known as Mars. Thus, Paul's sermon is often called the Sermon at Mars Hill.[43]

DOXOLOGY

by Thomas Ken

Praise God, from whom all blessings flow;
Praise him, all creatures here below;
Praise him above, ye heavenly hosts;
Praise Father, Son, and Holy Ghost!
Amen.

Paul Sees Jesus—Again!

Acts 18:5–11

Paul worked very hard preaching and teaching everyone he could about Jesus. Some people believed him and were baptized. Other people would not believe. And still others wanted to hurt Paul or even kill him for teaching about Jesus. Jesus appeared to Paul in a dream with a very special message of encouragement. Let's read about it.

Silas and Timothy came from Macedonia
and joined Paul in Corinth. After this, Paul
used all his time telling people the Good
News. He showed the Jews that Jesus is the
Christ. 6But they would not accept Paul's
teaching and said some evil things. So he
shook off the dust from his clothes. He
said to them, "If you are not saved, it will
be your own fault! I have done all I can do!
After this, I will go to non-Jewish people!"
7Paul left the synagogue and moved into
the home of Titius Justus. It was next to the
synagogue. This man worshiped the true
God. 8Crispus was the leader of that synagogue. He and all the people living in his
house believed in the Lord. Many others
in Corinth also listened to Paul. They too
believed and were baptized.
9During the night, Paul had a vision.
The Lord said to him, "Don't be afraid!
Continue talking to people and don't be
quiet! 10I am with you. No one will hurt
you because many of my people are in this
city." 11Paul stayed there for a year and a
half, teaching God's word to the people.

Let's Pray!

Dear God, give me courage when I suffer because of the bad choices of other people. In Jesus' name, amen.

Going Deeper

Read It! Jesus told Paul, "I am with you." To whom else did God say this? Find out in Genesis 28:10–15.

Do It! Are there things that you are afraid of? Remember Jesus' words to Paul: "I am with you." Jesus is with you too.

Quote of the Day:
A simple, childlike faith in a Divine Friend solves all the problems that come to us by land or sea.
—Helen Keller

Priscilla, Aquila, and Apollos

Acts 18:24–19:5

Just as Mary, Martha, and Lazarus were good friends of Jesus, so Priscilla and Aquila were good friends of Paul. They gave him a welcome place to stay and rest from his journeys. Priscilla and Aquila also helped others find their way to Jesus. One of them was a man named Apollos.

A Jew named Apollos came to Ephesus. He was born in the city of Alexandria. He was an educated man who knew the Scriptures well. [25]He had been taught about the Lord. He was always very excited when he spoke and taught the truth about Jesus. But the only baptism that Apollos knew about was the baptism that John taught. [26]Apollos began to speak very boldly in the synagogue, and Priscilla and Aquila heard him. So they took him to their home and helped him better understand the way of God. [27]Now Apollos wanted to go to the country of Southern Greece, so the believers helped him. They wrote a letter to the followers there, asking them to accept him. These followers had believed in Jesus because of God's grace. When Apollos went there, he helped them very much. [28]He argued very strongly with the Jews before all the people. Apollos clearly proved that the Jews were wrong. Using the Scriptures, he proved that Jesus is the Christ.

[19:1]While Apollos was in Corinth, Paul was visiting some places on the way to Ephesus. There he found some followers. [2]Paul asked them, "Did you receive the Holy Spirit when you believed?"

They said, "We have never even heard of a Holy Spirit!"

[3]So he asked, "What kind of baptism did you have?"

They said, "It was the baptism that John taught."

[4]Paul said, "John's baptism was a baptism of changed hearts and lives. He told people to believe in the One who would come after him. That One is Jesus."

[5]When they heard this, they were baptized in the name of the Lord Jesus.

LET'S PRAY!

If I go up to the skies, you are there.
  If I lie down where the dead are, you are
    there.
If I rise with the sun in the east,
  and settle in the west beyond the sea,
even there you would guide me.
  With your right hand you would hold me.

—Psalm 139:8–10

Did You Know?
Carved inscriptions in the catacombs (underground burial places) suggest that Priscilla's family had great wealth and social standing. Because her name is always given first, Priscilla must have been a woman of great intelligence and talent.[44]

Going Deeper

READ IT! Priscilla and Aquila held church meetings in their homes in Ephesus and in Rome. Read about it in 1 Corinthians 16:19 and Romans 16:3–5.

DO IT! Use sheets and chairs to make a tent in your room. Use it for your prayer time today.

The Peacemaker

Acts 19:23–30, 32–39, 41

"Those who work to bring peace are happy. God will call them his sons," Jesus said (Matthew 5:9). But it isn't always easy to be a peacemaker. It often takes a great deal of courage. In today's story, Demetrius is a silversmith. He and many others in the city of Ephesus made their living by making silver idols. But when they realized the Christians would not need their idols, they were afraid they would lose their way of making a living. So they started a riot. Who would be brave enough to try to bring peace to this crowd?

There was some serious trouble in Ephesus about the Way of Jesus. 24There was a man named Demetrius, who worked with silver. He made little silver models that looked like the temple of the goddess Artemis. The men who did this work made much money. 25Demetrius had a meeting with these men and some others who did the same kind of work. He told them, "Men, you know that we make a lot of money from our business. 26But look at what this man Paul is doing! He has convinced and turned away many people in Ephesus and in almost all of Asia! He says the gods that men make are not real. 27There is a danger that our business will lose its good name. But there is also another danger: People will begin to think that the temple of the great goddess Artemis is not important! Her greatness will be destroyed. And Artemis is the goddess that everyone in Asia and the whole world worships."

28When the men heard this, they became very angry. They shouted, "Artemis, the goddess of Ephesus, is great!" 29The whole city became confused. . . . Then all the people ran to the theater. 30Paul wanted to go in and talk to the crowd, but the followers did not let him. . . . 32Some people were shouting one thing, and some were shouting another. The meeting was completely confused. Most of the people did not know why they had come together. 33The Jews put a man named Alexander in front of the people. . . . Alexander waved his hand because he wanted to explain things to the people. 34But when they saw that Alexander was a Jew, they all began shouting the same thing. They continued shouting for two hours: "Great is Artemis of Ephesus!"

35Then the city clerk made the crowd be quiet. He said, "Men of Ephesus, everyone knows that Ephesus is the city that keeps the temple of the great goddess Artemis. All people know that we also keep her holy stone that fell from heaven. 36No one can say that this is not true. So you should be quiet. You must stop and think before you do anything. 37You brought these men here, but they have not said anything evil against our goddess. They have not stolen anything from her temple. 38We have courts of law, and there are judges. Do Demetrius and the men who work with him have a charge against anyone? They should go to the courts! That is where they can argue with each other! 39Is there something else you want to talk about? It can be decided at the regular town meeting of the people." . . . 41After the city clerk said these things, he told the people to go home.

Did You Know?
Artemis was one of the most widely worshiped of the Greek gods. As Apollo's twin, she was the goddess of fertility and childbirth.

Let's Pray!

Father, I praise you for being the one true God. Please help me never to have any idols in my life, but to always put you first. In Jesus' name, amen.

Going Deeper

Read It! Some people have the gift of being a peacemaker. But there are many different kinds of gifts, and each of them is important. Read about some of those gifts in Romans 12:6–8.

Do It! God gives each of us talents, but it is up to us to choose to use them for his glory. What are your talents—the things you are especially good at? Write them down and ask God to show you ways to use them for him this week!

Don't Sleep in Church!

Acts 20:7–12

Have you ever seen someone fall asleep in a strange place? Does your dad sometimes fall asleep in his chair after dinner? Do your friends doze off in class? Have you ever seen someone fall asleep in church? In today's story, a young man fell asleep while Paul was speaking—and learned that it's very important to be careful where you take a nap!

On the first day of the week, we all met
together to break bread. Paul spoke to the
group. Because he was planning to leave
the next day, he kept on talking till midnight. 8We were all together in a room
upstairs, and there were many lamps in
the room. 9A young man named Eutychus
was sitting in the window. As Paul continued talking, Eutychus was falling into a
deep sleep. Finally, he went sound asleep
and fell to the ground from the third floor.
When they picked him up, he was dead.
10Paul went down to Eutychus. He knelt
down and put his arms around him. He
said, "Don't worry. He is alive now." 11Then
Paul went upstairs again, broke bread, and
ate. He spoke to them a long time, until
it was early morning. Then he left. 12They
took the young man home alive and were
greatly comforted.

LET'S PRAY!

Two little eyes to look to God;
Two little ears to hear his Word;
Two little feet to walk in his ways;
Two little lips to sing his praise;
Two little hands to do his will
And one little heart to love him still.

—Traditional

Lord, I don't want to miss a single word of what you want to tell me today. Give me ears to hear what you want to say! In Jesus' name, amen.

Special Words:
The name Eutychus
means "fortunate."
Eutychus was very fortunate that Paul was there![45]

Going Deeper

Read It! In Galatians 5:22–23, Paul talked about the fruit of the Spirit. These aren't fruits to eat, but rather fruits to live. Find out what they are!

Do It! Make a fruit salad and name a different fruit of the Spirit with each bite you take!

Paul Says Good-Bye

Acts 20:17–38

Paul spent about twelve years on his three missionary journeys (AD 45–57). He traveled to all the places where Christianity had begun to grow throughout Asia and Greece. The work was hard and, at times, dangerous. In this story, Paul said good-bye to his friends at Ephesus. He didn't know whether or not he would ever see his friends again. So he left them with this message of encouragement.

Paul sent to Ephesus and called for the
elders of the church. [18]When they came to
him, he said, "You know about my life from
the first day I came to Asia. You know the
way I lived all the time I was with you. . . .
But you know that I always served the Lord.
I never thought of myself first, and I often
cried. [20]You know I preached to you, and I
did not hold back anything that would help
you. You know that I taught you in public
and in your homes. [21]I warned both Jews
and Greeks to change their lives and turn
to God. And I told them all to believe in our
Lord Jesus. [22]But now I must obey the Holy
Spirit and go to Jerusalem. I don't know
what will happen to me there. [23]I know
only that in every city the Holy Spirit tells
me that troubles and even jail wait for me.
[24]I don't care about my own life. The most
important thing is that I complete my mis-
sion. I want to finish the work that the Lord
Jesus gave me—to tell people the Good News
about God's grace.

[25]"And now, I know that none of you will
ever see me again. All the time I was with
you, I was preaching the kingdom of God.
[26]. . . If any of you should be lost, I am not
responsible. [27]This is because I have told
you everything God wants you to know. [28]Be
careful for yourselves and for all the people
God has given you. The Holy Spirit gave you
the work of caring for this flock. You must
be like shepherds to the church of God.
This is the church that God bought with his
own death. [29]I know that after I leave, some
men will come like wild wolves and try to
destroy the flock. [30]Also, men from your
own group will rise up and twist the truth.
They will lead away followers after them.
[31]So be careful! Always remember this: For
three years I never stopped warning each
of you. I taught you night and day. I often
cried over you.

[32]"Now I am putting you in the care of
God and the message about his grace. That
message is able to give you strength, and
it will give you the blessings that God has
for all his holy people. [33]When I was with
you, I never wanted anyone's money or fine
clothes. [34]You know that I always worked to
take care of my own needs and the needs
of those who were with me. [35]I showed you
in all things that you should work as I did
and help the weak. I taught you to remember the words of Jesus. He said, 'It is more
blessed to give than to receive.'"

[36]When Paul had said this, he knelt down
with all of them and prayed. [37–38]And they
all cried because Paul had said that they
would never see him again. They put their
arms around him and kissed him. Then
they went with him to the ship.

Let's Pray!

Thank You for the friends I meet;
And for neighbors down the street.
But most of all, dear Lord above,
I thank You for Your precious love.
—Unknown

Quote of the Day:
Only one life, yes only one,
Now let me say, "Thy will be done";
And when at last I'll hear the call,
I know I'll say 'twas worth it all;
Only one life, 'twill soon be past,
Only what's done for
Christ will last.
—*C. T. Studd*

Going Deeper

Read It! Paul left his friends in Ephesus so he could follow God's will for him to keep telling others about Jesus. Read about someone else who left the place he knew to follow God's command. Find out who in Genesis 12:1.

Do It! Pretend you are traveling to a new land to tell others about Jesus. Where will you go? What kind of people will you meet? How will you tell them about Jesus?

Paul Is Warned

Acts 21:7–14

Paul first met the prophet Agabus in Antioch when the prophet warned him of a coming famine (Acts 11:27–28). In today's story, the old prophet met with Paul again. This time it was to warn Paul not to return to Jerusalem because the Jews there would hand him over to the Gentiles. But would Paul listen?

We continued our trip from Tyre and
arrived at Ptolemais. We greeted the
believers there and stayed with them for
a day. 8We left Ptolemais and went to the
city of Caesarea. There we went into the
home of Philip and stayed with him. Philip
had the work of telling the Good News. He
was one of the seven helpers. 9He had four
unmarried daughters who had the gift of
prophesying. 10After we had been there
for some time, a prophet named Agabus
arrived from Judea. 11He came to us and
borrowed Paul's belt. Then he used the
belt to tie his own hands and feet. He said,
"The Holy Spirit says, 'This is how the Jews
in Jerusalem will tie up the man who wears
this belt. Then they will give him to the
non-Jewish people.'"

12We all heard these words. So we and
the people there begged Paul not to go to
Jerusalem. 13But he said, "Why are you crying and making me so sad? I am ready to be
tied up in Jerusalem. And I am ready to die
for the Lord Jesus!"

14We could not persuade him to stay away
from Jerusalem. So we stopped begging
him and said, "We pray that what the Lord
wants will be done."

Let's Pray!

God, thank you for your apostles who fearlessly spread your Word, even in the face of death. Help me remember in my prayers those who are suffering because they believe in you. In Jesus' name, amen.

SPECIAL WORDS:
"One of the seven helpers" (Acts 21:8 refers to the deacons named in Acts 6:2–3. But verse 21:8 also tells us that Philip's main job was to share the good news.

GOING DEEPER

READ IT! People make many plans for their lives, but who really controls them? Find out in Proverbs 16:9.

DO IT! Grab some friends and play a game of Follow the Leader. As you play, remember to always let Jesus be your leader in real life.

The Plot Against Paul

Acts 23:12–18, 31–35

When Paul's nephew overheard that the Jews were plotting to kill Paul, he hurried to tell his uncle. Would he make it in time?

In the morning some of the Jews made a
plan to kill Paul. They made a promise that
they would not eat or drink anything until
they had killed him. 13There were more
than 40 Jews who made this plan. 14They
went and talked to the leading priests and
the older Jewish leaders. They said, "We
have made a promise to ourselves that we
will not eat or drink until we have killed
Paul! 15So this is what we want you to do:
Send a message to the commander to bring
Paul out to you. Tell him you want to ask
Paul more questions. We will be waiting to
kill him while he is on the way here."

16But Paul's nephew heard about this plan.
He went to the army building and told Paul
about it. 17Then Paul called one of the officers and said, "Take this young man to the
commander. He has a message for him."

18So the officer brought Paul's nephew
to the commander. The officer said, "The
prisoner, Paul, asked me to bring this
young man to you. He wants to tell you
something."...

31"The soldiers . . . took Paul and brought
him to the city of Antipatris that night.
32The next day the horsemen went with Paul
to Caesarea. But the other soldiers went
back to the army building in Jerusalem.
33The horsemen came to Caesarea and gave
the letter to the governor. Then they turned
Paul over to him. 34The governor read the
letter. Then he asked Paul, "What area are
you from?" He learned that Paul was from
Cilicia. 35He said, "I will hear your case
when those who are against you come here
too." Then the governor gave orders for
Paul to be kept under guard in the palace.

LET'S PRAY!

A gentle answer will calm a person's anger.
But an unkind answer will cause more
anger.

—Proverbs 15:1

When I feel angry, God, help me not to try to get even or to speak hatefully. Help me to forgive instead. In Jesus' name, amen.

Quote of the Day:
Whatever is begun in anger ends in shame.
—Benjamin Franklin

Going Deeper

READ IT! There are two things that God cannot do. Find out what they are in Numbers 23:19.

DO IT! In today's story, Paul's enemies promised not to eat until he was dead. Have you ever promised something without thinking—and then been sorry for it? Talk with your parents about the importance of promises.

Paul Speaks to Agrippa and Bernice

Acts 25:23–26:8

Because Paul was a Roman citizen, he had special rights in the Roman courts. Paul was brought before the Roman governor of Judea, Felix. But Paul's words made Felix so uncomfortable that he ordered that Paul be held there at Caesarea. Paul stayed there for two years (Acts 24:27). Finally, Paul appealed to the emperor as a way to break free of Felix. He was then brought before King Agrippa and his sister Bernice. Would Agrippa allow Paul to continue on to Rome at last?

Agrippa and Bernice, the army leaders,
and the important men of Caesarea went
into the judgment room. Then Festus ordered the soldiers to bring Paul in. 24Festus
said, "King Agrippa and all who are gathered here with us, you see this man. All the
Jewish people, here and in Jerusalem, have
complained to me about him. They shout
that he should not live any longer. 25When
I judged him . . . I found no reason to order his death. But he asked to be judged by
Caesar. So I decided to send him. 26But I
have nothing definite to write the Emperor
about him. So . . . I hope that you can question him and give me something to write.
27I think it is foolish to send a prisoner to
Caesar without telling what the charges are
against him."

26:1Agrippa said to Paul, "You may now
speak to defend yourself."

Then Paul . . . said, "King Agrippa, I will
answer all the charges that the Jews make
against me. I think it is a blessing that I
can stand here before you today. 3I am very
happy to talk to you, because you know so
much about all the Jewish customs and the
things that the Jews argue about. Please listen to me patiently.

4"All the Jews know about my whole life.
. . . 5They have known me for a long time.
If they want to, they can tell you that I was
a good Pharisee. And the Pharisees obey
the laws of the Jewish religion more carefully than any other group of Jewish people.
6Now I am on trial because I hope for the
promise that God made to our ancestors.
7This is the promise that the 12 tribes of
our people hope to receive. For this hope
the Jews serve God day and night. My king,
the Jews have accused me because I hope
for this same promise! 8Why do any of you
people think it is impossible for God to
raise people from death?" . . .

29Paul said, "Whether it is a short or a
long time, I pray to God that not only you
but every person listening to me today
would be saved and be like me—except for
these chains I have!"

30Then King Agrippa, Governor Festus,
Bernice, and all the people sitting with
them stood up 31and left the room. They
were talking to each other. They said,
"There is no reason why this man should
die or be put in jail." 32And Agrippa said to
Festus, "We could let this man go free, but
he has asked Caesar to hear his case."

Quote of the Day:
The Lord will lead his people.
—Micah 2:13

Let's Pray!

Dear Lord God, fill me with your Word. Let it change my heart so everyone I meet will see Jesus shining in me. In Jesus' name, amen.

Going Deeper

Read It! Paul said many things to King Agrippa, teaching him about Jesus. Read all that Paul said in Acts 26.

Do It! It's very important to choose godly leaders for our government. This week, as a family, find out who all of your elected representatives are. Write one (or more!) of them a letter about something important to you—or just to let them know you are praying for them.

Shipwrecked!

Acts 27:33–44; 28:1

Paul was headed for Rome at last. But it was too late in the year to sail to Rome from Judea. The weather was stormy that time of year, and the seas were too rough. Paul warned the ship's crew, but they would not listen. The centurion, the pilot, and the owner of the ship were determined to sail anyway (Acts 27:10–12). Then the storms hit! For fourteen days, they battled to keep the ship together, and then things went from bad to worse. Would anyone survive?

Just before dawn Paul began persuading all
the people to eat something. He said, "For
the past 14 days you have been waiting and
watching. You have not eaten. 34Now I beg
you to eat something. You need it to stay
alive. None of you will lose even one hair
off your heads." 35After he said this, Paul
took some bread and thanked God for it
before all of them. He broke off a piece and
began eating. 36All the men felt better. They
all started eating too. 37(There were 276
people on the ship.) 38We ate all we wanted.
Then we began making the ship lighter by
throwing the grain into the sea.

39When daylight came, the sailors saw
land. . . . They wanted to sail the ship to
the beach, if they could. 40So they cut the
ropes to the anchors. . . . Then they raised
the front sail into the wind and sailed toward the beach. 41But the ship hit a sand-
bank. The front of the ship stuck there and
could not move. Then the big waves began
to break the back of the ship to pieces.

42The soldiers decided to kill the prisoners so that none of them could swim away
and escape. 43But Julius, the officer, wanted
to let Paul live. He did not allow the soldiers
to kill the prisoners. Instead he ordered
everyone who could swim to jump into the
water and swim to land. 44The rest used
wooden boards or pieces of the ship. And
this is how all the people made it safely to
land.

28:1When we were safe on land, we learned
that the island was called Malta.

Let's Pray!

Dear God,
Be good to me,
The sea is so wide
And my boat is so small.

—Prayer of a Breton Fisherman

Going Deeper

Read It! Sometimes, even though we know the right thing to do, we still choose to do the wrong thing instead. Read James 4:17 to find out what God calls this.

Do It! Does your family have an emergency plan in case of fire, storm, or other disaster? If not, spend some time this week putting together a plan. You could even put together an emergency first aid kit. Check online for what should go in it for your part of the country.

Snakebite!

Acts 28:1–6, 10–14

Paul and all the other survivors of the shipwreck made it to the island of Malta. There, the natives welcomed them, but Paul wasn't out of danger yet! Would Paul live through a deadly snakebite?

The island was called Malta. 2It was rain-
ing and very cold. But the people who lived
there were very good to us. They made us a
fire and welcomed all of us. 3Paul gathered
a pile of sticks for the fire. He was putting
them on the fire when a poisonous snake
came out because of the heat and bit him
on the hand. 4The people living on the
island saw the snake hanging from Paul's
hand. They said to each other, "This man
must be a murderer! He did not die in the
sea, but Justice does not want him to live."
5But Paul shook the snake off into the fire.
He was not hurt. 6The people thought that
Paul would swell up or fall down dead. The
people waited and watched him for a long
time, but nothing bad happened to him. So
they changed their minds about Paul. Now
they said, "He is a god!". . .

10–11The people on the island gave us many
honors. We stayed there three months.
When we were ready to leave, they gave us
the things we needed.

We got on a ship from Alexandria. The
ship had stayed on the island during the
winter. On the front of the ship was the sign
of the twin gods. 12We stopped at Syracuse
for three days and then left. 13From there
we sailed to Rhegium. The next day a wind
began to blow from the southwest, so we
were able to leave. A day later we came to
Puteoli. 14We found some believers there,
and they asked us to stay with them for a
week. Finally, we came to Rome.

Let's Pray!

Others went out to sea in ships.
They did business on the great oceans.
They saw what the Lord could do.
They saw the miracles he did.
He spoke, and a storm came up.
It blew up high waves.
The ships tossed as high as the sky and fell low in the waves.
The storm was so bad the men lost their courage.
They stumbled and fell like men who were drunk.
They did not know what to do.
In their misery they cried out to the Lord.
And he saved them from their troubles.
He made the storm be still.
He calmed the waves.
They were happy that it was quiet.
And God guided them to the port they wanted.

—Psalm 107:23–30

Lord, I will trust you to calm the storms in my life. I love you, Lord. In Jesus' name, amen.

Going Deeper

Read It! Did you know that your body is God's temple? Read about it in 1 Corinthians 6:19–20.

Do It! Because your body is God's temple, it's important to take good care of it. Exercise, eat lots of fruits and vegetables, and get plenty of sleep—every day!

Do all the good you can.
By all the means you can.
In all the ways you can.
In all the places you can.
At all the times you can.
To all the people you can.
As long as ever you can.

—John Wesley

Rome at Last!

Acts 28:16–23, 30–31

God said, "Go and tell this to the people: 'You will listen and listen, but you will not understand. You will look and look, but you will not learn'" (Isaiah 6:9). These words of the prophet Isaiah describe the men who had been trying to kill Paul for so long. They saw Paul and listened to the words he spoke, but they did not understand. In today's story, Paul attempted to reach the Jews of Rome. Paul spent two years there, trying to get them to believe in Jesus.

Then we arrived at Rome. There, Paul was
allowed to live alone. But a soldier stayed
with him to guard him.
[17]Three days later Paul sent for the Jewish
leaders there. When they came together, he
said, "Brothers, I have done nothing against
our people. I have done nothing against the
customs of our fathers. But I was arrested in
Jerusalem and given to the Romans. [18]The
Romans asked me many questions. But
they could find no reason why I should be
killed. They wanted to let me go free, [19]but
the Jews there did not want that. So I had to
ask to come to Rome to have my trial before
Caesar. But I have no charge to bring against
my own people. [20]That is why I wanted to
see you and talk with you. I am bound with
this chain because I believe in the hope of
Israel."
[21]The Jews answered Paul, "We have
received no letters from Judea about you.
None of our Jewish brothers who have
come from there brought news about you or
told us anything bad about you. [22]We want
to hear your ideas. We know that people
everywhere are speaking against this religious group."
[23]Paul and the Jews chose a day for a meeting. On that day many more of the Jews met
with Paul at the place he was staying. Paul
spoke to them all day long, explaining the
kingdom of God to them. He tried to persuade them to believe these things about
Jesus. He used the law of Moses and the
writings of the prophets to do this. . . .
[30]Paul stayed two full years in his own
rented house. He welcomed all people who
came and visited him. [31]He preached about
the kingdom of God and taught about the
Lord Jesus Christ. He was very bold, and no
one tried to stop him from speaking.

Let's Pray!

Dear Lord, I'd like to pray for all the people
that I love but who live far away.
Tonight with them my thoughts I share.
Please keep them in your loving care,
each night and every day.

—Traditional

Quote of the Day:
Good works do not make a good man, but a good man does good works.
—Martin Luther

Going Deeper

Read It! Just as we grow in height, we should also grow in wisdom, knowledge, and understanding. Read Proverbs 2:6 to see who gives us those things.

Do It! Think of something you can do this week to bless someone. But keep it a secret—just between you and God—and he will bless you!

This Is My Body

1 Corinthians 11:23–28

At the Last Supper, Jesus gave his apostles a special way to remember him. In today's story, Paul explained this to the church at Corinth. But Paul's message was not just for them; we should remember Jesus in this way too.

The teaching that I gave you is the same
teaching that I received from the Lord: On
the night when Jesus was handed over to be
killed, he took bread [24]and gave thanks for
it. Then he broke the bread and said, "This
is my body; it is for you. Do this to remember me." [25]In the same way, after they ate,
Jesus took the cup. He said, "This cup shows
the new agreement from God to his people.
This new agreement begins with the blood
of my death. When you drink this, do it to
remember me." [26]Every time you eat this
bread and drink this cup, you show others
about the Lord's death until he comes.
[27]So a person should not eat the bread
or drink the cup of the Lord in a way that
is not worthy of it. If he does he is sinning
against the body and the blood of the Lord.
[28]Everyone should look into his own heart
before he eats the bread and drinks the cup.

LET'S PRAY!

Lord, try me and test me.
Look closely into my heart and mind.
—Psalm 26:2

Father, we glorify your name and worship and adore you. Thank you for giving your body to save us. In Jesus' name, amen.

Special Words:
"In a way that is not worthy" means taking the Lord's Supper without believing that Jesus died for your sins and then rose from the grave so you could join him in heaven.

Going Deeper

Read It! In the Old Testament, God saved his people from physically starving with bread from heaven (Exodus 16:4, 31). In the New Testament, God saved his people from spiritually starving with this bread of heaven. Check it out in John 6:32–35.

Do It! Ask your parents to help you prepare your own Lord's Supper, using crackers and grape juice. As you take the Supper, think about all that Jesus did to save you from the consequences of your sin.

We Are the Body of Christ

Ephesians 1:3–7, 13–23

Did you know the Bible tells us we are God's adopted sons and daughters? The book of Galatians says, "When the right time came, God sent his Son. His Son was born of a woman and lived under the law. God did this so that he could buy freedom for those who were under the law. His purpose was to make us his children. And you are God's children. That is why God sent the Spirit of his Son into your hearts. The Spirit cries out, 'Father, dear Father'" (4:4–6). And so, we—along with all the other Christians who have ever lived—are part of God's family. In today's reading, Paul told us even more about the wonderful blessing of being a child of God.

Praise be to the God and Father of our Lord
Jesus Christ. In Christ, God has given us
every spiritual blessing in heaven. [4]In
Christ, he chose us before the world was
made. In his love he chose us to be his
holy people—people without blame before
him. [5]And before the world was made,
God decided to make us his own children
through Jesus Christ. That was what he
wanted and what pleased him. [6]This brings
praise to God because of his wonderful
grace. God gave that grace to us freely, in
Christ, the One he loves. [7]In Christ we are
set free by the blood of his death. And so we
have forgiveness of sins because of God's
rich grace. . . .

[13]You heard the true teaching—the Good
News about your salvation. When you heard
it, you believed in Christ. And in Christ, God
put his special mark on you by giving you the
Holy Spirit that he had promised. [14]That
Holy Spirit is the guarantee that we will get
what God promised for his people. This will
bring full freedom to the people who belong
to God, to bring praise to God's glory.

[15–16]That is why I always remember you in
my prayers and always thank God for you. I
have always done this since the time I heard
about your faith in the Lord Jesus and your
love for all God's people. [17]I always pray to
the God of our Lord Jesus Christ—to the
glorious Father. I pray that he will give you a
spirit that will make you wise in the knowledge of God—the knowledge that he has
shown you. [18]I pray that you will have greater
understanding in your heart. Then you will
know the hope that God has chosen to give
us. I pray that you will know that the blessings God has promised his holy people are
rich and glorious. [19]And you will know that
God's power is very great for us who believe.
That power is the same as the great strength
[20]God used to raise Christ from death and
put him at his right side in heaven. [21]God
made Christ more important . . . than anything in this world or in the next world.
[22]God put everything under his power. And
God made him the head over everything for
the church. [23]The church is Christ's body.
The church is filled with Christ, and Christ
fills everything in every way.

LET'S PRAY!

"I Surrender All"

All to Jesus I surrender;
All to him I freely give;
I will ever love and trust him,
In his presence daily live.
I surrender all,
I surrender all,
All to thee, my blessed Savior,
I surrender all.

—J. W. Van Deventer

GOING DEEPER

READ IT! When David was in the wilderness, he wrote a song of joy and worship to God. Read David's praise in Psalm 63:1–8.

DO IT! Go on a nature walk, and thank God for all the blessings you see.

The Armor of God

Ephesians 6:10–20

Can you imagine being a police officer or a soldier and going off to work in your pajamas? That's silly, isn't it? You might be more comfortable, but you wouldn't be protected! And you wouldn't have the tools you needed to do your job well and safely. In the same way, we Christians need protection from evil and effective tools to share God's light. These things are called the "armor of God"—and we need to put them on every day. Let's find out what they are!

Be strong in the Lord and in his great power. 11Wear the full armor of God. Wear God's armor so that you can fight against the devil's evil tricks. 12Our fight is not against people on earth. We are fighting against the rulers and authorities and the powers of this world's darkness. We are fighting against the spiritual powers of evil in the heavenly world. 13That is why you need to get God's full armor. Then on the day of evil you will be able to stand strong. And when you have finished the whole fight, you will still be standing. 14So stand strong, with the belt of truth tied around your waist. And on your chest wear the protection of right living. 15And on your feet wear the Good News of peace to help you stand strong. 16And also use the shield of faith. With that you can stop all the burning arrows of the Evil One. 17Accept God's salvation to be your helmet. And take the sword of the Spirit—that sword is the teaching of God. 18Pray in the Spirit at all times. Pray with all kinds of prayers, and ask for everything you need. To do this you must always be ready. Never give up. Always pray for all God's people.

19Also pray for me. Pray that when I speak, God will give me words so that I can tell the secret truth of the Good News without fear. 20I have the work of speaking that Good News. I am doing that now, here in prison. Pray that when I preach the Good News I will speak without fear, as I should.

LET'S PRAY:

Loving Shepherd of Thy sheep,
Keep Thy lamb, in safety keep;
Nothing can Thy power withstand;
None can pluck me from Thy hand.

—Jane Elizabeth Leeson

GOING DEEPER

READ IT! Jesus taught us to pray for protection. Check it out in Matthew 6:13.

DO IT! Put on your armor every morning! Pull on your pants, and pray that you remember God's truth. Button your shirt, and ask God to help you live right. Tie your shoes, and pray for ways to share God's Word. Put on your jacket, and ask God to protect you from the evil one. Comb your hair, and ask God to protect your thoughts. And don't forget your sword. Read a verse in God's Word before you go out to play!

Live as Children of Light

Philippians 2:12–16

The church at Philippi was the first church Paul established in Europe. It was early in his second missionary journey (Acts 16). Luke, who wrote both the gospel of Luke and the book of the Acts, was its leader for the first six years. In Paul's letter to the church at Philippi, he told them how to live as children of God. Paul's message wasn't just for them, though; it's for us too. Let's read his message.

My dear friends, you have always obeyed. You obeyed God when I was with you. It is even more important that you obey now while I am not with you. Keep on working to complete your salvation, and do it with
fear and trembling. [13]Yes, God is working in you to help you want to do what pleases him. Then he gives you the power to do it.
[14]Do everything without complaining or
arguing. [15]Then you will be innocent and without anything wrong in you. You will be God's children without fault. But you are living with crooked and mean people all around you. Among them you shine
like stars in the dark world. [16]You offer to them the teaching that gives life. So when Christ comes again, I can be happy because my work was not wasted. I ran in the race and won.

LET'S PRAY!

Holy Spirit, give us
Each a lowly mind;
Make us more like Jesus,
Gentle, pure, and kind.

Holy Spirit, brighten
Little deeds of toil,
And our playful pastimes
Let no folly spoil.

Holy Spirit, help us
Daily by Thy might
What is wrong to conquer
And to choose the right. Amen.

—Anonymous

Quote of the Day:
You are never in the wrong place to serve God. Even if no one acknowledges your efforts, God sees and knows. Bloom where you are planted.
—Unknown

Going Deeper

Read It! Remember, no matter what you are doing—worshiping God or cleaning your room—you are working for the Lord. Check it out in Colossians 3:23.

Do It! The Bible commands us to "do everything without complaining or arguing." That can be tough! Are there chores you complain about? Try to see them as a chance to bless and serve your family. Getting your heart in the right place can make even your worst chores a little better!

Run to Win the Prize

Philippians 3:8–17

On your mark . . . Get set . . . Go!" With that, you're off and running as fast as you can, pushing toward the finish line. And isn't it wonderful to reach the finish line and win the prize? God's Word says that's what it's like to live a Christian life—to arrive at the finish line and win the prize. Let's read about how we should run.

I think that all things are worth nothing compared with the greatness of knowing Christ Jesus my Lord. Because of Christ, I have lost all those things. And now I know that all those things are worthless trash. This allows me to have Christ [9]and to belong to him. Now that I belong to Christ, I am right with God and this being right does not come from my following the law. It comes from God through faith. God uses my faith in Christ to make me right with him. [10]All I want is to know Christ and the power of his rising from death. I want to share in Christ's sufferings and become like him in his death. [11]If I have those things, then I have hope that I myself will be raised from death.

[12]I do not mean that I am already as God wants me to be. I have not yet reached that goal. But I continue trying to reach it and to make it mine. Christ wants me to do that. That is the reason Christ made me his. [13]Brothers, I know that I have not yet reached that goal. But there is one thing I always do: I forget the things that are past. I try as hard as I can to reach the goal that is before me. [14]I keep trying to reach the goal and get the prize. That prize is mine because God called me through Christ to the life above.

[15]All of us who have grown spiritually to be mature should think this way, too. And if there are things you do not agree with, God will make them clear to you. [16]But we should continue following the truth we already have.

[17]Brothers, all of you should try to follow my example and to copy those who live the way we showed you.

Let's Pray!

I ask only one thing from the Lord.
  This is what I want:
Let me live in the Lord's house
  all my life.
Let me see the Lord's beauty.
  Let me look around in his Temple.

—Psalm 27:4

Lord, my goal is to live with you in heaven forever. But I know that I can't get there on my own. Thank you for sending Jesus to save me. In Jesus' name, amen.

Quote of the Day:
But the people who trust the Lord will become strong again. They will be able to rise up as an eagle in the sky. They will run without needing rest. They will walk without becoming tired.
—Isaiah 40:31

Going Deeper

Read It! When sins trip you up, don't quit running the race. Pray a prayer like the one found in Psalm 25:6–7. Then keep on running!

Do It! Run for the prize! As a family, participate in a local walk or run that benefits a charity.

Think About This!

Philippians 4:4–13

Paul learned a wonderful secret—the secret of being happy. No matter what happened to him—the beatings, stonings, shipwreck, and even being thrown into prison—Paul was a man who was truly happy. How? Paul had discovered the source of true happiness. Let's find out what, or who, it is!

Be full of joy in the Lord always. I will say again, be full of joy.

5Let all men see that you are gentle and kind. The Lord is coming soon. 6Do not worry about anything. But pray and ask God for everything you need. And when you pray, always give thanks. 7And God's peace will keep your hearts and minds in Christ Jesus. The peace that God gives is so great that we cannot understand it.

8Brothers, continue to think about the things that are good and worthy of praise. Think about the things that are true and honorable and right and pure and beautiful and respected. 9And do what you learned and received from me. Do what I told you and what you saw me do. And the God who gives peace will be with you.

10I am very happy in the Lord that you have shown your care for me again. You continued to care about me, but there was no way for you to show it. 11I am telling you this, but it is not because I need anything. I have learned to be satisfied with the things I have and with everything that happens. 12I know how to live when I am poor. And I know how to live when I have plenty. I have learned the secret of being happy at any time in everything that happens. I have learned to be happy when I have enough to eat and when I do not have enough to eat. I have learned to be happy when I have all that I need and when I do not have the things I need. 13I can do all things through Christ because he gives me strength.

LET'S PRAY!

Dear God, please help me control what I say. Let me speak only words that are helpful and bring joy to others. In Jesus' name, amen.

Going Deeper

Read It! Did you know that your words can be like golden apples? Check it out in Proverbs 25:11.

Do It! Play the "Telephone" game with your friends or as a family. Sit in a circle. The first person whispers a joke or a little story to the next person, who then whispers the same thing to the next person, and so on. The last person in the circle repeats what he or she heard to the whole group. How close was it to the original? What does this experiment tell us about gossip and whether we should always believe everything we hear?

Quote of the Day:
*Watch your thoughts;
they become words.
Watch your words;
they become actions.
Watch your actions;
they become habits.
Watch your habits;
they become character.
Watch your character;
it becomes your destiny.
—Unknown*

Jesus Will Return

1 Thessalonians 4:13–5:2, 4–5

Do you ever wonder what heaven will be like? Will there be high, puffy clouds with big mansions sitting on top? A giant zoo filled with every kind of animal that has ever lived? There is much about heaven that we won't know until we get there. But there is also a lot about heaven that we do know, and the most important thing is that we will get to see Jesus face-to-face! While we don't know exactly when Jesus is coming back, we do know that he is coming back! Let's read about his return.

Brothers, we want you to know about those
who have died. We do not want you to be sad
as others who have no hope. [14]We believe
that Jesus died and that he rose again. So,
because of Jesus, God will bring together
with Jesus those who have died. [15]What we
tell you now is the Lord's own message. We
who are living now may still be living when
the Lord comes again. We who are living
at that time will be with the Lord, but not
before those who have already died. [16]The
Lord himself will come down from heaven.
There will be a loud command with the
voice of the archangel and with the trumpet
call of God. And those who have died and
were in Christ will rise first. [17]After that,
those who are still alive at that time will be
gathered up with them. We will be taken up
in the clouds to meet the Lord in the air.
And we will be with the Lord forever. [18]So
comfort each other with these words.

[5:1]Now, brothers, we do not need to write
to you about times and dates. [2]You know
very well that the day the Lord comes again
will be a surprise like a thief that comes in
the night. . . . [4]But you, brothers, are not
living in darkness. And so that day will not
surprise you like a thief. [5]You are all people
who belong to the light. You belong to the
day. We do not belong to the night or to
darkness.

LET'S PRAY!

Come, Lord Jesus!

—Revelation 22:20

GOING DEEPER

READ IT! Did you know that Jesus is preparing a place for you in heaven? Read all about it in John 14:1–3.

DO IT! Let each family member share the answer to this question: If you knew Jesus was coming back tomorrow, what would you do today?

DID YOU KNOW?
Like most believers back then, Paul believed that Jesus would come back to earth in his own lifetime. But Jesus will come like a thief in the night; we won't know the day or the time (1 Thessalonians 5:1–2).

Passing on the Faith

1 Timothy 4:6–5:2

Most early Christians believed that Jesus would return to earth in a short time. Many of them were tempted to stop doing the normal, daily things of life and just wait for Jesus. In this letter to Timothy, Paul urged his young friend to "teach yourself only to serve God" (v. 7) and "do not let anyone treat you as if you were not important" because "you are young" (v.12). Instead, Paul told Timothy to be an example to those around him, to help others grow in faith and stay away from sin. In that way—whether Jesus returned right away or not—they would all be living in a way that pleases God.

Tell these things to the brothers. This will
show that you are a good servant of Christ
Jesus. You will show that you are made
strong by the words of faith and good teaching that you have been following. 7People
tell silly stories that do not agree with
God's truth. Do not follow what those stories teach. But teach yourself only to serve
God. 8Training your body helps you in some
ways, but serving God helps you in every
way. Serving God brings you blessings in
this life and in the future life, too. 9What I
say is true, and you should fully accept it.
10For this is why we work and struggle: We
hope in the living God. He is the Savior of
all people. And in a very special way, he is
the Savior of all who believe in him.

11Command and teach these things. 12You
are young, but do not let anyone treat you
as if you were not important. Be an example
to show the believers how they should live.
Show them with your words, with the way
you live, with your love, with your faith, and
with your pure life. 13Continue to read the
Scriptures to the people, strengthen them,
and teach them. Do these things until I
come. 14Remember to use the gift that you
have. That gift was given to you through a
prophecy when the group of elders laid
their hands on you. 15Continue to do those
things. Give your life to doing them. Then
everyone can see that your work is pro-
gressing. 16Be careful in your life and in
your teaching. Continue to live and teach
rightly. Then you will save yourself and
those people who listen to you.

5:1Do not speak angrily to an older man,
but talk to him as if he were your father.
Treat younger men like brothers. 2Treat
older women like mothers, and younger
women like sisters. Always treat them in a
pure way.

LET'S PRAY!

Lord, every morning you hear my voice.
Every morning, I tell you what I need.
And I wait for your answer.

—Psalm 5:3

Special Words:
The "silly stories" in verse 7 may have been the tales told by the false teachers named Hymenaeus and Alexander. They were tossed out of the church for their "silly stories that do not agree with God's truth."[46]

Going Deeper

Read It! There was another young man who did not let his age keep him from obeying God. Read about him and his friends in Daniel 1.

Do It! You are never too young to serve God and to be a good example to others. Be extra careful what you say and do today. You never know who is watching!

Onesimus the Runaway

Philemon vv. 10–19

This little book of the Bible—Philemon—was Paul's attempt to smooth the way for a runaway slave to return to his master. Onesimus was a slave. He had stolen from his master, Philemon, and run away to Rome. But while he was in Rome, Onesimus met Paul and became a believer in Christ. Philemon was also a believer. So Paul wrote this letter, asking Philemon to forgive and to accept Onesimus as a brother in Christ. But Paul's words aren't just good advice for Philemon; they are good advice for us today, in all our relationships—as parents and children, as husbands and wives, as friends, bosses, and workers. Let's read what Paul said.

I am asking you a favor for my son
Onesimus. He became my son while I was
in prison. 11In the past he was useless to
you. But now he has become useful for both
you and me.
12I am sending him back to you, and with
him I am sending my own heart. 13I wanted
to keep him with me to help me while I
am in prison for the Good News. By helping me he would be serving you. 14But I did
not want to do anything without asking you
first. Then any favor you do for me will be
because you want to do it, not because I
forced you to do it.
15Onesimus was separated from you for
a short time. Maybe that happened so that
you could have him back forever—16not to
be a slave, but better than a slave, to be a
loved brother. I love him very much. But
you will love him even more. You will love
him as a man and as a brother in the Lord.
17If you think of me as your friend, then
accept Onesimus back. Welcome him as
you would welcome me. 18If Onesimus has
done anything wrong to you, charge that to
me. If he owes you anything, charge that to
me. 19I, Paul, am writing this with my own
hand. I will pay back anything Onesimus
owes. And I will say nothing about what you
owe me for your own life.

Let's Pray!

Lord, every day is a gift from you. And so I give my day back to you—every moment, every hour—with the hope that you will be pleased with what I do, what I say, and where I go. I want to do your will, O God! In Jesus' name, amen.

Did You Know?
The Bible doesn't tell us if Onesimus was welcomed back by his master or if he was punished. But there is a tradition that says Onesimus went on to become a leader in the church at Berea.[47]

GOING DEEPER

READ IT! Onesimus appears one other time in the Bible. Read about him in Colossians 4:9.

DO IT! The name *Onesimus* means "profitable or useful." In Rome, he learned to be "useful" to God. What does your name mean? Ask your parents to help you check it out on the Internet. How can you use the meaning of your name to help you serve God?

What Is Faith?

Hebrews 11:6–10, 13–16; 12:1–3

Hebrews 11 is often called the "Hall of Faith." One after another, the great heroes of the faith are praised. These great examples help us understand what true faith is. They also remind us that God's faithfulness has been unchanging from one generation to the next, all the way up to today!

Without faith no one can please God. Anyone who comes to God must believe that he is real and that he rewards those who truly want to find him.

7It was by faith Noah heard God's warnings about things that he could not yet see. He obeyed God and built a large boat to save his family. By his faith, Noah showed that the world was wrong. And he became one of those who are made right with God through faith.

8It was by faith Abraham obeyed God's call to go to another place that God promised to give him. He left his own country,
not knowing where he was to go. 9It was by
faith that he lived in the country God promised to give him. He lived there like a visitor who did not belong. He lived in tents with Isaac and Jacob, who had received that same
promise from God. 10Abraham was waiting
for the city that has real foundations—the city planned and built by God. . . .

13All these great men died in faith. They did not get the things that God promised his people. But they saw them coming far in the future and were glad. They said that they were like visitors and strangers
on earth. 14When people say such things,
then they show that they are looking for a
country that will be their own country. 15If
they had been thinking about that country they had left, they could have gone back.
16But those men were waiting for a better country—a heavenly country. So God is not ashamed to be called their God. For he has prepared a city for them. . . .

12:1So we have many people of faith around us. Their lives tell us what faith means. So let us run the race that is before us and never give up. We should remove from our lives anything that would get in the way. And we should remove the sin that so easily catches
us. 2Let us look only to Jesus. He is the one who began our faith, and he makes our faith perfect. Jesus suffered death on the cross. But he accepted the shame of the cross as if it were nothing. He did this because of the joy that God put before him. And now he is sitting at the right side of God's throne.
3Think about Jesus. He held on patiently while sinful men were doing evil things against him. Look at Jesus' example so that you will not get tired and stop trying.

Let's Pray!

Lord, your love reaches to the heavens.
Your loyalty goes to the skies.
Your goodness is as high as the mountains.
Your justice is as deep as the ocean.
Lord, you protect both men and animals.
God, you love is so precious!
You protect people as a bird protects her young under her wings. . . .
Continue to love those who know you.
And continue to do good to those who are good.

—Psalm 36:5–7, 10

Quote of the Day:
Faith of our fathers, living still.
In spite of dungeon, fire and sword;
O how our hearts beat high with joy
Whene'er we hear that glorious word!
Faith of our fathers, holy faith!
We will be true to Thee till death!
—Frederick W. Faber

Going Deeper

READ IT! Who was the "father of many nations"? Find out in Romans 4:18.

DO IT! Who is your favorite hero of the faith? Look up his or her story and read it today.

Jesus paid it all,
All to Him I owe;
Sin had left a crimson stain,
He washed it white as snow.

—Elvina M. Hall

Jesus of Nazareth
King of the Jews

How to Please God

James 1:19–27

The first chapter of James was written for the Christian who is of two minds—who wants to live with one foot planted firmly in the stuff of this world and the other foot headed toward heaven. What a disaster! It's enough to split a person in two! And so, in this chapter, James reminded us how to live as a true child of God: to listen more than you speak, to put away evil things, to obey God's Word, and to care for those who need help. This is who God wants us to be.

My dear brothers, always be willing to listen and slow to speak. Do not become angry
easily. 20Anger will not help you live a good
life as God wants. 21So put out of your life
every evil thing and every kind of wrong
you do. Don't be proud but accept God's
teaching that is planted in your hearts. This
teaching can save your souls.
22Do what God's teaching says; do not just
listen and do nothing. When you only sit
and listen, you are fooling yourselves. 23A
person who hears God's teaching and does
nothing is like a man looking in a mir-
ror. 24He sees his face, then goes away and
quickly forgets what he looked like. 25But
the truly happy person is the one who carefully studies God's perfect law that makes
people free. He continues to study it. He
listens to God's teaching and does not
forget what he heard. Then he obeys what
God's teaching says. When he does this, it
makes him happy.
26A person might think he is religious.
But if he says things he should not say, then
he is just fooling himself. His "religion" is
worth nothing. 27Religion that God accepts
is this: caring for orphans or widows who
need help; and keeping yourself free from
the world's evil influence. This is the kind
of religion that God accepts as pure and
good.

LET'S PRAY!

Lord of the loving heart, may mine be
    loving too.
Lord of the gentle heart, may mine be
    gentle too.
Lord of the willing feet, may mine be
    willing too,
So I may grow more like you
    In all I say and do.

—Unknown

Quote of the Day:
Expect great things from God.
Attempt great things for God.
—William Carey

Going Deeper

Read It! Pleasing God doesn't mean you have to be perfect. In fact, the one of whom God said, "He is the kind of man I want" made lots of mistakes. Find out who he was in Acts 13:22.

Do It! Today's reading urges us to care for "orphans and widows who need help." Think of one way to do that this week: help a widow with her yard work, donate toys to a children's home, or volunteer at a shelter.

The Christian Life

James 5:7–20

Do you remember the story of Job? He had everything taken away from him, yet he still trusted God. Just like Job, we must trust God even in hard times—that is the message of today's Scripture reading. No matter what happens on this earth, our God is always faithful.

Brothers, be patient until the Lord comes
again. A farmer is patient. He waits for his
valuable crop to grow from the earth. He
waits patiently for it to receive the first rain
and the last rain. 8You, too, must be patient.
Do not give up hope. The Lord is coming
soon. 9Brothers, do not complain against
each other. If you do not stop complaining,
you will be judged guilty. And the Judge
is ready to come! 10Brothers, follow the
example of the prophets who spoke for the
Lord. They suffered many hard things, but
they were patient. 11We say they are happy
because they were able to do this. You have
heard about Job's patience. You know that
after all his trouble, the Lord helped him.
This shows that the Lord is full of mercy
and is kind.

12My brothers, it is very important that
you not use an oath when you make a promise. Don't use the name of heaven, earth, or
anything else to prove what you say. When
you mean yes, say only "yes." When you
mean no, say only "no." Do this so that you
will not be judged guilty.

13If one of you is having troubles, he
should pray. If one of you is happy, he
should sing praises. 14If one of you is
sick, he should call the church's elders.
The elders should pour oil on him in
the name of the Lord and pray for him.
15And the prayer that is said with faith will
make the sick person well. The Lord will
heal him. And if he has sinned, God will
forgive him. 16Confess your sins to each
other and pray for each other. Do this so
that God can heal you. When a good man
prays, great things happen. 17Elijah was a
man just like us. He prayed that it would
not rain. And it did not rain on the land
for three and a half years! 18Then Elijah
prayed again. And the rain came down
from the sky, and the land grew crops
again.

19My brothers, one of you may wander
away from the truth. And someone may
help him come back. 20Remember this:
Anyone who brings a sinner back from the
wrong way will save that sinner's soul from
death. By doing this, that person will cause
many sins to be forgiven.

Let's Pray!

Gentle Jesus, meek and mild,
Look upon a little child . . .
Lamb of God, I look to Thee;
You shall my example be.
You are gentle, meek, and mild,
You were once a little child.
Let me, above all, fulfill
God my heavenly Father's will. . . .
Loving Jesus, gentle Lamb,
In Your gracious hands I am.
Make me, Savior, what You are,
Live Yourself within my heart.

—Charles Wesley

GOING DEEPER

READ IT! Sometimes you may not know what to pray. Maybe you are too happy or too sad or too angry. Maybe you just don't know what to ask for. Take heart! God has taken care of that. Read how in Romans 8:26–27.

DO IT! Spend some time just listen for God today. Find a quiet, comfortable spot. Then simply sit and listen to what God's Spirit says to your heart!

QUOTE OF THE DAY:
No pain, no palm;
no thorns, no throne;
no gall, no glory;
no cross, no crown.
—William Penn

Respect Your Spiritual Leaders

1 Peter 5:4–11

Do you have a hard time saying yes when someone—a teacher or parent—asks you to do something you don't want to do? Ephesians 6:2 tells us that we must honor our fathers and mothers. That is, we must respect those in authority. This is true in family life, and it is also true in the church. God wants us to grow closer to him. He gives us Bible teachers and preachers to help us grow closer to him.

When Christ, the Head Shepherd, comes,
you will get a crown. This crown will be glorious, and it will never lose its beauty.
5In the same way, younger men should be
willing to be under older men. And all of
you should be very humble with each other.
"God is against the proud,
but he gives grace to the humble."
Proverbs 3:34
6So be humble under God's powerful
hand. Then he will lift you up when the
right time comes. 7Give all your worries to
him, because he cares for you.
8Control yourselves and be careful! The
devil is your enemy. And he goes around like
a roaring lion looking for someone to eat.
9Refuse to give in to the devil. Stand strong
in your faith. You know that your Christian
brothers and sisters all over the world are
having the same sufferings you have.
10Yes, you will suffer for a short time. But
after that, God will make everything right.
He will make you strong. He will support
you and keep you from falling. He is the
God who gives all grace. He called you to
share in his glory in Christ. That glory will
continue forever. 11All power is his forever
and ever. Amen.

LET'S PRAY!

For this reason, all who obey you
  should pray to you while they still can.
When troubles rise like a flood,
  they will not reach them.
You are my hiding place.
  You protect me from my troubles.
  You fill me with songs of salvation.

—Psalm 32:6–7

Thank you, Lord, for protecting me and for filling me with your songs. I sing my praises to you! In Jesus' name, amen.

QUOTE OF THE DAY:
God sends no one away empty except those who are full of themselves.
—Dwight L. Moody

Special Words:
Humility is understanding that everything we have is a gift from God.

GOING DEEPER

READ IT! We can trust God to lead us. Read his promise in Proverbs 3:5–6.

DO IT! To be humble is to think more of God and others than of yourself. How can you be humble today? Let someone else go first, spend time with God before you play, or do a chore for someone else.

Confess Your Sins

1 John 1:1–10

God's Word tells us why it is important to confess our sins. First John 1:9 says, "If we confess our sins, he will forgive our sins." Not one of us is perfect. God understands that, and he provides a way for us to be forgiven—by confessing our sins to him. Confessing is more than just telling God you are sorry. To confess is to be so sorry that you will try very hard not to commit that same sin again.

We write you now about something that has always existed.

We have heard.
We have seen with our own eyes.
We have watched,
and we have touched with our hands.

We write to you about the Word that gives
life. 2He who gives life was shown to us.
We saw him, and we can give proof about it. And now we tell you that he has life that continues forever. The one who gives this life was with God the Father. God showed
him to us. 3Now we tell you what we have
seen and heard because we want you to have fellowship with us. The fellowship we share together is with God the Father and
his Son, Jesus Christ. 4We write this to you
so that you can be full of joy with us.

5Here is the message we have heard from
God and now tell to you: God is light, and
in him there is no darkness at all. 6So if we
say that we have fellowship with God, but we continue living in darkness, then we are
liars. We do not follow the truth. 7God is in
the light. We should live in the light, too. If we live in the light, we share fellowship with each other. And when we live in the light, the blood of the death of Jesus, God's Son, is making us clean from every sin.

8If we say that we have no sin, we are fooling ourselves, and the truth is not in us.
9But if we confess our sins, he will forgive
our sins. We can trust God. He does what is right. He will make us clean from all the
wrongs we have done. 10If we say that we
have not sinned, then we make God a liar. We do not accept God's true teaching.

LET'S PRAY!

Lord, listen to me and answer me.
I am poor and helpless.
Protect me, because I worship you.
My God, save me, your servant.
I trust in you.
Lord, be merciful to me.
I have called to you all day.
Give happiness to me, your servant.
Lord, I give my life to you.
Lord, you are kind and forgiving.
You have great love for those who call to you.
Lord, hear my prayer.
Listen when I ask for mercy.
I call to you in times of trouble.
You certainly will answer me.

—Psalm 86:1–7

Quote of the Day:
Be kind and loving to each other. Forgive each other just as God forgave you in Christ.
—Ephesians 4:32

Going Deeper

Read It! God knew we needed a way to escape our sins. That's why he sent Jesus. Read about it in John 3:16–18.

Do It! Each night before you go to sleep, search your heart for any sins you may have committed that day. Ask God to forgive you. He already knows what you've done; he just wants you to admit it. Then you will be able to sleep in peace.

John's Vision

Revelation 1:9–18

The book of Revelation is one of the most mysterious books in the whole Bible. It has inspired all kinds of imaginative, and sometimes frightening, ideas about the end of the world. This book was first written to the seven churches in Asia, which are in present-day Turkey. While Revelation was written for those early churches, its wonderful descriptions of heaven are for us too!

I am John, and I am your brother in Christ. We are together in Jesus, and we share in these things: in suffering, in the kingdom, and in patience. I was on the island of Patmos because I had preached God's message and the truth about Jesus. [10]On the Lord's day the Spirit took control of me. I heard a loud voice behind me that sounded like a trumpet. [11]The voice said, "Write what you see and send that book to the seven churches: to Ephesus, Smyrna, Pergamum, Thyatira, Sardis, Philadelphia, and Laodicea."

[12]I turned to see who was talking to me. When I turned, I saw seven golden lampstands. [13]I saw someone among the lampstands who was "like a Son of Man." He was dressed in a long robe. He had a gold band around his chest. [14]His head and hair were white like wool, as white as snow. His eyes were like flames of fire. [15]His feet were like bronze that glows hot in a furnace. His voice was like the noise of flooding water. [16]He held seven stars in his right hand. A sharp two-edged sword came out of his mouth. He looked like the sun shining at its brightest time.

[17]When I saw him, I fell down at his feet like a dead man. He put his right hand on me and said, "Do not be afraid! I am the First and the Last. [18]I am the One who lives. I was dead, but look: I am alive forever and ever! And I hold the keys of death and where the dead are."

Let's Pray!

Hold me fast and guide me
In the narrow way;
So, with Thee beside me,
I shall never stray.

Daily bring me nearer
To the heavenly shore;
May my faith grow clearer.
May I love Thee more!

—Thomas Benson Pollock

Going Deeper

Read It! John is not the only person to have a vision of heaven. Read about Isaiah's vision in Isaiah 6:1–8.

Do It! Today's reading is very dramatic! Draw a picture of how you believe Jesus looked to John.

Jesus Is Knocking

Revelation 3:14–22

We can learn a great deal from the church of Laodicea, which was scolded for being lukewarm and spiritually poor. Sometimes, as people become richer and able to provide what they need for themselves, they forget that they still need God. In today's Scripture reading, the Spirit urged people to remember that true riches—heavenly riches—are only found in following God and his Son, Jesus.

"Write this to the angel of the church in Laodicea:

"The Amen is the One who is the faithful and true witness. He is the ruler of all that God has made. He says this to you: [15]I know what you do. You are not hot or cold. I wish that you were hot or cold! [16]But you are only warm—not hot, not cold. So I am ready to spit you out of my mouth. [17]You say you are rich. You think you have become wealthy and do not need anything. But you do not know that you are really miserable, pitiful, poor, blind, and naked. [18]I advise you to buy gold from me—gold made pure in fire. Then you can be truly rich. Buy from me clothes that are white. Then you can cover your shameful nakedness. Buy from me medicine to put on your eyes. Then you can truly see.

[19]"I correct and punish those whom I love. So be eager to do right. Change your hearts and lives. [20]Here I am! I stand at the door and knock. If anyone hears my voice and opens the door, I will come in and eat with him. And he will eat with me.

[21]"He who wins the victory will sit with me on my throne. It was the same with me. I won the victory and sat down with my Father on his throne. [22]Everyone who has ears should listen to what the Spirit says to the churches."

Let's Pray!

Lord, you have blessed me with so much. I am thankful for all your many gifts to me. But help me remember that my greatest blessings are your love and mercy and faithfulness. I love you, Lord! In Jesus' name, amen.

Quote of the Day:
The best and most beautiful things in the world cannot be seen or even touched. They must be felt with the heart.
—Helen Keller

Going Deeper

Read It! Treasures are what we love most. Is God your treasure, or are the things of this world? Read Matthew 6:19–21 to see what Jesus said about the treasures of this world.

Do It! Movie Night! Watch *The Miracle Worker*, and talk about Helen Keller's journey.

The Lion and the Lamb

Revelation 5:1–14

In today's Scripture reading, a mysterious scroll appears. Only Jesus, the Lamb of God, can open it and reveal its secrets. This image reminds us that our lives and our futures are safe in the hands of Jesus. There is no need to fear the future as long as we trust it and ourselves to Jesus' care.

Then I saw a scroll in the right hand of the One sitting on the throne. The scroll had writing on both sides. It was kept closed with seven seals. 2And I saw a powerful angel. He called in a loud voice, "Who is worthy to break the seals and open the scroll?" 3But there was no one in heaven or on earth or under the earth who could open the scroll or look inside. 4I cried and cried because there was no one who was worthy to open the scroll or look inside. 5But one of the elders said to me, "Do not cry! The Lion from the tribe of Judah has won the victory. He is David's descendant. He is able to open the scroll and its seven seals."

6Then I saw a Lamb standing in the center of the throne with the four living things around it. The elders were also around the Lamb. The Lamb looked as if he had been killed. He had seven horns and seven eyes. These are the seven spirits of God that were sent into all the world. 7The Lamb came and took the scroll from the right hand of the One sitting on the throne. 8After he took the scroll, the four living things and the 24 elders bowed down before the Lamb. Each one of them had a harp. Also, they were holding golden bowls full of incense. These bowls of incense are the prayers of God's holy people. 9And they all sang a new song to the Lamb:

"You are worthy to take the scroll
and to open its seals,
because you were killed;
and with the blood of your death you bought men for God
from every tribe, language, people, and nation.
10You made them to be a kingdom of priests for our God.
And they will rule on the earth."

11Then I looked, and I heard the voices of many angels. The angels were around the throne, the four living things, and the elders. There were thousands and thousands of angels—there were 10,000 times 10,000. 12The angels said in a loud voice:

"The Lamb who was killed is worthy
to receive power, wealth, wisdom and strength,
honor, glory, and praise!"

13Then I heard every living thing in heaven and on earth and under the earth and in the sea. I heard every thing in all these places, saying:

"All praise and honor and glory and power forever and ever
to the One who sits on the throne
and to the Lamb!"

14The four living things said, "Amen!" And the elders bowed down and worshiped.

Let's Pray!

Holy, holy, holy is the Lord of heaven's armies.
His glory fills the whole earth.

—Isaiah 6:3

Special Words:
The "lion from the Tribe of Judah" and "David's descendant" both mean Jesus.

Going Deeper

Read It! True faith is the greatest praise we can give God. Read about it in 1 Peter 1:7.

Do It! Make a scroll by taping a pencil to the top and another pencil to the bottom of a six-inch-wide piece of paper. Write a prayer of praise on the paper. Roll the paper up on the pencils. Read your scroll at dinner tonight!

A Sea of Martyrs

Revelation 7:9–17

In this world, there are trouble and sickness, and sin and sadness, and death. But in heaven, all of these things will be gone. Today's Scripture tells us that those who suffered on earth will never again suffer. Let's read about this wonderful place!

Then I looked, and there was a great number
of people. There were so many people that
no one could count them. They were from
every nation, tribe, people, and language
of the earth. They were all standing before the throne and before the Lamb. They
wore white robes and had palm branches
in their hands. [10]They were shouting in a
loud voice, "Salvation belongs to our God,
who sits on the throne, and to the Lamb."
[11]The elders and the four living things were
there. All the angels were standing around
them and the throne. The angels bowed
down on their faces before the throne
and worshiped God. [12]They were saying,
"Amen! Praise, glory, wisdom, thanks,
honor, power, and strength belong to our
God forever and ever. Amen!"

[13]Then one of the elders asked me, "Who
are these people in white robes? Where did
they come from?"

[14]I answered, "You know who they are, sir."

And the elder said, "These are the people
who have come out of the great suffering.
They have washed their robes with the
blood of the Lamb. Now they are clean and
white. [15]And they are before the throne of
God. They worship God day and night in his
temple. And the One who sits on the throne
will protect them. [16]Those people will never
be hungry again. They will never be thirsty
again. The sun will not hurt them. No heat
will burn them. [17]For the Lamb at the center of the throne will be their shepherd.
He will lead them to springs of water that
give life. And God will wipe away every tear
from their eyes."

LET'S PRAY!

Be near me, Lord Jesus, I ask Thee to stay
Close by me forever, and love me, I pray;
Bless all the dear children in Thy tender
care,
And fit us for heaven to live with Thee
there.

—John Thomas McFarland

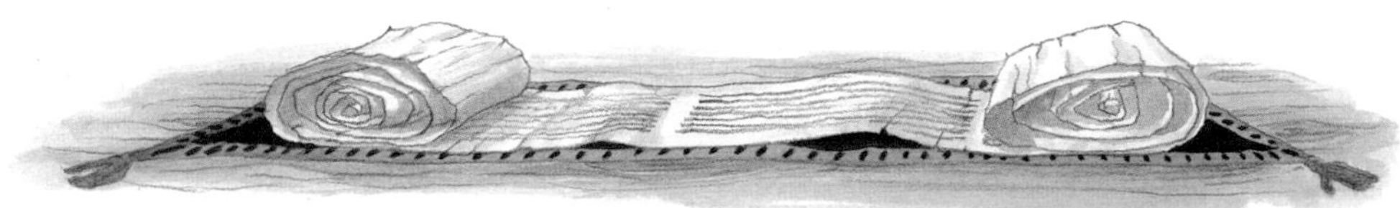

Quote of the Day:
Eternity to the godly is a day that has no sunset; eternity to the wicked is a night that has no sunrise.
—Thomas Watson

Going Deeper

READ IT! When God forgives our sins, it's as if we've been washed whiter than snow. Read about it in Psalm 51:7.

DO IT! In this world, some people may make fun of you for believing in God. But don't let them stop you! With your parents' help, practice what you will do and say if that happens to you.

A New Heaven and Earth

Revelation 21:1–4, 10–12; 22:12–13, 20–21

Heaven will be an amazing place, more wonderful than anything we could ever imagine. Today's reading gives us just a glimpse of what heaven will be like.

Then I saw a new heaven and a new earth.
The first heaven and the first earth had
disappeared. Now there was no sea. [2]And
I saw the holy city coming down out of
heaven from God. This holy city is the new
Jerusalem. It was prepared like a bride
dressed for her husband. [3]I heard a loud
voice from the throne. The voice said,
"Now God's home is with men. He will live
with them, and they will be his people. God
himself will be with them and will be their
God. [4]He will wipe away every tear from
their eyes. There will be no more death,
sadness, crying, or pain. All the old ways
are gone." . . .
[10]The angel carried me away by the Spirit
to a very large and high mountain. He
showed me the holy city, Jerusalem. It was
coming down out of heaven from God. [11]It
was shining with the glory of God. It was
shining bright like a very expensive jewel,
like a jasper. It was clear as crystal. [12]The
city had a great high wall with 12 gates.
There were 12 angels at the gates. On each
gate was written the name of 1 of the 12
tribes of Israel. . . .
[22:12]"Listen! I am coming soon! I will
bring rewards with me. I will repay each
one for what he has done. [13]I am the Alpha
and the Omega, the First and the Last, the
Beginning and the End." . . .
[20]Jesus is the One who says that these
things are true. Now he says, "Yes, I am
coming soon."
Amen. Come, Lord Jesus!
[21]The grace of the Lord Jesus be with all.
Amen.

LET'S PRAY!

Holy Father, help me live for Jesus. Let him be the King of my heart every day. In Jesus' name, amen!

GOING DEEPER

READ IT! This man dreamed of a ladder to heaven with angels going up and down it. Find out who he was in Genesis 28:12–15.

DO IT! Which Bible hero are you most looking forward to meeting in heaven? Is it Noah, Ruth, Moses, Peter, or someone else? Why?

Index

People, Places, and Things

Verse References

Day is done.
Gone the sun,
From the lake,
From the hills,
From the sky.
All is well,
Safely rest.
God is nigh.
—Unknown

Notes

1. "Facts," Olympus Mons, http://www.olympusmons.com/mars/facts.html (accessed June 2, 2012).
2. Ronald F. Youngblood, F. F. Bruce, and R. K. Harrison, *International Children's Bible Dictionary* (Nashville: Tommy Nelson, 2006), 62.
3. Traci Watson, "86 Percent of Earth's Species Still Unknown?" National Geographic Daily News, August 24, 2011, http://news.nationalgeographic.com/news/2011/08/110824-earths-species-8-7-million-biology-planet-animals-science/ (accessed June 2, 2012).
4. Youngblood, Bruce, and Harrison, *International Children's Bible Dictionary*, 174.
5. Ibid., 2, 172.
6. Ibid., 89–90.
7. "Arabian (Dromedary) Camel, NatGeo Wild, http://animals.nationalgeographic.com/animals/mammals/dromedary-camel/ (accessed June 2, 2012).
8. Youngblood, Bruce, and Harrison, *International Children's Bible Dictionary*, 23.
9. Ibid., 90.
10. Ibid., 55, 116.
11. Ibid., 110, 145.
12. Lawrence Richards, *International Children's Bible Field Guide* (Nashville: Tommy Nelson, 1989), 47.
13. Henry H. Halley, *Halley's Bible Handbook* (Grand Rapids: Zondervan, 2007), 173.
14. Ibid., 177.
15. Youngblood, Bruce, and Harrison, *International Children's Bible Dictionary*, 101.
16. Halley, *Halley's Bible Handbook*, 189.
17. Youngblood, Bruce, and Harrison, *International Children's Bible Dictionary*, 34, 120.
18. Ibid., 72.
19. Ibid., 52.
20. Halley, *Halley's Bible Handbook*, 228.
21. Ibid., 261.
22. Ibid., 259.
23. Youngblood, Bruce, and Harrison, *International Children's Bible Dictionary*, 165.
24. Ibid., 7.
25. Ibid., 148.
26. Halley, *Halley's Bible Handbook*, 384, 393–94.
27. Ibid., 409.
28. Ibid., 446.
29. Ibid., 587.
30. Ibid., 531.
31. Ibid., 627.
32. Ibid., 631.
33. Youngblood, Bruce, and Harrison, *International Children's Bible Dictionary*, 68.
34. Ibid., 33.
35. Halley, *Halley's Bible Handbook*, 635.
36. Youngblood, Bruce, and Harrison, *International Children's Bible Dictionary*, 48.
37. Ibid., 84.
38. Ibid., 69; Richards, *International Children's Bible Field Guide*, 163.
39. Halley, *Halley's Bible Handbook*, 559.
40. Youngblood, Bruce, and Harrison, *International Children's Bible Dictionary*, 170.
41. Richards, *International Children's Bible Field Guide*, 174.
42. *Wikipedia*, s.v.,"Tyrian Purple," http://en.wikipedia.org/wiki/Tyrian_purple (accessed June 2, 2012).
43. *Wikipedia*, s.v., "Areopagus," http://en.wikipedia.org/wiki/Areopagus (accessed June 2, 2012).
44. Halley, *Halley's Bible Handbook*, 677.
45. Youngblood, Bruce, and Harrison, *International Children's Bible Dictionary*, 57.
46. Halley, *Halley's Bible Handbook*, 762.
47. Ibid., 778.